ANCIENT AND MODERN RELIGION AND POLITICS

Previous Publications

Ethics and Creativity in the Political Thought of Simone Weil and Albert Camus, John Randolph LeBlanc (2004)

Teaching African American Religion, Carolyn M. Jones Medine and Theodore Trost, Eds. (2005)

ANCIENT AND MODERN RELIGION
AND POLITICS
NEGOTIATING TRANSITIVE SPACES
AND HYBRID IDENTITIES

John Randolph LeBlanc and Carolyn M. Jones Medine

ANCIENT AND MODERN RELIGION AND POLITICS
Copyright © John Randolph LeBlanc and
Carolyn M. Jones Medine, 2012.

First published in 2012 by
PALGRAVE MACMILLAN®
in the United States—a division of St. Martin's Press LLC,
175 Fifth Avenue, New York, NY 10010.

Where this book is distributed in the UK, Europe and the rest of the
World, this is by Palgrave Macmillan, a division of Macmillan Publishers
Limited, registered in England, company number 785998, of
Houndmills, Basingstoke, Hampshire RG21 6XS.

Palgrave Macmillan is the global academic imprint of the above
companies and has companies and representatives throughout the world.

Palgrave® and Macmillan® are registered trademarks in the United
States, the United Kingdom, Europe and other countries.

ISBN: 978–0–230–34084–8

Library of Congress Cataloging-in-Publication Data

LeBlanc, John Randolph.
    Ancient and modern religion and politics : negotiating transitive
    spaces and hybrid identities / John Randolph LeBlanc,
    Carolyn M. Jones Medine.
        p.   cm.
    ISBN 978–0–230–34084–8
    1. Religion and politics.   2. Peace.   I. Medine, Carolyn
    M. Jones.   II. Title.
    BL65.P7L42625 2012
    201'.72—dc23   2012015243

A catalogue record of the book is available from the British Library.

Design by Integra Software Services

First edition: October 2012

10 9 8 7 6 5 4 3 2 1

To our parents, who as black and white Southerners, knew the meaning of transitivity from experience
and
to our mentors and teachers who helped shape our minds and our beings

CONTENTS

ACKNOWLEDGMENTS

The authors would like to acknowledge those who, through their support, made this volume possible. We would especially like to thank the people of the Honors College at Louisiana State University as it was from 1991–1999. We taught with a group of scholars—Dr. James D. Hardy, Jr., Christine Cowan, Dr. Kenneth Kitchell, and Dr. Bainard Cowan—who were marvelous conversation partners, mentors, and are and always will be friends. From these people in this environment, we learned the real meaning of scholarly collaboration. Dr. Billy Seay, who headed the Honors College during those years, shaped and protected this environment and was a marvelous support for both of us, young scholars trying to find our voices. In addition to his many intellectual contributions, Dr. Cecil L. Eubanks of the LSU Department of Political Science also generously shared his calm insight and wisdom to our development as scholars and people.

We would also like to thank the Mid-South Peace and Justice Center in Memphis, Tennessee. This organization brings together scholars and activists for fruitful dialogue on some of the more pressing issues in our culture. It was at their conferences that we began to think through the issues in this book. We delivered several of these papers at their annual Gandhi-King Conference where we received support for and encouragement in our work.

We would like to thank Jessica Couch and Caroline Maria Piotrowski. These two young scholars contributed significantly to the production of this volume. We are very grateful for their careful reading of the manuscript and for the preparation of the index and bibliography.

Finally, we would like to thank our editor at Palgrave, Burke Gerstenschlager, for his enthusiastic support of this project, and Kaylan Connally, editorial assistant with Palgrave, without whose patience and persistence, this project would never have reached completion.

Introduction: Negotiations
in Transitive Spaces

The co-authored chapters in this volume are the result of over a decade of ongoing conversation. While our training is in the distinct disciplines of religious studies and political theory, our concerns overlap in several places including, but not restricted to, cultural criticism; the role, function, and power of discourse; the "other," in all the forms that it can take, particularly in literature and literary criticism; and, more generally, "meaning" in all human activity. These diverse mutual interests coalesce around a shared concern with narratives of otherness and dislocation. In this book, we read these narratives not merely as critiques of existing structures, but, more significantly, for what they bring forward from the traditions in which they are embedded and how they challenge those traditions, both political and religious. We also read these narratives for what they tell us about either overcoming those structures or creating meaning within them, for while we cannot live outside meta-narratives, our interdisciplinary approach seeks new spaces in which answers to questions of meaning are made possible. This relation between "tradition and the individual talent," as T. S. Eliot would put it, or between tradition and the "other(s)," as we would put it, is the site where culture develops.[1]

The title of this book, *Transitive Identities*, indicates the theme that binds the chapters together. The transitive is key to understanding what we do, suggesting movement, across and through space and in time. Our concern with the transitive demands that we attend to the delicacies and difficulties of movement, both external and internal. Consequently, movement of both people and ideas is one element of our work. In addition, however, the term *transitive* suggests multiple modes of relation. A transitive verb, for example, is incomplete without a direct object. In mathematics, the transitive suggests order and relation. As we use the term, however, it need not predetermine the character of relation.

In either the concrete circumstances of human life or the discourses we use to negotiate those circumstances, we also encounter another sense of the term *transitive*, one that may lead to violence. In *Totality and Infinity*, Emmanuel Levinas writes, "The notion of act involves a violence essentially: the violence of transitivity."[2] So while transitivity suggests that something is carried from one place to another, this transmission, or movement, always risks the difficulty, even the probability, of transgression and/or destruction. This risk and its possibilities are what we work through in the chapters of this volume.

The notion of transitivity lies at the intersections of several theoretical notions. Transitivity involves passage, which necessitates an examination of the ritual process and rite of passage. Consequently, the idea of the *limen* informs, but does not exhaust, our work. The "crossing status" of the *limen* involves the erasure of stable identity. As Victor Turner writes in *The Ritual Process*, those in the *limen* are "threshold people"; that is, they are "betwixt and between the positions assigned and arrayed by law, custom, convention and [ceremony]."[3] They occupy an ambiguous status, existing in a realm that "has few or none of the attributes of the past or coming state." The word Turner uses for these people is *passenger*, suggesting that they, though dislodged, are nevertheless being transported.[4] Societal or religious rites of passage, therefore, do not maintain the *limen* indefinitely. The neophyte is "crossing" into a new social or religious role. Ritual, therefore, is carefully controlled, with (re)integration as its aim. The *communitas* of rite of passage is powerful in its capacity to level social status, gender, race, and other distinguishing social markers, but, in the end, it is temporary.

The *limen*, then, is a kind of contact zone, a second theoretical model with which we work. Mary Louise Pratt defines contact zones as "social spaces where disparate cultures meet, clash, and grapple with each other."[5] In the contact zone, persons and cultures face an asymmetry in their power relations to each other. Since the contact zone is liminal, one may not cross out of it into another space or role. Instead, one may either have to live with what W. E. B. Du Bois calls "double consciousness" or become what Giorgio Agamben calls "bare life," life that has been determined by the sovereign to have no social or religious value and that can be "killed" but not "sacrificed."[6] Identity, whether group or individual, is unsettled.

In this book, we have attempted to capture the fluidity of fundamentally unsettled environments in which contemporaries wander in search of meaning, both religious and political. That the religious and political are so readily conflated in our post-Enlightenment environment signals the crisis of meaning that Nietzsche diagnosed but with which we have yet to come to grips. In this introduction, we articulate our starting point, a place only now identifiable, in any coherent sense, after the dominance of the discourses of postmodern and postcolonial theory and after the postcolonial moment of emergent states. Weaving together the concerns of modernity with the insights and criticisms of both postmodernity and the classical, we demonstrate both how we proceed and the assumptions upon which we do so. We know ours is only a reading or, better, a series of readings. They are ongoing, speculative, and open to questions, but always grounded in experience, reflection, and scholarship. We are keenly aware of the incompleteness of this project and hope our readers will engage us with that awareness, entering the text in a dialogic mode.

Our conversations and, therefore, these chapters explore the intersections of religion and politics, particularly at sites of literary and philosophical expression. We work with both ancient and modern literatures, contending that the West has not moved so far beyond the categories first articulated in Greek tragedy as it would like to think. As with the Greeks, our contemporaries long for stability, but in the encounter with otherness, as Judith Butler has so poignantly remarked, "We are undone by each other. And if we're not, we're missing something."[7] We contend with Butler that we can no longer afford to miss this "something," this undoing that reminds us that we are selves separate from but intimately connected to one another. The challenge for the contemporary West lies not just in seeing and listening (often for the first time) to those who have been marginalized historically, but also in negotiating the otherness in ourselves generated by the encounter. To "be" in the presence of another is a very different thing than to "be" in one's absence or in what we have deemed is one's "insignificance." Over literatures, discourses, and histories, we identify and interrogate enduring issues the West has faced as it thinks about self and other, individual and community, race and gender, home and homelessness.

Above all, each of us is drawn to the idea of story. For us, narrative constructions—literary, religious, philosophical, and political—are simultaneously coherent and contingent, necessary and negotiable. Our close attention to narrative—to story—and, therefore, to language and memory, however, marks us as children not only of the postmodern and the postcolonial, but also and especially of the world before the Enlightenment. While many have breathed a sigh of relief that the postmodern seems to be coming to an end, we argue that it cannot. If, as Jean-Francois Lyotard suggests, memory and narrative mark the pre-modern, the modern, *and* the postmodern, then they (and we) are intimately connected.[8] The problem of modernity,

Lyotard argues, is its insistence that some stories, those of science, for example, are universal and that "local" narratives are to be corrected or abandoned in light of this universality. The postmodern and, we argue, the postcolonial mark the recovery of these lost or oppressed stories. This recovery is dangerous because it threatens to undermine our epistemologies. These recovered stories de-center what has been called the master narrative, contextualizing our assumptions and commitments. A mature sensibility, however, can reflect upon its own self-understanding. The child, as Piaget reminds us, lacks this self-reflexive ability[9]; the adult has the ability, but inasmuch as we refuse its challenge, we can only remain immature. Kant thought this self-reflective tendency was the essential characteristic of the Enlightenment.[10] We have seen otherwise. Consequently, the recovery of previously disrespected stories precipitates a recognition of dislocation—where our very selves and the very possibility of being at home are called into question.

The idea of dislocation, so prevalent in ancient literature and so symptomatic of modernity's shortcomings, goes largely unexamined by our popular culture and news accounts. We live in Guy Debord's "society of the spectacle," in which pace and newness substitute for connection.[11] On our reading of Debord, when dislocation appears, it takes a human form, in the figure of the refugee, the stateless person, or the homeless person, but what spectacle suggests is "nothing human"; dislocation is something that "happens" only to others. It appears as an event rather than a state of being and, indeed, marks "those" people as others and their experiences as alien and transitory.

Yet we simultaneously live in a culture that values the transitory through perpetual acquisition (of stuff and recognition) and alteration (of physical self through plastic surgery and emotional self through psychotropic medications). We chase an ideal that we have not considered, let alone taken the time to articulate. In this context, it seems imperative to attend to stories of dislocation as we seek to recover our selves. The project is dangerous as it threatens what we think we know about ourselves. But, we are arguing, it might bring us to the recognition of our own dislocation, of being in that space of undoing that we share with those we define as alien "others." The transformation of both self- and other-understanding requires and, we hope, points to a rethinking and expansion of our notions of selfhood and community.

The structure of this book reflects these concerns and works through them in a variety of contexts. In the first section, we examine the complexities of "Home and Homelessness." The chapters in this section represent attempts to approach the difficulties of displacement and diaspora from the perspective of home and its absence. The massive destruction and dislocation of populations in the past century is but a mirror of the displacement of the human from conceptions of community. In response to these dislocations, an active nostalgia for home developed, of which the "nation" is one major form, in both postcolonial revolutions and established liberal political environments. This nostalgia, however, did not manage the liberation of human beings from their technical creations, but a retrenchment into older forms of belonging (e.g., *jus soli* and *jus sanguinus*). These revanchist formations only masked, temporarily at least, what "home" has always been: in addition to a base from which to develop our "selves," home can be a site of terror, a space where violations of intimacy are passed over in order to preserve neat legal distinctions between private and public spaces and to keep racial, gender, and other cultural hierarchies in place. The inadequacies (to say the least) of these elder forms of home seem to demand that we abandon home as we thought we knew it and re-conceive it, in many instances, from positions of dislocation and exile.

The question emerges whether this project demands that we abandon old narratives and take on "new" ones in their place. In these chapters, our contention is that we should not abandon these narratives because to do so would be to lose sight of how we got here and the possibilities of where we might go. Self-diagnosis rather than denial is called for. Like our experience, our language is ours—that is, the one with which we must work—thus our sympathies with the Greeks and Christians, in addition to the postmoderns and postcolonials, who remind us of the limitations of language and open us to transgressive readings and realizations.

The first chapter of this section, "Culture, Location, and the Problem of Transitive Identity," utilizes Homi Bhabha's analysis of the interplay between culture and location to read Caryl Phillips's memoir and travelogue *The Atlantic Sound* as a text that firmly locates us in what Mary Louis Pratt calls the "contact zone."[12] In it, we see the fruits of diaspora, both wonderful and terrible. The diasporic experience leads to a sense of the fragility of our self-understandings. It leads to what we call here "transitive identity," that is, a sense of self-in-place that is never "in place." Here, we intend the term *transitive* to capture both the movement and the development of human consciousness as it is buffeted about from place to place, from awareness to awareness, from uncertainty to uncertainty—seeking rest while being permanently displaced from the complex site of its origins. Bhabha's attempt to articulate this fluidity meshes well with Phillips's text, allowing us to examine these issues through alternative stories.

The second chapter, "Going Home in the Works of Charles H. Long and Ashis Nandy," explores the roots from which we in the West understand diaspora and its elements of power. The chapter discusses G. W. F. Hegel's *Phenomenology* from the point of view of two racial-ethnic scholars, the African American historian of religions Charles H. Long and the Indian psychologist and politician Ashis Nandy. Both Long and Nandy interrogate Hegel's "master-slave" relation and how the oppressed "other" has resisted its implications. Their analyses are particularly sensitive to the fact that diasporic homelessness generates anger and despair. The value of the dialectic is in the slave's taking of agency, of naming himself and his experience. In doing so, the "slave" generates a dialogic situation in which before there had been only the master and the silenced. In this dynamic, there is also the possibility that the diaspora itself can, through this agency, be deemed transitive—a space or phase in which to move and to learn rather than submit to master or circumstance Our work rejects the inevitability of the violence implicit in the Hegelian dialectic as a locus of home. Instead, we embrace the relational reading of Nandy. The liminal self improvises the space of home in terms of intimacy, transgressions, the interdependence of the multiplicity of selves, and, by attending to detail, "intimate things in place."

In the final chapter of this section, "The Politics of Statelessness: Edward Said and the Ambiguities of Liberal Nationalism," we argue that the emergence of a liberal form of nationalism at the end of the past century may be seen in part as an attempt by stateless communities to stake a claim to international legitimacy. Taking statelessness as a collective, political form of homelessness or exile, we examine the vulnerability of the stateless in both the physical and the discursive realm through the work of Palestinian-American cultural critic Edward Said. In his efforts to articulate the Palestinian position, Said made a late (and temporary) nod in the direction of what is called "liberal nationalism." His suggestions for the future of the question of Palestine/Israel bear close resemblance to the body of liberal nationalist thought, particularly as articulated by the Israeli political philosopher Yael Tamir in her work *Liberal Nationalism*.[13] Despite Said's postcolonial methodology of "reading back" to the assumptions of Western social, political, and literary theory, this late turn represents an intriguing, if partial, embrace of those assumptions as a practical—if deeply problematic—response to the statelessness of the Palestinians.

The second section, "Mediations of Religion and Politics," begins by recognizing that overcoming dislocation means critically reexamining our sources of meaning and self. The chapters in this section seek those sources in the intersections of ancient and modern literature and theory. We return to the ancients—especially, but not exclusively, to the Greek tragedians—for their deeply psychological understandings of human character. The cliché, "living with others means first knowing how to live with oneself," was no cliché at all for the Greeks or their inheritors, the Stoics. Among the many other things that tragedy represents is a working through of the possibilities—both enlightened and dark—of the human being by seriously examining sources of self-understanding. By bringing these elder narratives into dialogue with more recent works, we attempt to interrogate our own frames of reference and to argue that the way we have framed our own experiences in community has implications for the way we understand new presences. More importantly, the narratives we use mark revisionings of these elder narratives often by those "new presences," and these encounters of classical and, usually, colonial suggest possibilities for transformed communities. Our work here insists that we must come to terms with older narratives, and, while we recognize that this project risks making those narratives subject to circumstances they did not anticipate, it is precisely their value that they still speak with authority in those new circumstances, taking as their object the human presence wandering in an often-alien universe.

In the first chapter of this section, "Self-Cultivation and the Practice of Peace: Foucault and the Stoics," we look at Michel Foucault's final work, *The Care of the Self,* to explore its unfinished implications for postmodern life.[14] We find, in Foucault, the recognition that the cultivation of the particular can hold out the possibility of a functional, creative, and healthy commonality. We are drawn to the Aristotelian notion that a human self, let alone a peaceful one, requires existence in a community of others. The postmodern difficulty is that those others are not necessarily chosen. Therefore, the application of Aristotelian moderation, self-understanding, and balance is insufficient to meet the exigencies of the presence of those others, but can serve as a model for (re)conciliation and coexistence. The Stoics' Aristotelian inheritance reminds us that structures are never finally sufficient, that any kind of purposeful cohabitation depends upon a willingness of human beings to work at balance and never rest upon the cohabitation as something achieved once and for all.

With this philosophical prelude, the next three chapters in this section turn to classical tragedy, specifically the work of Sophocles and Euripides, discussing have used them and understood and they inform current political and spiritual relationships. In " 'The Better Angels of our Nature': Sophocles' *Antigone* and the Crisis of Union," we explore the tensions between self and community, individual and union, through the lens of Abraham Lincoln's *Second Inaugural Address*. The images invoked by Lincoln reflect those difficult places where a community's original sin, emerging from political and religious convictions, must be negotiated using the language of both. Here Lincoln confronts the relation of self to others in the context of intimate violence—slave/free and North/South. Civil war is always a violation of intimacy, and Lincoln understood that this was particularly true in the American case in which slavery was the central issue. The emphasis here, as it was *in absentia* in *Antigone*, is on practical wisdom. Lincoln's rhetoric here is tragic in the Aristotelian sense— aimed at the deepest parts of the human conscience with the purpose of generating catharsis. The purging of America's original sin—slavery, long perpetuated in Oedipal blindness—could be paid for only in the blood of intimates and in self-mutilation.

In the third chapter of this section, "*Oedipus at Colonus* and *The Gospel at Colonus*: African American Experience and the Classical Text," we turn to the final play of Sophocles' Oedipus trilogy, *Oedipus at Colonus*, to explore an African American displacement of that play. The chapter interrogates the value of ritual, story, and divine grace in generating the connectedness inherent in the experience of peace. We use the encounter between these two texts and the experiences they represent to explore the meaning of sanctuary (another form of home) and its potential place in the world of politics. Generating sanctuary and the peace it represents, as with Aristotelian ethics, must be an ongoing, conscious, and intensely creative process. Consequently, while the chapter attempts to come to grips with the complexities (and inevitable shortcomings) of trying to institutionalize social and political justice, it points us in the direction of working to instantiate the values represented by the idea of peaceful sanctuary in a functioning community.

The chapter "The Power of Horror: Variations and Re-framings of *The Bacchae*" concludes this section; it includes three readings of the work of Euripides. It examines how literary critic Robert Detweiler, African playwright and theorist Wole Soyinka, and American novelist Toni Morrison understand Euripides' *The Bacchae*, particularly its images of rendering, as metaphors for modernity. Euripides understood the power of the darkness of the human *psyche* and would have been least surprised of the tragedians by the violence that marked the twentieth century. Taken in one place, the readings given *The Bacchae* by Detweiler, Soyinka, and Morrison remind us that the dark sides of the *psyche*, of the imagination, are critical and must be taken into account. If we deny them, as Nietzsche well understood, we forget what we are capable of and risk stumbling blindly into horror. To take ourselves and our fellows seriously, we must reinforce what we know but often reject without thinking: that darkness is a seductive presence both in our personal lives and especially in our public, political lives where we may be joined, supported, and encouraged by others in our madness. Human beings have consciences; mobs do not.

The concluding section of the book, "The Possibility of Peace and the 'Beloved Community,' " begins by revisiting the lessons to be taken from the encounter of our contemporaries with classical narratives. What we learn is that the kinds of human meaning represented by politics, on the one hand, and religion, on the other, are mutually self-destructive when pitted against each other and equally perilous when confused for each other. Both religion and politics suffer from inner conflict as well as from the external collisions they have with each other. We would like to suggest that it is one thing for meanings to be transitive and quite another for them to be relative, having little or no communicable meaning at all, or fixed and dogmatic, so certain of their own truths as to be incapable of any other perspective. The task of the postmodern is to give transitivity substance without hardening it into an ideological or dogmatic weapon to be used against the other or turned upon the self. The resort to violence—physical or discursive—is a concession, not to the incommunicability of these forms of meaning, but to our unwillingness to make them communicable: our unwillingness to speak or hear with our "other" either in mind or in the room. Without listening, there is no hearing; without hearing, there is no communication; without communication, there is no community—let alone a "beloved" community in which intimacy is valued as a reasonable and worthwhile risk. Put another way, giving substance to our spiritual and political lives means reimagining ourselves in relationship to others and refashioning the way we carry out and perform those relationships.

The first chapter in this section, " 'In-Between' Culture and Meaning: Voegelin, Bhabha, and the Intervention of the Political," examines the power of symbols to define and delimit values, bringing a voice we heard earlier, Homi Bhabha's, into a discussion of political identity and the role of the minority voice in its formation, with neo-Hegelian political philosopher Eric Voegelin. We ask whether Voegelin's insistence on categories like "transcendence" precludes a consideration of the messy politics of our present, particularly, the politics of cultural confrontation and transformation. We make a case that the verticality of Voegelin's work must not necessarily exclude Bhabha's horizontal concerns or it risks not being able to speak to lived human lives. We argue that their mediation point is Bhabha's insistence that we look to the margins, not just of individual human existences, but of those of the community itself, in order to see who makes it up.

The second chapter, "Negotiating Space(s): Reframing Political Conflict in Walzer and Lyotard," explicates the distinct, but not entirely unrelated, versions of the space in which politics takes place in the work of Michael Walzer and Jean-Francois Lyotard.[15] This chapter underlines our concern with political space: with who names it, who occupies it, and the permissible activities therein. Liberal political theorists like Walzer emphasize boundaries and the distribution of goods when speaking of justice. The postmodern approach of Lyotard emphasizes discourse and the extension of the rules of Wittgensteinian language games. What Lyotard's perspective adds to the admittedly confining conception of Walzer is a stipulation to the need for rules while detaching them from ontological or epistemological certainties. In other words, while political order requires some contingent certainties, if our concern is speaking with others about and creating justice across boundaries, across the divides of space, of language and of expectation, the key to such speech is a willingness to "play" with our assumptions, engaging them with a serious, ongoing openness.

The last two chapters of this section take up the theme with which we wish to close: the reconstitution of community. In "Alice Walker's *The Color Purple* and Beyond: Suffering and the Reconstitution of Community," we argue for the need to move beyond structure and ideology to some healing bond of human commonality as the prelude to reconstituting community. Human commonality would seem to be the sticking point, but the Greek tragedians remind us that suffering is what we share, and Walker's work reiterates that the oppressor is every bit as subject to suffering as the oppressed. Our work on Walker, this revolutionary artist, points to the need for the suffering of all to be expressed in both everyday language and within the framing concepts of our political discourse. These stories must be told, but in a form and forum in which they can be heard and the experience can be shared. The sharing of these stories of suffering—the speaking and the listening—marks the beginning of the human commonality that holds out the possibility of human community.

The final chapter revisits the issue of reconstituting community by insisting upon and explicating the distinction between
"reconstitution" and "reconstruction." In "The Limits of Reconstruction: Reconstituting Community in Martin Luther King, Jr.," we
isolate the tension between the two terms, arguing that reconstruction means rebuilding materiality while reconstitution is the infinitely
more difficult task of (re)building relationships. To emphasize reconstruction polarizes and inhibits the possibility of true community by
focusing the discussion on physical damage, on only tangible destruction. We argue that Martin Luther King, Jr., understood that community must be built from human relationships, from *agape* and practice,
and on the assumption of the other's goodwill. King's work echoes
Lincoln's, suggesting the need for a "more perfect union" between
people as a prerequisite to a functioning, nutritive human community.
This community is unavailable if the focus is on mere reconstruction,
for the reconstructed community resembles a Frankenstein's monster.
Despite positive developments in race and other relations, King knew
as we do, that we still face the perilous work of creating a community
that must be reconstituted and remixed before it can be restored.

Such relation ties our work to that of Levinas. In the face of the
other, we, Levinas argues, yield, making—not discourse—but multiple modes of conversation, witness, and testimony, for example, and
perhaps, opening up love between previously unacknowledged others.
These modes of speaking open us to a future,[16] one that does not deny
the past, but faces it and recovers its best attributes. Truth is fraternal,
pointing us to the political, and in the face of the other, we sense
something beyond, though impossible to name, pointing us to the
religious. In the transitive movement, these loci of meaning-making
can dance.

SECTION I

HOME AND HOMELESSNESS

CHAPTER 1

CULTURE, LOCATION, AND THE
PROBLEM OF TRANSITIVE IDENTITY

"Identity politics" misunderstands the nature and, therefore, the importance of its subject matter. Far from being something fixed and exclusive, identity is the transitive or motive element that negotiates meaning between settled understandings and the fluidity of cultural development. A self, in this mode, is a being who can articulate a sense of identity—in other words, one who can narrate self-consciousness—within a set of ideas, moral and ethical, that locate that self in the larger human endeavor of community or culture. Making clear-cut definitions of identity is complicated by the experience of diaspora. Diaspora, initially, is an identity detour, a movement or shift away from the traditional understanding of the linear journey of the self from beginning to end of life within established structures, which allows us to make meaning along the way. Diaspora takes us out of those structures, creating dead ends that stop movement and establish new borders, new spaces of contact and interactions that lead either to reinforcement, maintenance of the "old" self, or the mixing, creolization, or hybridity, a remaking/remixing of identity and self in the new place in relation to new "others." This remixing is further complicated by factors of race and ethnicity. In this chapter, we will look at manifestations of this remixing and the complications that arise in the context of diaspora, particularly confronting issues of race, identity, and culture, using, primarily, the work of Homi K. Bhabha in *The Location of Culture* and Caryl Phillips's travelogue/memoir *The Atlantic Sound*.[1]

HOMI K. BHABHA: THE PERFORMANCE OF SELF
AND NATION

We are accustomed to claiming and living out in an unconscious way what we think are fixed identities—selves—in relation to better or more poorly defined "others." Such claims come easily, whether we fancy ourselves either oppressor or oppressed, or neither. These claims, however, may make sense only in reference to that carefully defined "other." If the question of authentic identity is set in terms of "purity," however, negotiation is interrupted. In this sense, identity is necessarily negative and prone to the inanity of syllogism of the kind deployed in some places after the terror attacks of September 11: "they" are bad; "we" are not them; therefore, we are good.[2] The interactions of cultural differences, however, are rarely, if ever, that clear-cut. The "bad" and "good" that emerge in any particular circumstance have a history that, probably, is a checkered one indeed. In more "stable" political and religious environments, cultural differences ordinarily are ignored or negotiated until something sparks a confrontation, at which point we assert identities from a space of cultural-political power or powerlessness.

As Paul Gilroy expresses it in *The Black Atlantic: Modernity and Double Consciousness*, race is central in such power-driven situations of "cultural insiderism."[3] Cultural insiderism "distinguishes people from one another and at the same time acquires an incontestable priority over all other dimensions of their social and historical experience, culture, and identities."[4] In such a construction, racial ethnic people are always "other" in order that a pure national identity may be articulated. Creolization, mestissage, mestizaje, and hybridity represent, from the point of view of power, "a litany of pollution and impurity."[5]

In other words, at the point of cultural contact or confrontation, we realize—often suddenly—that borders look solid but that what occurs on borders is full of movement and exchange: we find ourselves as transitive beings. Points of interaction become contact zones. Relying on cultural-political power as the source of our national identity in the contact zone is problematic in at least two ways. First, the melange of cultures that is the modern nation-state is never a multicultural paradise of cooperating cultures. A national culture, in the political sense, makes the rules, defines the virtues, and decides whether to accommodate difference or not. Identities that depend on political hegemony quantify (votes, power, money, the value of social goods defined as such by those who possess them) important questions of meaning and generate discussions that are zero-sum conflicts, which is to say, no discussions at all. Second, more or less global communication technologies either homogenize our experiences across cultures or exclude altogether those without access to the technologies. Identities that depend on technological "superiority" devalue the human presence on both ends. That is to say, either "others" are less human because they do not have the "stuff" (or know how to operate it), or the humanity of the "other" and its possibilities are limited to *only* having and knowing the "stuff." Given the rate of technological turnover, even this latter assumption of humanness is precarious at best. With the glaring inadequacies of politics and technology as sources of identity, it is little wonder that we are returning to the concept of culture in order to reopen discussions about identity.

The return to culture as a source of identity troubles some who fear that the older conceptions of the role of culture resemble in their purity and exclusivity the way we think about political and technological differences. A role for culture like that offered by Homi K. Bhabha, however, in which culture is situated within and without a more fluid conception of a larger community, the "nation," offers the opportunity to rethink the crucial relationships among terms like "self," "nation," and "identity" and, as we will argue, in Phillips's work, the connections and corresponding problems of race and diaspora.

Bhabha's work is an intervention and exemplar in the attempt among theorists to revive nationalism in a more humane form than that which emerged in the twentieth century. He eschews the historical certainty of the discourse of nationalism preferring to write of the Western nation as an obscure and ubiquitous form of *living the locality* of culture.[6] Far from being a settled source of identity, the nation is now the site of a discursive liminality: a transitive entity. Bhabha builds on W. E. B. Du Bois's notion of the double consciousness articulated in post-Reconstruction America. For Du Bois, double consciousness is the idea that African American people, understood as a social "problem," live out a double identity:

One ever feels his twoness,—An American, a Negro; two souls, two thoughts, two unreconciled strivings; two warring ideals in one dark body, whose dogged strength alone keeps it from being torn asunder.[7]

In Du Bois, this is, ultimately, an issue that involves both consciousness, that is, how African American people construct identity, and lived experience. It emerges from the "unhappy symbiosis" between thinking (the racially particular), being (the nationalistic), and seeing (the diasporic) as functions of the human consciousness.[8] Bhabha, working from the concept of double consciousness, accepts this fragmentation as constitutive of the postcolonial self and, given that we all live in a situation of postcoloniality, applies the double consciousness to the nation itself. For Bhabha, the modern nation is home to a people only now beginning to recognize their doubleness:

> the nation's people must be thought in double-time; the people are the historical "objects" of a nationalist pedagogy, giving the discourse an authority that is based on the pre-given or constituted historical origin *in the past*; the people are also the "subjects" of a process of signification that must erase any prior or originary presence of the nation-people to demonstrate the prodigious, living principles of the people as contemporaneity.[9]

The nation, as double, is two. First, it exists as a stable entity. It is recognized as the product of a pedagogy that may or may not reflect the experience of the (non-)member; in other words, it articulates national memory (history), sets national rituals (ordinary religion, like the Fourth of July in America), and structures interaction (law and custom) for a supposed homogenous whole.

The stability of this narrative, in double-time, is undercut by what Bhabha calls the performative "agency of a people," the narrations of the actual, lived cultural experience of those in the nation, those who are politically narrated. The result, for Bhabha, is that the people of the nation come to represent the cutting edge between the totalizing powers of the nation as homogeneous, consensual community, and the forces that signify the more specific address to contentious, unequal interests and identities within the population.[10] In short, the emergence of this/these more complicated cultural consciousness(es) means that the pot is no longer hot enough to melt its contents and that no single spoon is big enough to stir it. Melting pot becomes gumbo pot. In the mixture, therefore, is where the processes of ordinary politics, chiefly characterized by conflicts and their systemically nonthreatening outcomes, meet their limit in questions of meaning. Such questions, situated within an increasingly heterogeneous nation, are reopened by the people in lived experience so that, Bhabha writes, "no political ideologies [can] claim transcendent or metaphysical authority for themselves."[11]

From his postcolonial perspective, Bhabha reconceives the politics of conflict as a politics of negotiation in the contact zone. There are at least two dimensions of this reconception: location and the concept of interstices. *Location* has to do with what we might call "ordinary" politics, while the concept of *interstices* is the recognition of a political space for "extraordinary" politics. First, for Bhabha, our location is the more or less fixed point from which we speak and act. It is the conception of identity we referred to earlier in this chapter, the one that we take for granted and that is most effective when not interrogated. It is the source of our public (i.e., political) voice—the one with which we speak with and to the homogenous nation. Bhabha, however, does not mean to confine us to this point: he insists that we recognize that what we become and what we say are colored permanently by our location, whether we like it or not. The responsible member of the community knows from where he or she speaks and does not avoid the implications of that location. Bhabha intends by this device to preserve us in our public selves, but also to remind us that our public selves are only part of a larger community, limited in experience, knowledge, and understanding.

Part of our location is the way we have learned, internalized, and come to understand the language of our social, political, and cultural inheritances. Location, as a term of ordinary politics, is vulnerable to affiliation with the older colonialist order in which the "other" is carefully defined and restricted to his location. Bhabha is not content to remain where the colonizer would place him. He recognizes what theorists and critics often forget: that once a term or subject is defined, the signifier ceases to concern himself with the subtleties of the signified. In other words, the way a term or subject is understood is limited, potentially liberating the subject by leaving a space in which she may define her self in creative, useful, and politically empowering ways. The terms of ordinary politics, therefore, generate critical spaces from which the dominant discourse and its institutional manifestations may be challenged, changed, and rewritten.

Bhabha's analysis suggests that since politics, as we understand it, is about the strategic allocation of resources, there is an inevitable fluidity to the meaning of our political language and the uses to which we put it. The monolithic meta-narrative exists only as a tool or shorthand and should not be seen as the only or ultimate repository of communal meaning. He wants what he describes as a "shift" of attention away from the political as pedagogical, ideological practice to politics as the stressed necessity of everyday life, that is, politics as performance.[12] The politics of seeking or claiming a permanent, authoritative, and universal cultural meaning embodied in similarly permanent institutional and social arrangements should no longer be the focus of either functional theory or political praxis. Concerning ourselves with the content of civilizational meaning detracts from the real problem of political existence on this side of diaspora: negotiating and living with differences in cultural self-understanding(s). Bhabha's political thought finds freedom and possibility on borders where cultural self-understandings meet and even clash. Rather than obsessing over either winning or overcoming the "other" in these situations, our understandings would benefit more from focusing on the moments produced in the articulation of those cultural differences, that is, on the performance of politics, not on some ostensibly "final" outcome.

Bhabha's real interest, then, is in the spaces wherein cultural differences encounter one another, "the overlap and displacement of domains of difference," which he calls *interstices*.[13] This second dimension of Bhabha's political thought is, in fact, central to a functional conception of politics. Bhabha writes,

The challenge lies in conceiving of the time of political action and understanding as opening up a space that can accept and regulate the differential structure of the moment of intervention without rushing to produce a unity of the social antagonism or contradiction. This is a sign that history is happening within the pages of theory, within the systems and structures we construct to figure the passage of the historical.[14]

Political disputes, to the degree that they rush "to produce a unity of the social antagonism or contradiction," are set up as zero-sum situations, to be won or lost rather than negotiated. In this default political context, cultural difference is seen as a threat to be co-opted or otherwise eradicated ("cleansed") with profound and permanent consequences for both cultures. In both domestic and international clashes, each side portrays the other as static, a permanent threat to the native culture, leaving life or death (for culture or individual) as the only possible outcomes. This is what Jean-Francois Lyotard, extending perhaps from Mircea Eliade's idea of the "terror of history," calls the terror of politics.[15]

Bhabha uses theory to move beyond the conflict model of politics. He finds, in fact, that the function of theory or critique is to open up a space of translation, by which he means that the representations of the sides in an encounter are both on the table for negotiation. Neither can be seen as authoritative in any final sense. Negotiation counters the very idea of the meta-narrative as a necessarily stable generality.

From the perspective of negotiation and translation...there can be no final discursive closure of theory. It does not foreclose on the political even though battles for power-knowledge may be won or lost to great effect. The corollary is that there is not a first or final act of revolutionary social (or socialist) transformation.[16]

For Bhabha, the "other's" culture always appears as the "closure of grand theories."[17] In other words, rather than being seen as a threat, as the beginning of the cycle of destructive terror with which we associate politics, this appearance demands a negotiation, a rethinking, in which the claims of the "other" are taken every bit as seriously as those who claim the right to sanction by invoking a grand theory.

Bhabha's work suggests that political meanings, even those grounded in grand theories, like the liberal, capitalist, Christian, white, male West, are always fluid though they are rarely depicted as such. It is in the interest of the powerful that these meanings are seen as settled, universal, sacred, and so on, so that when they come into question, the questioning can be portrayed as an attack with the fate of "civilization itself" hanging in the balance. The strategic, political, often contradictory uses to which these meanings are put, however, suggest that they are not, in fact, settled, universal, or sacred. The very use of the language means that all political meaning is subject, therefore, to negotiation. Heretofore, the negotiations have taken place among the powerful in a language shared, if not commonly understood, by the negotiators. In Bhabha's postcolonial context, cultural differences and the theoretical translations of those differences can forge a place for new voices and new languages in these negotiations. Between the "I and the You," Bhabha suggests, the production of meaning now must pass through a Third Space that "constitutes the discursive conditions of enunciation that ensure that the meaning and symbols of culture have no primordial unity or fixity."[18] Assuming the unity or fixity of a cultural reading as once and for all authoritative traps us into a politics of conflict mediated only by power assumed and exercised. Such a politics denies the more sacramental I-Thou relation available only between whole selves. Bhabha's politics of performed identity demands that negotiation on the level of culture, rather than political power exercised as one can, must be the center of political activity and the foundation of contact or conversation.

CARYL PHILLIPS: *THE ATLANTIC SOUND* AND THE COMPLEXITY OF SELF IN NATION

Paul Gilroy, in *The Black Atlantic*, opened a discussion of the Atlantic as both a space of experience and a discourse, and in doing so, works out in concrete form Bhabha's notions of location and concept of the interstices. Movement across the transitive space of the Atlantic shattered location, Gilroy argues, and was a curse in the slave trade. In diaspora, however, someone like Phillips is able to "repossess" movement.[19] The journey he undertakes reconstructs diaspora as an informative location, "as the basis of a privileged standpoint from which certain useful and critical perceptions about the modern world become more likely."[20] Movement that is chosen represents a response to the forced diaspora that characterizes black life. Such movement, Gilroy argues, transgresses the boundaries of nations. Caryl Phillips undertakes such movement in *The Atlantic Sound*. Phillips travels from Guadeloupe, to Liverpool, to Ghana and the slave fort at Elmina, and finally, to Charleston, South Carolina. He follows the trade routes opened by Europeans—routes that, eventually, became the routes of the slave trade, as goods from Liverpool were delivered in Ghana and traded for slaves, who were transported on the second leg of the journey, the Middle Passage, to the Americas, where they were sold for other goods. This commodification of persons points to the doubleness that Du Bois, Bhabha, Gilroy, and Phillips explore, naturally placing one in the interstices, in a space of negotiation between cultures.

To unpack double consciousness, Phillips interweaves his own story with the stories of others who have crossed the "Black Atlantic." How, he asks, did and do people live out this double diasporic identity? How do I? To see what diaspora has meant, Phillips undertakes the reverse Middle Passage willingly and consciously. In general, he does not analyze or explain the complex identities he finds. He simply records what he sees with little commentary. What he shows us is that the Atlantic and the countries involved in the slave trade are in the interstices. The "Black Atlantic" is a space of trade, of transaction, and of transitivity that complicates notions of culture and home, of self and identity. The Atlantic "sound" is multiple; it is polyphonic. First, sound means healthy, whole, correct, and forceful. Phillips asks where such soundness is in diaspora. Second, it also means to "sound out": to measure the depths, intentions, opinions, will, and desires of another—that is, to fathom, which is Phillips's task. Finally, sound is that which is heard, both something made and an effect; it is call and response.

Phillips's work is incredibly rich. We can focus here only on his trip to Ghana and on the stories he tells to parallel his own journey. As his memoir begins, he leaves Liverpool, a center of the slave trade, disillusioned. He parallels his time in Liverpool with that of John Ocansey, who came to Liverpool in 1881 to try to discover why his father, William Ocansey, had not received the ship he ordered from Robert W. Hickson, a Liverpool businessman. Like Ocansey, who wanders the streets of Liverpool and who leaves the city knowing that his family has been cheated but finds no resolution, Phillips explores Liverpool and leaves the city in sad wonder. He writes:

It is disquieting to be in a place where history is so physically present, yet so glaringly absent from people's consciousness. But where is there any different? Maybe this is the modern condition, and Liverpool is merely acting out this reality with an honest vigour. If so, this dissonance between the two states seems to have engendered both a cynical wit and a clinical depression in the souls of Liverpool's citizens.[21]

Double consciousness creates dissonance—cynicism and depression—when lived without examining its sources. Escaping the depression that is both psychic and economic, Phillips travels from Liverpool to Ghana to an event called Panafest: a homecoming for diasporic peoples to West Africa and to the Elmina slave fort. There, in an event advertised as an opportunity to celebrate cultural unity and values of the "family" of black people returning to "Mother Africa," Phillips hopes to find a more conscious evaluation of diaspora.[22]

What he finds is a fascinating combination of persons with a variety of agendas about Africa as a location. His driver, Mohammed Mansour Nassirudeen, is back in Ghana after having been imprisoned in England. Mansour desperately desires diaspora; he wants to leave Ghana for America. With Mansour as his guide, Phillips begins to seek an answer to the question of what we should "do with" the past, and he gets several answers.

First, Mansour introduces Phillips to Dr. Mohammed Ben Abdallah, a Ghanaian politician and writer, who is an organizer of Panafest. His name suggests another layer of postcoloniality, one that predates the slave trade and, in a sense, originates it: the presence of Muslims in Africa. Abdallah believes that Africa should look back to a "useful past." He wants the continent to recover a form of "African democracy" that he believes exists in a pure past. He argues that those who were sold into slavery are not part of this "purity." They were not "good" people and, therefore, got what they deserved.[23] For him, the slave forts that are the location of Panafest's activities are sites of African *history* and, therefore, are worth preserving and restoring, but the *memory* of slavery is a different thing. For Abdallah, memory is the responsibility of black Americans.[24]

Phillips also meets Dr. Robert Lee, an African American dentist named after a Confederate general, who has settled in Ghana. While Abdallah places the responsibility for slavery on black Americans, Lee places it on the Africans. Lee tried to buy Abanze, one of the slave "castles," in order to educate Africans about their "brokenness,"[25] a condition brought about by their participation in the slave trade. Lee is the cynic, contemptuous of both sides, seeing Africans, both in the slave trade and in the present, as exploitative businessmen and those blacks returning to Africa—with the exception of himself—as misguided romantics. Among those returning are a third group Phillips encounters. These are black Jews who understand themselves as "African Hebrew Israelites." They emerge from the "Back to Africa" movements in early-twentieth-century America. Theirs is an imaginative reality that links them to two diasporic peoples. They desire to restore Hebrew practices they believe were once done purely in Africa.

In contrast to these conflicting voices of ideological purity is a lived messiness. At the Western European-style hotel where Phillips stays is an additional assortment of peoples, from Jamaica, the United States, South Africa, and other places. They represent a cacophony of languages, cultural customs, and motivations. Kate, the African desk clerk, struggles, in an amusing and unsettling vignette, with the Jamaican delegation. They are cooking in the rooms, building fires in the middle of the tile floors[26] and using the hotel's decorative landscaping, sweet lemon grass, for seasoning and to make tea. They are also ingesting "certain substances" that the hotel is unhappy about.[27] Kate tells Phillips that they will probably have to leave. Meanwhile, the Americans are present, wearing, of course, the various versions of the official tee shirt.

The Panafest, as sincere as it might be, is a reconstruction of somebody's idea of African identity, from the sacrifice of a ram to the "Thru the Door of No Return" ceremony. It is a semi-disaster, at least for Phillips. Nothing starts on time and nothing is truly African. It is a conglomeration of staged events, souvenir booths, and confusion. What is it for? Phillips decides that the focus of Pan-Africanism has changed. After the slave trade, blacks in diaspora wanted to cultivate a relationship to the motherland for the purposes of location and self-definition that was not based on race and on their identity as "other," but as part of a family, though one with a fractured history, to which one could return, recovering a pure blackness, or, as Phillips writes, "to put it more accurately, they were not white. There was engendered in their souls a romantic yearning to return 'home' to a family and a place where they could be free from the stigma of race. They would be 'home' again, albeit in a strange and forbidding region where the language, climate and culture were now alien to them, but at least they would be 'home.'"[28] The direction, Phillips suggests, has changed

since the days of the nineteenth-century black missionaries and intellectuals and the twentieth-century yearnings of Marcus Garvey and
others. Now, Africans crave a "new unity" with those they originally
sold into slavery. This is partly economic, as a conversation Phillips has
on the plane with Ben, an African businessman, suggests. Ben says:

> "I go to England to do business, maybe three times a year. That is all England
> is good for these days. Make some money and leave. They don't want to know
> us anymore."
>
> "Any more?"
>
> "Since independence. We have to survive by ourselves."
>
> "But isn't that the purpose of independence?" Ben seems momentarily
> offended, so I press on. "Britain's primary relationship is now with Europe.
> That's just how it goes."
>
> "But what about us?" Ben twists around in his seat to face me. "You
> think it's fine to just forget us? . . . . You think it's fine to forget the
> Commonwealth?"[29]

The conversation with Ben adds another layer to the complexity of
the interdependence created in the colonial situation and denied in
the postcolonial one. As Europe pulls away from the "Africa" it politically and ideologically constructs, the borders it makes and enforces
for economic gain, "Africa," which never existed, must redefine and
relocate itself in the international world as this false unity. The interaction with the Americas and Americans, who have lost tribal specificity
but desire the identity connection, is part of this repositioning.

If the old structures that drove the original slave trade—those of
capitalism, religion, and territory—drive the new relationships, where
is "authentic" identity to be found? Phillips, within each of his chapters, records the life of a particular person, a fellow pilgrim. At each of
the sites of encounter—Liverpool, Elmina, and Charleston—Phillips
explores a life lived there. We have already mentioned John Ocansey,
in Liverpool to help his father. In a similar way, Phillips narrates the
story of Philip Quaque (an anglicized version of Kweku, a Fante
name), an African priest who "worked and resided on the coast [and
who] occasionally took temporary command of the lesser forts of
Dixcove, Sekondi, and Komenda."[30]

Quaque, identified as an African prodigy, was educated in England,
married an English woman, and became a missionary to his own
people. He "joined the staff of an active slave fort, and he was
allotted accommodation by the Governor."[31] In what Phillips calls
"the remarkable twilight world of interdependence and fusion that
characterized the relationship between the native and the European

in this period before the concrete formality and racial separation of the colonial period,"[32] Reverend Quaque was to minister to the spiritual needs of the British slavers in the slave fort. This was a difficult job; they were not interested. Neither was the indigenous population. Quaque, then, started a school in an upstairs room in the slave fort where he taught both academic subjects and religion. He seems, Phillips tells us, remarkably unconcerned about what was happening below him, in the slave trade. In none of his letters does he mention his African brothers and sisters held below; he is interested in doing his job effectively. When, Phillips asks, did he make this shift in identity from Kweku to Quaque? Does that shift suggest his becoming a "hollow man," like the officials in Conrad's *Heart of Darkness*? Whenever the shift was and however it played out, Phillips seems to see Quaque as more whole than hollow and to respect Quaque, for reasons we will explore in a moment. He takes care, as he leaves Panafest, "to step over, and not on, the tomb of Philip Quaque."[33]

In Charleston, the slave port where about a third of all slaves that came to America entered at Sullivan's Island, Phillips visits another grave and gives us another story. It is the story of Judge J. Waties Waring, who accepted exile from his social group—the elite Charleston SOBs who reside "south of Broad Street"[34]—to uphold the rights of African Americans in South Carolina. Phillips points out that Waring's work set the groundwork for Thurgood Marshall's argument in *Brown v. Board of Education*. For this, Waring earned the eternal hatred of his class—those Phillips interviews simultaneously admire and despise him—and permanent exile. He finally left Charleston, for it "was simply too burdensome to be among those who openly hated you in a place you called 'home.' "[35] Phillips visits Waring's and his wife's graves, on the edges of Charleston's Magnolia Cemetery. "The whole scene," he concludes, "is elegant in its simplicity and heartbreaking in its loneliness."[36] After leaving the cemetery, he thinks about Waring as he attends an African/African American festival in Charleston and speculates, given Waring's life, on what home might mean in this modern world:

The rhythms of Africa floating over Charleston...Somewhere in the distance...Sullivan's Island. And before Sullivan's Island? Africa. And the vessel's European point of departure? Its home port? Its home? White men and women dancing to the rhythms of Africa in the street behind the United States Custom House. Magnolia cemetery on a bright moonlit night, some distance to the north. Home. African drums...Ghosts walking the streets of Charleston. Ghosts dancing in the streets of Charleston.[37]

Stable and "pure" locations, like home or Africa, seem far in the past and irretrievable. The meaning is in the mixture and in those who live in it with integrity. In all the confusion, what stands out are these three lives: Ocansey, Quaque, and Waring. Theirs are located lives lived transitively in Bhabha's interstices. Each lived within his location but changed it as well, in small and large ways. These three represent the three domains of interaction in the colonial nation/space: economics, religion, and law. As Bhabha suggests, these are constitutive of the nation, but change on the level of culture as the individual moves in transitive modes. The actions and experiences of Ocansey, Quaque, and Waring—and by extension, Phillips—leave them both most located and most alienated. Theirs are the lonely and complicated lives of men just doing their jobs, facing the facts of diaspora alone and in the best ways they can. They search for a moral and ethical place to stand. As such, their lives are, if not authentic, at least real.

There is, therefore, nothing to say, only a way to be. Phillips, in the end of his memoir, chooses the silence of the complication. He ends in the desert, with the Black Jews. Urged to look at the beautiful landscape during a cultural performance that includes double-dutch jump rope, Marvin Gaye, and majorettes, Phillips thinks of cultural baggage that cannot be tucked neatly beneath the seat in front of you.[38] Given that we all carry that baggage, what is the "Atlantic sound" and how do we know and make it? It is unfathomable. It means to accept that we are not sound. It is to be silent in the face of, living with the facts of diaspora, to hear, first, rather than to make sound. It is to live, as well and happily as one can, on the ragged, jagged edge of experience, and with memory:

I say nothing. There is nothing I can say. You were transported in a wooden vessel across a broad expanse of water to a place which rendered your tongue silent. Look. Listen. Learn. And as you began to speak, you remembered fragments of a former life. Shards of memory. Careful. Some will draw blood. You dressed your memory in the new words of this country. Remember. There were no round-trip tickets in your part of the ship. Exodus. It is futile to walk into the face of history. As futile as trying to keep the dust from one's eyes in the desert.[39]

CULTURE ON THE BORDERS

What we have tried to demonstrate here is that identity "in-between," in the interstices, is a function of making analogies: it is transitive.

As we see, Phillips thinks of his trips alongside, even intersecting with, the trips of Ocansey and others. The "others" he researches and encounters do not remain "other"; they become mirrors for and dimensions of his own self. This can function in both positive and negative ways. What Phillips encounters at Panafest is the negative. Those at Panafest are thinking, for black Americans, for example: I am black; therefore, I am African. This, we see, is not true, yet such an experience is not a wasted one.

Finding and seeking experiential commonality only to realize that you are not what you thought you were or that the experience is not what you thought it was can be formative of self. The danger is, as the Panafest illustrates, positing no difference: the "other" is the self. The Jamaicans, while originally African, are thoroughly Jamaican and the African Americans more American than African. The "other" cannot be kept, however, utterly distant from the self. Oneself is "as" another, though it is not the "other." Jamaicans and African Americans do, in one sense, share "Africanness," though not purely.

To move away from an idea of purity to the creole or the hybrid can lead to discoveries that reinforce an appreciation and acceptance of one's original location by adding depth to the understanding of it. There is value in knowing you are not what you claim, as much as knowing what you are. This returns us to Bhabha's performance of politics. We *should and do* seek these analogies as a process of self-definition; we play ourselves off against other human beings, places, and things and learn from and about them. This seeking and learning are our obligations as members of community and as human beings. They also widen our notions of what community and humanity are.

Performance, which is necessarily transitive, is, therefore, about recognition: about seeing the self clearly and coming to see the other clearly in the doing, in living. We have to recognize what we think we are in order to seek it, and we learn from seeking it and either finding or not finding it. Through this process, the way we see our identities becomes more lucid. We put the fixed self at risk, open it to new experiences of identity, and refashion the self.

Culture, therefore, is a creation, a sound made by polyphonic voices. The sense, at first, seems to be that the less consciously constructed, the better; the more culture is allowed to develop on its own, the better. Culture, however, should not be seen as something that happens to us. The self and/in its search for identity is the engine that drives culture.

Terror results when "stuff" is asserted as all there is: when we commodify self and "other." We are most willing to accept creolization in play: in carnival, like Mardi Gras; in music; and in food; we then want the "sign" of our participation in otherness: the tee shirt. Commodification gives us an excuse to stop searching, to allow ourselves to be named and then silenced.

We have tried to deconstruct name and silence, to add dimension to diaspora. In the twenty-first century, as Bhabha and Phillips show us, the categories of oppressor/oppressed are complicated and, perhaps, empty. To end where we began, identity politics misses its mark: it tries to keep these binaries in perpetual tension and to concretize what is not concrete. Waring, for example, shows us this is not the case. He abandons his privileged position as oppressor to do something larger than himself for community.

This is not to say, however, that great wrongs have not been done. They have. Phillips's silence as sound does not mean that the pain is gone. What we need, however, are new ways to deal with that pain.

Diaspora comes to us as a "bad thing imposed on others." Diaspora has been, however, a fact of human existence since there have been human beings: we are transitive beings who move, by choice and by force. Diaspora is, finally, another form of journey. We focus, as theorists and experiencing persons, on the dispersion; what Phillips and Bhabha show us is the meaning of the journey itself. In diaspora, whether this is good or bad, we are forced to construct selves and empower ourselves. The double identity of diaspora can mean, positively, a range of choices about ideological and actual movement represented in the telling of the story. Perhaps the lives Phillips shows us, then, are the statement of what culture might be, or has been in the interstices. Diaspora touches all, and creates a web of related stories, rather than a hierarchy of being. Phillips positions his story beside, and in relation to other stories, and that, perhaps, demonstrates, and performs, a new meaning of nation, community, and identity: that I cannot think and tell my story without thinking and telling yours.[40]

CHAPTER 2

GOING HOME IN THE WORK
OF CHARLES H. LONG
AND ASHIS NANDY

In *Culture and Imperialism*, Edward Said argues that, in looking at our overlapping histories, we need an alternative to the politics of blame and to the "even more destructive politics of confrontation." He writes:

A more interesting type of secular interpretation can emerge, altogether more rewarding than the denunciation of the past, the expressions of regret for its having ended, or—even more wasteful because violent and far too easy and attractive—the hostility between Western and non-Western cultures that leads to crisis. This world is too small and interdependent to let these passively happen.[1]

Like Said, Ashis Nandy, an Indian politician and psychologist, and Charles H. Long, an African American historian of religions, seek a response to the postcolonial dilemma, one that avoids anger, denunciation, nostalgia, and passivity. Nandy in *The Intimate Enemy: Loss and Recovery of Self Under Colonialism* and Long in the essays in *Significations: Signs, Symbols, and Images in the Interpretation of Religion* examine how the cultures of oppressor and oppressed intersect, often unconsciously cooperate, and repel each other.[2] Mary Louise Pratt calls such a space "the contact zone."[3] How does one construct new notions of freedom in a creolized space? Long, in "Freedom, Otherness, and Religion: Theologies Opaque," writes: "If this freedom is not to be simply the sentimental imitation of the lordship-bondage structure with a new set of actors, it would have to be a new form of freedom."⁴ In this chapter, we want to examine the possible forms that might emerge in an improvisational discourse on freedom. We will begin with Nandy, looking at the space in which "intimate" becomes "enemy." Next, we will suggest that intimacy might be not only a source or location of our problems in modern culture, but the answer to that problem. Indeed, rethinking intimacy might help us to articulate a notion of culture that could acknowledge the existence and interdependence of a multiplicity of selves and that could help us to create structures in which such free and mutual selves could interact. We call this structure, in line with much postmodern thinking, "home," recognizing all the problems that homes contain.

James Baldwin, in an essay on Martin Luther King, Jr., analyzed the silence that he encountered on an integrated bus not long after the Montgomery boycott ended:

This silence made me think of nothing so much as the silence which fol-lows a really serious lovers' quarrel: the whites, beneath their cold hostility, were mystified and deeply hurt. They had been betrayed by the Negroes, and not merely because the Negroes had declined to remain their "place," but because the Negroes had refused to be controlled by the town's image of them. And without this image, it seemed to me, the whites were abruptly and totally lost. The very foundations of their private and public worlds were being destroyed.⁵

The hegemonic construction of the American world—how it worked and what it meant—changed with the Montgomery Bus Boycott. Baldwin's insight expresses the very notion of Nandy's "intimate enemy." Social stability in colonial and postcolonial structures depends on cultural configurations and cultural arrangements that are often unacknowledged and that take for granted a silent and marginal presence—usually ethnic and female—to operate. When only the "majority" culture can authorize changes in the cultural arrangement, there is what Nandy calls a certain "style" for engaging dissent. The "majority" can insist that the "minority" remain silent and invisible, or, even more terribly, that the marginal presence can speak only in the voice and in/on the terms that the dominating culture dictates. The "majority" in this situation controls, as Nandy puts it, both the stereotypes it creates and, as it appropriates the language of defiance of the oppressed,⁶ the style of dissent. If, as Marx argued, control of the ideology means control of the world, then, we argue, interrogating, challenging, changing, and sometimes destroying language become a path to freedom.

Nandy, using Hegel, illustrates the sources of the kind of stalemate in which the intimate becomes enemy. He presents us, in *The Intimate Enemy*, with the Hegelian reflexive structure on which colonialism and, indeed, Western thought depend. Nandy, then, breaks out of that binary by arguing that colonialism is a shared culture, an imposed structure that meets with an "indigenous process released by external forces."[7] The Hegelian master-slave binary describes a world in which the self not only *confronts* the "other," but, in the attempt to establish the self as self, *creates* the other as well. In the West, the binary seems to be inescapable, except through nihilism or by falling into despair, both of which seem to us to be the end of some badly done poststructural thought. In the most extreme expression of the binary, we remain, forever, in the victim/victimizer world in which power, as Kojeve puts it in his *Introduction to the Reading of Hegel*, is self-creation through the "conscious negating Action" that makes one the master and that gives one the power to oppress the other, the slave.[8]

Hegel and Nandy shift the thesis (master) and its antithesis (slave) and, thereby, raise questions of what is margin and what is center—albeit in different ways. Hegel deposits meaning with the marginalized through work. The master loses his meaning as he or she loses the means of production and as the master refuses to confront the central meaning of his or her own existence: that the leisure and sustenance of the master is totally dependent on the slave as both producer and, ultimately, reproducing product. At Thomas Jefferson's Monticello, for example, there is a device in the dining room that, to us, symbolizes this denial. There is a revolving door, with shelves, that allowed food to be sent into the dining room without any slaves either being present or—more important—seen. This technology of camouflage, this strategy of innocence, is the essence of civilization caught in the Hegelian binary: so much can be hidden. This masking of truth allows an illusion of what Nandy calls homogeneity,[9] the sense that one, in fact, can fulfill the desire to rid oneself of the other on whom one is dependent. This is the master's illusion of freedom. As Long reminds us, however, concealment of the truth robs the master of access to his or her inner primordial existence.[10]

The slave, Hegel argues, has more freedom than the master because the slave can control and understand the methods of production, even if he or she cannot own those means or their final products. In that control, the slave has the capacity to change himself, whereas the master changes only through the slave. Therefore, the historical process, the process of becoming human, is the product of the working slave and not of the possessing master.[11] What Hegel does is to locate

freedom and consciousness in materiality. Yet central in Hegel's difficult thought is that the slave is still subject to violence. Hegel justifies
this violence by positing a teleology of the spirit that, while it flips
the power within the binary, still accepts violence and barbarity as the
means to establish meaning. Violence is justifiable, if the end is good.
This is in direct tension with, for example, Aeschylus, who, in the
Oresteia, makes a critique of such a stance. Though all try to convince
themselves that the end justifies the means, there are reminders in
the text that human beings must observe limits, as Clytaemestra prays
in the *Agamemnon*: "Let not their passion overwhelm them; let no
lust/seize on these men to violate what they must not."[12] One must
not violate "tender things," like women and children, custom, and
sacred places. The chorus reiterates this, saying that humans must not,
"[trample] down the delicacy of things/inviolable."[13] Agamemnon,
though insincere, knows that he should not be revered as a god: "I tell
you, as a man, not god, to reverence me./Discordant is the murmur
at such treading down/of lovely things."[14] Such a stance is also in
tension with most moral philosophy, for example, Catholic moral philosophy, which argues that a good end cannot justify bad means.[15] For
Hegel, there can be no liberation without a fight, without war. War
gives rise to the best in humans, as one of two rights gives way in conflict. Freedom achieved without conflict is, for Hegel, metaphysically
impossible.

We see the acceptance of Hegelian violence and its undoing in
Frederick Douglass's slave narrative, *Narrative of the Life of Frederick
Douglass, An American Slave* (1845).[16] In his fight with the slave
breaker Covey, Douglass fights him almost two hours, and only
Douglass draws blood. This battle is the turning point, psychologi-
cally and actually, in Douglass's sense of self and freedom. He casts
the moment in terms of resurrection:

I felt as I had never felt before. It was a glorious resurrection, from the tomb
of slavery, to the heaven of freedom. My long-crushed spirit rose; cowardice
departed, bold defiance took its place; and now I resolved that, however long
I might remain a slave in form, the day had passed when I could be a slave in
fact.[17]

In this Hegelian struggle, done in body and confirmed in spirit, the
slave ceases to be a slave when he will fight, when he ceases to fear
death. The moment is so important that Douglass returns to it in
great detail in his second autobiography, *My Bondage and My Freedom*, written in 1855. In that volume, the fight gets more complex.

Douglass adds dialogue. He tells Covey that he had been "treated by him like a *brute* . . . and that [he] should stand it *no longer*."[18] When Douglass wins the struggle, he declares, "I was *nothing* before; I WAS A MAN NOW."[19]

What comes after in the 1845 *Narrative* undercuts, however, the Hegelian moment. Douglass's manhood cannot make him master; he does not lead a rebellion, for example. He uses his internalized freedom for other purposes. He moves more forcefully into his community. For example, he teaches other slaves to read. He writes that a spirit moves through the people, and that this engagement in the community is "sweet."[20] He finds nobility, courage, and love, as he moves out of individual isolation and into communal cooperation. Doing so, he disrupts the definition that the master narrative has given him for himself. In teaching others to read, and in writing himself, he undoes the notion of slaves as less than human. As Henry Louis Gates and Charles Davis remind us in *The Slave's Narrative*, writing is the sign of reason, which marks Enlightenment equality.[21] Since the slave was understood to be without his own writing—that is to say, without a Hegelian collective cultural memory—he was understood to be without identity, unworthy of and incapable of freedom.[22]

Without writing, there could exist no repeatable sign of the workings of reason, of mind; without memory or mind, there could exist no history; without history, there could exist no "humanity," as was defined consistently from Vico to Hegel.[23]

Douglass's physical mastery leads to a cultural mastery: he takes himself out of the realm of nature or the company of children into adult selfhood and community—and takes others with him.

Here, with the uses of violence, Nandy breaks with Hegel and stands with Douglass. Nandy agrees, on one level, with Hegel's location of the transformative consciousness. He writes that we must "choose the slave" because he represents "a higher-order cognition which perforce includes the master as human, whereas the master's cognition has to exclude the slave except as a 'thing.' "[24] He sees, however, what Hegel and Hegel's master construct fail to understand: that no exchange—or conversion, as Jerry Bentley in *Old World Encounters* calls it, suggesting chemical process, monetary exchange, and religious conversion as models—is complete. Whether conversion takes place voluntarily, through pressure, or through assimilation,[25] there is always something left over, a remainder, an excess in which otherness is revealed: the otherness of both master and slave. That excess calls us beyond established structures to change and challenge discourse and structure, and into community.

Nandy offers a subtle reading of Hegel and opens a door to considerations of other paths for freedom, even paths that include the oppressor. If we do not read the master/slave as a static binary but as a reciprocal relationship, new things emerge. This doubling rather than devouring is what Nandy and Long work with in Hegel's thought. Colonial structures, Long has argued, are not as simple as "bad old oppressors" and "virtuous oppressed victims." The creolized forms that become authorized dimensions of culture are hybrids—or more— which emerge from a process of relationality between two defined cultures and self-defining consciousnesses. This is what Albert Murray discusses with white intellectuals as he travels *South to a Very Old Place*—the common, or as he calls it "mulatto," culture that the South is. Robert Penn Warren puts it best:

The wrongs of slavery are beyond words, simply beyond words. No question about that, and there is no way that any of it can be excused.... But another thing to remember, and now this you always have to remember. Always. And of course this is the horror of it too: that it was also a human thing, institution—not to say humane—a system made up of human beings, and in such a system—any system—where what is involved is human beings, every possible, every imaginable, every imaginable combination of human social relationship is likely to exist. And did exist.[26]

The first thing to face, as Warren's comment suggests, is that all are involved and implicated: all have been part of the structure, acting within it in both authorized and unauthorized ways. There are no innocent people here. The enemy, bound to us in every imaginable combination of relationship, is our intimate partner. In a structure in which we have been implicated, if not cooperative, whether consciously or not, in which self-definition goes on under even the most extreme circumstances, how do we break the victim-victimizer cycle? As we will see, Nandy's answer is symbolized in Gandhi, who transformed memory and myth, religious forms, into a counter-political force to undo an empire.

We are not arguing that systems cannot perpetuate real terror, inducing trauma that is difficult, if impossible, to overcome. This, too, is part of the issue in language and structure. Jenny Edkins in *Trauma and the Memory of Politics* reminds us that, in situations that produce trauma, we are facing situations beyond language and normal, linear political time. As trauma disrupts linearity, the event does not fit the authorized story. It cannot be symbolized.[27] Trauma, Edkins argues, reveals intimacy: it reflects a particular form of intimate bond between personhood and community. When that bond is violated, it makes transparent the workings of power.[28] Thus, trauma is revelation; it reveals the power of language as well as structure. What we can say about the traumatic event does not make sense in the ordinary language of the culture; the order has betrayed the sufferer and he or she cannot speak.[29] What we want to say is the language of the culture may not be able to articulate. The question is how to have "fidelity to the ontological crack in the universe."[30]

Edkins sees in memorials a mode of representation, beyond words, that lets the traumatized speak, albeit in a culturally authorized way. Nandy, however, believes that there is a counter-strain, which postmodern thinkers will call "counter-memory" that always already speaks. Nandy argues that in every culture there exists "the marginalized reflective strain that must underlie—or, to protect one's own sanity and humanity, must be presumed to underlie—every culture that goes rabid."[31] This strain challenges structure and the false homogeneity that colonialism, for example, tries to assert. In deconstructing hegemony and homogeneity, this counter-force generates new forms. Nandy, in his discussion of Gandhi, calls such forms "androgynous." These androgynous forms signal a reconstitution that allows for, at least, survival and, at best, the ability to transform social situations. These forms have all the characteristics, Nandy argues, of what he calls the "liminal Hindu."[32] We will return to this designation at the end of the chapter.

What might these androgynous forms look like and do? Modernist and postmodern theorists and artists have suggested a number of metaphors for such a mode of being.

Edward Said describes a self that is multiple, a self that can live with cultural ambiguity and with ambiguity in the self. In an interview called "Criticism, Culture, and Performance," Said argued that this is a form of self that does not claim a single identity. Instead, it recognizes that we all perform "multiple identity, the polyphony of many voices playing off against each other, without . . . the need to reconcile them, just to hold them together."[33] In the postcolonial world, we experience "[m]ore than one culture, more than one awareness, both in its positive and negative modes."[34] How can identity hold irreconcilable opposites together?

Albert Murray, in *The Hero and the Blues* and other works, like *The Blue Devils of Nada*, points to improvisation as a mode of identity. Murray, who admires artists like Ralph Ellison, Romare Bearden, and Ernest Hemingway, sees in the artistic endeavor a mode of living.

Ellison, Bearden, and Hemingway demonstrate a mastery of an art. Such mastery, Murray suggests, can translate into life. He argues that one can develop a mode of identity that, given that one knows well the instrument of self, "enables [one] to extemporize under pressure and in the most complicated circumstances" and is, therefore, the ultimate skill.[35]

Through improvisation, W. E. B. Du Bois's structure of the double consciousness can become, as Nandy puts it, "a controlled inner schism" that becomes a source of "robust realism."[36] The double consciousness, instead of being only a sign of inner division and a source of pain, is also self-protective. It shields that self that the other did not create. As Richard Hardack puts it in his discussion of double consciousness in Toni Morrison's *Jazz*, Morrison "uses fragmentation to resituate the improvisational against the inevitable. She reenvisions the use of...fragmentation to transcend fragmentation, and double consciousness to undo double consciousness."[37] This mode of reconstituting the self, if successfully accomplished, becomes a way of engaging the historical and political realities of oppression. Such a mode of individual identity is located, yet transitive. As such it is capable of negotiating multiple tasks, of managing and creating a world. That capacity insures survival and that is, for Nandy, Long, Morrison, Murray, and Said the essential issue.

Violence, as Nandy suggests, may crown an immediate victor, but "perhaps, freedom is survival: adapting, staying on the stage, appearing dead in somebody's eyes, so as to be alive for one's own self."[38] This "passive power" is, Long writes, the "power to be, to understand, to know even in the worst historical circumstances, and it may often reveal a clearer insight into significant meaning of the human venture than the power possessed by the oppressor."[39] To the "majority" culture, this might look like "Toming," clowning, or standing silent and, therefore, cooperative, in the face of oppression. But this public self gives the private self the space in which it can, as Ralph Ellison put it, "change the joke and slip the yoke."[40]

Such a self opens up relationality on different levels. Nandy uses Gandhi as his example. Nonviolent resistance is the self that stays on the stage and adapts. That self may appear or become dead, but such staying power transforms, as we have seen, by confounding. It challenges and changes discourse and structure. Thus, the oppressed, perhaps through Gandhi's method of *satyagraha*, which is Martin Luther King's method of nonviolent resistance, beats the oppressor at his own game simply by revealing and reflecting back who he or she is. To be sure, such methods forge a model of autonomy that accepts suffering. Such a method is scary, because it risks all, even death, as do those who resist nonviolently. Charles Long calls this the freedom to undergo willingly what we have been forced to undergo in the past.[41] The courageous human being willingly suffering is a challenge to the oppressor who creates that suffering, making him or her "crawl back through history."[42] In that autonomous suffering, the master/slave dichotomy is broken. The master sees that he or she is the slave; the self becomes "other" and "self" at once, forcing the oppressor into a kind of double consciousness. The terms of the war model, which Hegel could not escape—winner/loser—may dissolve along with the question of the possession of virtue—who is "good" and who is "bad"? In this deconstructive encounter, reconstruction becomes possible.

The hermeneutical time/space, the interstices, as we saw Homi Bhabha call it in our first chapter, between self and other, master and slave, and so on, therefore, potentially becomes a transitive space. That is, it creates a moment, a fold, an opening to the border in which improvisation, transformation, and even meaningful, reflective silence can emerge. This space may be one of silence. Such silence, Long writes, "is radically ironic...[It] forces us to realize that our words, the unities of our naming and recognition in the world presuppose a reality which is prior to our naming and doing."[43] Silence is a "fundamentally ontological position...which though involved in language and speech exposes us to a new kind of reality and experience."[44]

Reality and experience force us into a new relationship with self and other, history and memory. Identity is not formed, therefore, in the simple recovery of the past, but in the way in which we position ourselves in relation to that past and rename ourselves and our realities. This renaming becomes layered, opaque, complex. Storytelling, memory, is one modality of this renaming. Nandy confirms the importance of storytelling and myth-making. Myths, he tells us, contain history while being open to invention. They widen human choices and allow us to "remember in an anticipatory fashion."[45] They let us, he argues, remake the past.[46] Community, myth, and individual story are the "other language" that incorporate the West and remain outside it at once. Story can make what Said calls a "contrapuntal" reading of history and of the master narrative, undercutting and extending their meaning. Myth and story can contain opposites without having to reconcile them. What Robert Detweiler calls the "erotic" power of narrative is its capacity to form relationships—communities—between nonrelated selves.[47] What kind of communities?

To attempt an answer, let us turn back to the "intimate other/enemy." Toni Morrison's phrase "intimate things 'in place' " lets us think about communal and individual space. In an interview with Robert Stepto, Morrison talks about the meaning of place to her in her novel *Sula*. She says that place for her is detail:

I think some of it is just a woman's strong sense of being in a room, a place, or in a house. Sometimes my relationship to things in a house would be a little different from, say, my brother's or my father's or my sons'. I ... do very intimate things "in place": I am sort of rooted in it, so that writing about being in a room looking out or being in a world looking out, or living in a small definite place is probably very common among most women anyway.[48]

Morrison indicates two meanings of her phrase: that women do intimate things in a located space and that, in located space, they put intimate things "in place," where they belong. Morrison uses the example of black women who, moving across the boundaries of intimate spaces—homemaking and housekeeping, in both their own and white women's homes—have dealt most directly with the excess, with what is left over in exchanges between and conversions in cultures. Morrison believes that in this movement, and the concomitant responsibility for putting things in place, is freedom and a model for living. Yet, simultaneously, black women have not been able to avoid locating meaning in particular people, places, and things, even when that meaning is terrible. This is what Morrison does in the novel, in her storytelling: she offers us knowledge that has been called local and particular. It is knowledge that has been disparaged, appropriated, and, most of all, misunderstood but that has continued to speak, even in trauma. She sees this discredited knowledge as not just local, but universally useful, revealing the extraordinary in the ordinary. And, in telling stories, she suggests places we might locate ourselves imaginatively so that we can relocate ourselves humanly.

This transitive location does not defeat the master narrative of the West; instead, it acknowledges the West within us all and, as Nandy puts it, "domesticates" it.[49] This location does not deny history; instead, it affirms myth in history and, thereby, orders history in a new way. This location does not deny suffering and trauma; it embraces suffering and reminds trauma of old languages that might give it voice. This location does not rule; it hides, remains private until it can speak. It is home—or as bell hooks more accurately calls it, "homeplace," stressing particularity as well as function. hooks hopes for homeplace to be a safe, revitalized community of human persons in mutual interactions. Homeplace is not homogeneous; at homeplace, voice is born, as Charles Hartmann puts it in *Jazz Text*, "from a matrix of voices."[50] Such voice is, he argues, "authorial but not exactly authoritative"; it is an activity or space in which voice's function depends on others,[51] as in the jazz band. The community, like the jazz band, is an extension of voice that "emphasizes the possibility of the multiplicity of voice."[52] Homeplace is multiple. There, we accept differences, negotiate conflicts, and, most important, love one another.

This is not easy. Home is always the site of our first wounds, our first understandings of the self as separate from the other. What hooks and others recognize is that, though we bring all those traumas with us, all of us are transitive; none of us is in our original home—hence, "homeplace" and not "home."[53] We find ourselves, as postmodern and postcolonial people, in multiple communities of affiliation, some permanent and some temporary. This leads us back to Nandy's notion of the liminal Hindu.

Hindu, Nandy reminds us, is a made-up term. It "was first used by the Muslims to describe all Indians who were not converted to Islam. Only in recent time have the Hindus begun to describe themselves as Hindus."[54] Reading this, one can contemplate the power of renaming, and of, as Charles Long reminded us, willingly embracing what we have been forced to undergo, and in that acceptance, signifying and finding power. For Nandy, accepting the definition of "Hindu" opens up a past of multiple resources, such as the ones Gandhi used. One can see Hindu as Hebrew as black as Palestinian as Indian; all these peoples are named by others, and are remnants, left-overs, and survivors, whose experiences tell, despite their apparent fragmentation, a whole story. They are, as June Jordan puts it, "a surging latticework inside the merciless detritus of diaspora."[55]

Diaspora has generated the need for a new covenant, a renewed consensual association of previously unrelated persons who share an experience of suffering and survival, articulated in a variety of stories, and who take responsibility for each other's stories in community. Toni Morrison ends her monumental novel *Beloved* with the image of putting stories side-by-side to become a "friend" of the other's mind. In this image, homeplace is the space in which conversation is shared, in which confession is made, in which the witness testifies and is acknowledged. Homeplace recognizes that we have suffered, yes, but also that, as voices as separate in time as St. Paul and Maya Angelou remind us, we have also been paid for and now we are free to be, to love.

Perhaps it is time, as June Jordan tells us in "Moving Towards Home," to accept the transitive, and be on the way. This poem is one that is transitive itself, having been taken up by many in the Middle East to express their situation. Jordan writes:

> I intend to speak about home...
> I intend to speak about living room
> Where the talk will take place in my language
> . . .
> ...against the relentless laughter of evil
> there is less and less living room...
> It is time to make our way home.[56]

CHAPTER 3

THE POLITICS OF STATELESSNESS:
EDWARD SAID AND THE
AMBIGUITIES OF LIBERAL
NATIONALISM

We have a common self-consciousness of not the most, but one of the most interesting twentieth century experiences of dispossession, exile, migration.... That's where I feel I have tried to place my emphasis. To speak our case, when we suffer and go through all the terrors of exile and dispossession and the absence of rights. People write to me and say, look, I don't have a passport. If you live on the West Bank, it says on the passport "Identity unconfirmed or indeterminate." If you have a refugee's piece of paper in Lebanon, it says, "Nationality: Stateless." The name [Palestinian] is never mentioned. When you look and see Palestinians, as I do all the time, it's very difficult to say that this is just metaphorical, because it's terrible, it's lived.

—Edward Said[1]

Statelessness is a political form of transitivity, one that usually involves violence and displacement. The state is a different structure from community or the *polis* that we have explored previously. The state, as Arjun Appadurai shows us in *Fear of Small Numbers: A Geography of Anger*, is an overarching or meta-system.[2] It involves order, norms, protocols, legislation, territory, and symbols (like flags). Appadurai writes that the state sees itself as complete. He calls this system "vertebrate" to contrast it with the "cellular" systems of, for example, terrorist groups.[3] The "fantasy" of the nation-state is its trust in its systemic wholeness: it trusts that it is sovereign and complete.[4]

The "War on Terror" and the Israeli-Palestinian conflict are two manifestations of what Appadurai calls the "cellular." The cellular, in contrast to the nation-state's "vertebrate" structure, is "laboratory," mobile, and denationalized.[5] Al-Qaeda, for example, exploits the advantages of the cellular in which information, people, technology, and money move across fractal boundaries.[6] While the Palestinians have been forced to partake of this cellular level, they desire the vertebrate. As such, they illustrate the doubleness involved in the modern difficulty of negotiating statelessness. To try to make one's way in a global politics conducted by nation-states without a nation-state to call one's own is, in the words of John Dunn, "a profound misfortune."[7] This chapter will address the issue of Palestinian transitivity by situating the postcolonial critique of nationalism, specifically as it is found in the political thought of Edward Said, within the discourse of liberal nationalism, especially that found in the work of Yael Tamir. In doing so, we will explore the tension between identity, particularly communal identity, and statehood.

In terms of contemporary political discourse, the stateless are radically "other," the "small numbers" Appadurai writes about: unknown and unknowable. They are, therefore, both endangered and seen as dangerous for at least three different reasons. First, the stateless lack the standing to negotiate on "even" or "fair" or "just" terms. Second, the stateless lack the resources to make and defend their claims via traditional means (i.e., discursive, economic, military, etc.). Third, and in consequence, the stateless necessarily resort to nontraditional means of resistance, of self-defense, of provocation, thereby adding to the perception that they are, in fact, radically other. These modes of resistance, these demands for recognition, serve to unmask the nation-state itself, revealing the transitive character of that which is otherwise assumed to be static, thereby mobilizing anxieties of incompleteness.[8] They generate a fear that the "real world game" of nations has escaped the net of state sovereignty and international diplomacy.[9] In response, the "international community" of nation-states marks the stateless as outside and places the burden upon them to prove they are worthy of a state with the accompanying recognition and protections.[10] Yet the fluid condition of the stateless (i.e., the inability to provide for material needs or security, at least without interference) makes the kind of internal stability and coherence necessary for entrance into the family of nations a near impossibility. The circle is vicious, apparently unbreakable, and, as we have seen, increasingly dangerous.

We argue that, in terms of global politics, the "profound misfortune" of statelessness is a collective and overtly political form of homelessness. In his essay on "Homelessness and the Issue of Freedom," Jeremy Waldron argues that what characterizes the condition of the homeless is the lack of a space in which to be human.[11] Waldron contends that the Western commitment to property as an essential element of personhood finds its reflection in the legal structures of our communities. What property gives to those who possess it is a space in and from which to meet basic human needs (eating, sleeping, disposing of body waste, some physical autonomy, and security). To be homeless is to be without real property, and, therefore, without the space that is utterly required to be human. To be homeless is also to be without voice or positive legal identity, without legal or social protection. It is to be at the mercy of all others and, as Waldron argues, to have to keep moving so as not to run afoul of "rules that provide freedom and prosperity for some by imposing restrictions on others."[12]

Waldron's concern is the condition of homeless individuals, but there is a useful, if imperfect, analogy between the condition of the homeless and the plight of the stateless. For seven decades, Palestinians have been without a place, at least an even nominally secure one, in which to be Palestinian. Generations of Palestinians live in exile around the world with no hope of returning to their ancestral lands. Still more Palestinians, also to be counted in generations, have lived in refugee camps around the Middle East, where they have been neither safe nor welcome.[13] Even contemporary Gaza—where newly built luxury hotels are often touted as manifestations of great change for the better—is bordered by a "security barrier" that Palestinians are not free to move beyond without being harassed by Israeli security.[14] In addition, the ongoing blockade of Gaza (of building materials, some foodstuffs, etc.), violently enforced by the Israeli government, and the Israeli invasion and bombing of Gaza ("Operation Cast Lead") in late 2008 demonstrate the lack of security for ordinary Palestinians that is otherwise an expectation under international law and stated norms.[15] This vulnerability stems from many things, including a lack of what lawyers like to call "standing."

Like Waldron's homeless individual, dispossessed communities like the Palestinians are required to prove that they *exist* before they are worthy of legal recognition and protection. Yael Tamir writes of the stateless that "the pre-state fear that inspires national movements to strive for states of their own is one of having no voice, no status, of standing defenseless, dependent on the protection offered by others."[16] Said argued that Palestine/Israel was a hybrid form of imperialism/colonialism, and the circumstance of the Palestinians certainly suggests that, despite the nominal end of colonialism, a community's proving worthy of recognition usually involves a movement from community to nation, that is, the assertion of a coherent national identity and a corresponding, even coerced, commitment to liberal democratic political and free market economic institutions and values. In this context, Tamir's appeal to liberal nationalism from statelessness recognizes these prerequisites while, by preserving some cultural integrity, representing an attempt to resist the latent colonial impulse underlying them.[17] Said's seeming embrace of a form of liberal nationalism for Palestine/Israel, however, points to the inadequacies of relying on institutional solutions to conflicts that have to do with the survival of identities fearful for their very existence.

In the postcolonial situation, the apparent expulsion of the Western imperial presence left formerly disparate populations, united by and in their opposition to the colonial order, to assert a hitherto nonexistent national coherence upon which a state could be established and, thereafter, governed. The new regimes-to-be learned from the colonial powers that an asserted, articulated, coherent national identity was not only essential to resisting colonialism but would also be vital for garnering recognition from the international political community. In the work of Frantz Fanon, among others, postcolonial nationalism recognizes its effective agency, but also becomes aware of itself as a construct. Consolidating this construct into a unity of forms and meanings of the type necessary to govern hybrid communities has proven problematic. Nonetheless, the impulse to nationalism among the colonized is very real, and finds contemporary reflection among the unprotected stateless. A claim to national identity has become a problematic prerequisite to asserting a claim for statehood, for claiming a plot of land over which to exercise sovereignty, and for obtaining membership in the international community.

There is a difficult relationship between the assertion of a national identity and the claim to legitimate statehood, which this chapter addresses by situating the postcolonial critique of nationalism, specifically as it is found in the political thought of Edward Said, within the discourse of liberal nationalism, especially that found in the work of Yael Tamir. The postcolonial critique takes seriously the influence of Western political conceptions—especially regarding the forms of the state—on non-Western and diasporic or stateless communities. The emergent hybrid conceptions of political community are often at odds with Western expectations and generate the need for the negotiation of cultural understandings of "nation." Yet this negotiation requires a public space, an in-between transitive space in which the vertebrate and cellular can recognize their interdependence. Appadurai argues that the modern nation is a double: its "gray areas"[18] connect to and are complicit with the cellular. The necessary space of negotiation would be one in which different cultural meanings could be articulated, temporarily stripped of their authoritativeness, and brought into conversation.

Providing this space in the context of a respect and desire for cultural coherence is the impulse behind contemporary versions of liberal nationalism. The liberal nationalist seeks to preserve the all-too-human need undergirding nationalism, that is, to practice and preserve one's way of life in the context of others who share it, by using political structures associated with Western-style classical liberalism. The apparent contradiction, preserving an exclusive set of national cultural practices in a formal context grounded in liberal values like tolerance, will—the liberal nationalist contends—be mediated by liberal political structures (values, processes, etc.).[19] The existence of the liberal state becomes utterly essential in the preservation of national cultures.[20] The problem is that not everyone gets a state. Liberal nationalists differ on who gets a state, and why, how, and what it means to not have one, though mostly everyone gets a public space. It is at this point that Said's analysis asks after the recognition and protection of the dispossessed and the stateless. Even as he might express a postcolonial's skepticism about a project like the liberal nationalist one, Said's stateless voice comes to embrace the impulse behind it when speaking of the Israeli-Palestinian question. Drawing Said into more overt conversation with Tamir's liberal nationalism yields a constructive sense of what it means to negotiate statelessness.

THE APPEAL TO NATIONALISM

Few would contend that the impulse to nationalism is exclusive to the postcolonial period, but its postcolonial form is more readily associated with resistance and liberation than the earlier forms it took in the West. Nationalism brings with it the baggage not only associated with imperialism but also that of the xenophobic "nationalist" regimes of Nazi Germany and Mussolini's Fascist Italy among others. With the apparent breakdown of colonial and Cold War hegemonies, however, colonies appealed to nationalism in places as diverse as the Middle East,[21] the former Yugoslavia,[22] Australia,[23] and Canada.[24] Yet even these new nationalisms fall victim to the exclusivist tendencies of their elder European forebears. With what Michael Walzer calls the

"return of the tribes," necessary questions arise regarding how different "national" populations with claims to the same physical space are
to live together and under whose umbrella.[25] These questions are intimately related. Government requires institutions, and no institutional
arrangement is free of preferences for a particular set of values. The
problem is profound, because, as Walzer suggests, in each instance

> [w]hat is at stake is the value of a historical or cultural or religious community
> and the political liberty of its members. This liberty is not compromised, it
> seems to me, by the postmodern discovery that communities are social con-
> structions: imagined, invented, put together. Constructed communities are
> the only communities there are: they can't be less real or less authentic than
> some other sort. Their members, then, have the rights that go with member-
> ship. *They ought to be allowed to govern themselves*—insofar as they can do that,
> given their local entanglements.[26]

Walzer's liberal solution is to figure out a way in which political
structures can best accommodate the multiplication and division of
identities in these situations. He recognizes that "the negotiation
of difference will never produce a final settlement,"[27] but Walzer—
perhaps in an attempt to preserve his spheres of justice or, perhaps, in
order to avoid dealing with the impact of the creation of the state of
Israel on the "natives" of Palestine—too hastily passes over the importance of the fact that communities are constructed. If communities
are constructs, then the institutionally protected hierarchies therein
are grounded in a preferred—not to say immutable or final—set of
epistemological (or even ontological) certainties. Lacking the absolute authority of a mythical finality, they can and must be subject to
negotiation. This is difficult. It requires risk, sacrifice, and, ultimately,
trust. If the community comes to us as a given, born of a mystical, immutable past and this is certainly part of what is involved in
the creation of Israel, then the certainties that past carries forward as
authoritative are profound sources of power. In their "self-evidence,"
they serve as justification of anything from divine right, to "liberal
capitalist democracy," to many more dreadful things. Politics requires
order, but agreeing to disagree and then to live together in negotiation and compromise demand a corresponding concession: because
the community is a construct, its meaning, its values, and its social and
political arrangements are *all* subject to negotiation.

    Active participation in negotiation requires a standing that the
stateless do not enjoy. Whether actually or not, the stateless,
metaphorically, are "small numbers" and, therefore, generate
anxiety.[28] We see the attempt to negotiate this anxiety in the work

of Edward Said, whose political thought articulates a demand for formal recognition and political viability of his native Palestinian culture.
Said's awareness of Palestinian statelessness began in 1967, when he,
as a freshly minted and already successful Western intellectual, was
reminded how far he had come from a home he hardly knew. For
Said, the Six Day War marked a decisive moment in the Israeli dispossession of the Palestinian population, because the so-called Arab world
demonstrated its unwillingness to defend the cause of Palestinian self-
determination.[29] The cause of Palestinians would have to be taken up
by Palestinians everywhere, and Said was disturbed to find that was
not happening. The silence of Palestinians, particularly those thriving
in exile like Said himself, seemed to substantiate the "if-then" negation
of Golda Meir in which the West seemed complicit: if there were no
such people as Palestinians, they could not have been dispossessed.[30]
By their inaction, Palestinians were acquiescing in a denial of what
Said later identified as their "Permission to Narrate" their own story.[31]
Part of Said's motivation was his understanding that, as he wrote in
an essay of that name, "the idea of a Palestinian homeland would
have to be enabled by the prior acceptance of a narrative entailing
a homeland. And this has been resisted as strenuously on the imaginative and ideological level as it has been politically."[32] The problem
of Palestinian statelessness created a need for articulating an identity
upon which to base negative claims of injustices suffered, on the one
hand, and a positive demand for the security of statehood, on the
other. The initial assertion of a Palestinian identity, well documented
by Muhammad Y. Muslih and Rashid Khalidi, took the form of a
Palestinian nationalism situated within the larger phenomenon of Arab
nationalism.[33]

Said's work takes us from the dispossession of a people, their consequent realization of the need, as a stateless community, to construct
a national identity, through their ongoing confrontation with bitter
enmity, and, finally to understanding that the demands of history and
political exigency short-circuit any justification for and requirement of
an exclusively Jewish or Palestinian state. In *The Question of Palestine*,
Said demonstrated how important the idea of a homeland was in the
creation of the state of Israel. Palestinians, Said contends, were displaced by a unique form of postcolonial nationalism—the creation
of a state of, by, and for "the Jewish people" called "Israel." The
uniqueness of this colonial adventure was that, unlike other imperial projects, this one chose to proceed as if the "natives" did not
exist instead of using them as instruments, labor, etc. The Palestinians
were "disappeared" from their land, from history, etc. Said explored

how public discourse contributed to the perpetuation and power of this "disappearance" in *Covering Islam* (1981) and in the volume he co-edited with Christopher Hitchens called *Blaming the Victims* (1988).[34] In both, Said connects physical and political dispossession, suggesting that the denial of Palestinian existence by Israelis and the West was, and in some instances still is, a strategy devised to justify Israel's right to exclusive occupation of Palestine. It was to counter these denials, Said argues at various points in *The Politics of Dispossession* (1994) and later in collections like *The End of the Peace Process* (2000), that Palestinians should and did draw on the language of nationalism as a form of resistance, as a way to press their very existence as (a) people.[35]

The real source of Palestinian nationalism, Said's work suggests, is the requirement of making these counter-assertions: of being "a people," of possessing "a culture," and of calling others to witness their dispossession. At each step, the goal is "proving" that Palestinians are a viable national culture worthy of recognition by the international community.[36] The absurdity of having to prove one's existence, we argue, is a significant manifestation of political homelessness and thrusts one into a transitive state. Here, as Waldron's analysis of the condition of the homeless shows, the circle of assumptions is unbreakable: one cannot claim to be human unless one can claim a place to be human, and one cannot claim a place to be human unless one can claim to be human. Nationalism adds another layer in which one's humanity is tied to membership in the in-group. In defending the Palestinian claim to exist, Said sought international recognition that the destinies of the Israeli and Palestinian populations (including the millions in exile) are irrevocably bound together. In efforts to correct non- and misrepresentations of Palestinians and, he hoped, to create a fruitful dialogue on the question of Palestine, Said moved from an initial support of Arab nationalism, to a trenchant criticism of all such fundamentalisms (including cultural nationalisms, political ideologies, and religious fundamentalisms), to an uneasy and temporary embrace of the forms if not the language of liberal nationalism.

At its core, we are arguing, the assertion of nationalism is a rejection of the homelessness that statelessness represents. Said's understanding of nationalism, drawing on Fanon, recognizes that the emergence of postcolonial forms of nationalism may be traced to the need to oppose imperialism, and, therefore, the idea of nation can be used in a strategically essential way. Said argues that nationalism is "reactive," that is, a playing of the game that is being played. Nationalism is most effective where the rules of the political game require a national identity in order to claim a culture and engage in political action. This is why, he suggests, that early colonial struggles were cast in nationalist terms. "There is an emphasis upon forging a self-identity as a nation or a people that resists but has its own integrity (as in Cesaire's *negritude*). But it does seem to me that despite essential virtues, there are great limitations to that intellectually as well as politically."[37]

Said was cautious about identity, but knew he must engage the process. The essential virtues of nationalism, and thus its utility to the stateless, include its articulation of a communal meaning, that is, an assertion of the right to name oneself. The claims of nationalist communities mark the assertion of their existences and the specific expression of identities, grounded in common, if often neglected or suppressed, histories. The charge that such claims create nationalisms where none existed before is precisely the postcolonial point. The assertion of nationalism marks a distinction between us and them. The appeal to nationalism as the basis of a demand for statehood or, particularly, sovereignty over "non-members" of the national community is the layered residue of colonialist assumptions: (1) the emphasis on the nation-state as the most legitimate form of political community, the one most likely to receive international recognition and protection, and (2) the need for an asserted identity to justify sovereignty over territories enclosed by borders drawn or erased by the colonial powers. These conditions mark the permanent proximity of colonial assumptions and show the way for the assertion of postcolonial nationalisms.

As with other nationalisms, postcolonial nationalist identities are constructions put upon a set of experiences. These experiences are often divergent, but they converge in the fact of having been colonized. The methodology of Said's literary theory recognizes that all identities are constructed. His landmark *Orientalism* (1979) questions the assumptions underlying Western attitudes and approaches to "the Orient." He argues there that "the Orient" exists independently as a construct of the Western, particularly academic, mind.[38] This construct, he maintains, nonetheless creates a reality. When taken together with the construct of "the Occident" of which it is both a product and an interlocutor, the Orient obscures the lived realities it claims to represent. There is Foucauldian power in the ways these categories become a kind of damaging shorthand in which identities are constructed, imposed, and then authorized to become analytical assumptions.

These literary and cultural tendencies have their analogues in colonial practices like claiming already inhabited territories and redrawing borders. The consequent displacements of peoples and their cultures are then explained as being in the natural order of things. In *Culture and Imperialism*, Said seeks and finds the constructed presences and absences of whole groups of colonial "others" in authors as apparently diverse as Jane Austen and Albert Camus.[39] These invisible presences come to define the colonial order and, inevitably, to influence the postcolonial order. Said's strategy, which he formulates as a "writing back" to the canon, exhibits the doubleness characteristic of postcoloniality: his work is a response simultaneously *from* these constructed presences and absences and *to* the cultural mechanics that create and enable them. While his critical work attempts to give voices to those who are silenced or taken for granted, he does not forget that these voices and the identities they claim are also constructions. As such, they are no less vulnerable to the charge of circumscribed authenticity than the privileged voices of the canon.

In Said's work, recognizing constructed identities and recovering silenced voices are acts of resistance to colonizing and imperialist assumptions. Read this way, the emergence of postcolonial nationalisms becomes the political equivalent of "writing back" to colonialist assumptions. But, Said argues, these nationalisms find it difficult to avoid the linguistic temptations of the colonial, that is, justificatory claims to purity—of race, religion, and political ideology. Postcolonial nationalisms, he suggests, must resist—as they have not—the "temptation to essence" and recognize that these constructed identities are hybrids of the concerns of the colonized and the language of the colonizer (Fanon writes in French, Said primarily but not exclusively in English). As an exemplar, Said points to Arab nationalism, which initially gave voice to cultures ignored or silenced in the West, like the Palestinian nationalism born of that context.[40] While, however, Palestinian nationalism endures in Said's thought, he argues that it must transcend its birthplace because Arab states have abandoned its cause. Cynically, these regimes, like their Western counterparts, have turned nationalism and the temptation to essence into political tools with which to justify "the national security state, the repressive apparatus, the secret police, [and] the army, as an instrument of oppression."[41]

Any Palestinian nationalism, Said argues, must resist these temptations and function on two levels. First, it must give voice to

an urgent necessity for people, the large majority of whom today...enjoy no rights at all, precisely because of their national origins. For example, there are over four hundred thousand Palestinians in Lebanon, all of whom exist as stateless people, and who have pieces of paper saying "you are stateless."[42]

The awareness and frustration of having a national identity but being forced to live in statelessness makes the Palestinians a transitive population, multiply related. Such a placement generates a reaction, working what Said calls an "invidious nationalism." This is a negative form of identity-construction, now properly feared in the West and elsewhere, that generates exclusivist needs that it cannot meet and corresponding methodologies of desperation. It finds itself situated in the space between nation and cellular structure, having both a total and predatory identity and an incomplete one.[43] These tensions, Said argues, can be assuaged in a preliminary way by reframing the transitive position. That would be, as Said puts it, "founding a national identity [and] having a state,"[44] but, then, abandoning these claims to essence before they can take on a life of their own and become dangerous. If the Palestinian movement could remain focused on its principles and avoid degenerating into chauvinism, it could function, Said believed, on a second level as an exemplary movement. The Palestinian movement should assert itself, he says, as a "vanguard" movement undertaking "a secular struggle in a part of the world where religious nationalism is very, very powerful."[45]

Religion complicates the questions of nation. The regional presence of religious nationalism is a critical negative presence for Said and part of his suspicion of certainties, especially institutionalized and politicized certainties. "We are not a religious movement. We are a nationalist movement for democratic rights," Said insisted, "in a part of the world where there is no democracy."[46] Said's discomfort with the role and power that religious fundamentalism has in the region, manifest in misreadings of religious requirements all round with disastrous effects, shows in his insistence that "we are a secular struggle with democratic rights for all people, men and women, religions, creeds, and sects."[47] Along with the secular dimension, Said uses the language of democracy strategically—it is all too familiar to his Western audiences—in order to distinguish the Palestinian movement from the religious nationalisms of the region (Islamic in Iran, Algeria, and Jordan; Jewish in Israel; Christian in Lebanon). He wishes to avert the destructive presence of misunderstandings generated by Western ignorance and distrust of Islam as well as Arab ignorance and distrust of Judaism and Christianity. To do so, he distances himself from the use of religion in the negotiation of regional conflict. His methodological insistence on the worldliness of texts and ideas, articulated in *The World, the Text, and the Critic*, made Said a voice undergirding the "new secularism,"[48] and he articulates one political manifestation of it in his argument for the secular worldliness of the

Palestinian movement.[49] By limiting the role of religious and political fundamentalisms and trusting neither fundamentalism nor contemporary states in the region, Said hopes to create a space—a discursive one in advance of a physical one—for the Palestinians to engage the world quite apart from the ontological and epistemological difficulties involved in negotiating from the differences among fundamentalist religions.

Said's attempt to distance Palestinian nationalism from religious fundamentalism not only is a political necessity, but also goes to the heart of his critique of all fundamentalisms, including any nationalism grounded in the assertion of an immutable essence, a tyrannical "native identity" that "dissolves or occludes important questions as well as issues of class, race, gender, and property."[50] He seeks a non-exclusivist approach to identity formation as a prelude to a functional politics. This is the cornerstone of Said's vision of Israel/Palestine.

While nationalism may be valuable as a tool of liberation at the identity-formation stage, it becomes problematic when one tries to govern according to its necessities. It is part of the very nature of nationalism, he argues, that its "limitations have to do with the fetishization of national identity," which leads to "the rise of what I would call a kind of desperate religious sentiment."[51] This desperate religious sentiment takes the form of a transitivity of violence that excludes, homogenizes and terrorizes rather than including and opening up spaces of negotiation as a more Levinasian form of transitivity might. Nationalist chauvinism drives people to seek the comfort that comes from associating with their own kind, making the other the enemy.[52] Silencing difference and dissent marks the aggressiveness of all fundamentalisms—religious, ideological, nationalist. Relying upon false, dangerous assertions of purity and pure identities, fundamentalisms must deem any criticism to be a mortal danger to the "essence" they embody and exist to protect. The logic of fundamentalism dictates that these mortal threats must be eradicated. Thus, criticism of the policies of the Israeli government, *vis-à-vis* the Palestinians, risks making one *ipso facto* an anti-Semite.[53] Yet the policies of the Israeli government, to the degree that they have marginalized, dispossessed, and excluded the Semitic people known as Palestinians, seem immune from such a morally perilous, even fatal, danger. It is in this disjunction that we find an example of what Said calls the *telos* of nationalism. It emerges as a fundamental reinforcement of that which has been constructed for negative, defensive purposes, thus its limitations as the backdrop of a functional politics. Origins in negation and denial, he understands, make this kind of nationalism a problematic base from which to engage in creative, positive governance, and he hopes that Palestinians can avoid it and the Israelis can overcome it. But how?

THE APPEAL OF LIBERAL NATIONALISM

Against this fundamentalist form of nationalism, Said posits a secularism that attends to living human beings. Said's secular approach requires assigning religion to its proper place as a crucial source of communal identity, as an integral part of what Ibn Khaldun called *asabiyyah*.[54] One must resist projecting these primary associational commitments into the political arena. While one cannot be committed to all others equally, a disproportionate commitment to one's blood relations makes for bloody politics. Living together despite disparate cultural practices is the trick of a functional multicultural politics. Drawing on Giambattista Vico, Said argues that politics must be grounded in a human history that is understood as the product of living men and women rather than a function of divine intervention.[55] Neither religious fundamentalisms nor national identities of the sort posited by decolonization movements can be allowed to submerge the complexities of secular life into an artificial homogeneity.

Resisting the submergence of the strictly human means breaking down assumptions about the demographic and geographic stability of nationalisms embodied in nation-states that were products of both imperialism and the resistance to it. Grounded in liberal assumptions about the relationship between property and personhood, imperialism generated an equation between legitimate identity and the control or possession of physical space. In fact, Said argues, the past 300 years have been a struggle for territory with conquest resulting in a re-transcription of territorial meaning. He was "interested in antecedent justifications" for these reasons. In Australia, England, America, and Palestine, he wrote, "*what always happened was a conflict of these justifications with, you might say, the realities of the people there. Therefore it is a struggle over geography, but also over justification and philosophy and epistemology and whose land it is.*"[56] The physical space as a space of meaning is critical. As Waldron demonstrates in his analysis of homelessness, there is no more basic assumption in classical liberal theory than the Lockean idea that personality, indeed, personhood, is tied to the possession of property.[57] Imperialism rewrote the equation between legitimate identity and the possession or control of space and usually grounded it in some religious, historical, or philosophical (i.e., antecedent) justification. What is interesting about all of this is that postcolonial resistance movements and postcolonial nationalisms internalized these assumptions recreating the geography of the imperial borders, which hardened, Said argues, into "reified, stable entities and on them is built the usually repressive apparatus of the national security, one-party state."[58] The philosophical and finally political denial of the human occupants of colonial and postcolonial spaces generates the epistemological and nearly ontological differences between I and You, East and West, etc. The imperialist connection of geography to national identity is the liberal property trap writ large,[59] bequeathed to postcolonial nationalisms, obscuring the fundamental insight to be gleaned from the entire imperial experience: the world, Said insists after Homi K. Bhabha, "is mixed, we deal in a world of interdependent, mongrelized societies." Nations, with and without states, "are hybrids, they are impure."[60] Political or national homogeneity is a dangerous fiction.

Maintaining the diffusion of cultural particularities within these new old borders, without unduly threatening the substance or existence of those differences, is the challenge of postcolonial politics. It is a tall order. Communal identification, national, religious, cultural, etc., cannot be wished away, but must be "negotiated" in the sense articulated by Bhabha. All postcolonial communities—and this would seem to work for post-Cold War communities as well—are hybrids, that is, composed of pre-colonial, colonial, and postcolonial elements mixed together in ways not easily parsed out. For Bhabha, negotiation of these differences is the very stuff of politics. There are profound potential problems, however, including terrorism and neocolonial practices, in allowing national "truths" to collide in the zero-sum context of power politics in confined spaces. When truths collide, defeat, including coming up short in a negotiation, too often means repudiation. This kind of zero-sum negotiation can mean obliteration. Bhabha's scheme therefore demands the recognition of a Third Space in which no set of meanings is authoritative and new meanings must be created, agreed upon, and renegotiated. We are calling this a transitive space.

The generation and preservation of such a space would seem to be the response of liberal nationalism. National truths, the liberal nationalist contends, must be allowed to coexist and interact in a political space governed by the commitments of classical liberal theory. Some years ago, Neil MacCormick offered a nice summary of these commitments:

[I]ndividual human beings are the bearers of moral value and legal rights. I continue to affirm that the good society is one in which individuals—*each* individual—are taken seriously; in which each human person has that fair opportunity of material well-being and that just extent of civil liberty that are essential to the flourishing of each one's individuality as a person.[61]

Here, we want to draw the analogy to homelessness clearly. Denial of a space to meet basic human needs is a denial of personhood. Denial of these liberal fundamentals marks a denial of human being and of human community. Living these commitments, MacCormick suggests in an Aristotelian moment, requires a community of properly regarded human others. While he concedes that nationalism has been the justification for many atrocities, he also argues that it is one way of realizing a species of identity that is the necessary precondition of human individuality. A group with whom one can identify provides the context in which one develops as an appropriately distinct but rooted human being. To fear the impulse behind nationalism, our reading of his analysis suggests, is to fear ourselves and the identities we create and have created for ourselves. In the absence of totalitarian or other hegemonic regimes to suppress these identities, he argues, "there ought to be respect for national differences, and that there ought to be an adoption of forms of government appropriate to such differences."[62]

Reconciling particularistic cultural differences to the needs of establishing and maintaining an orderly political life that respects those differences is the problem addressed by liberal nationalism. As articulated by Yael Tamir, liberal nationalism situates itself between two alternatives available in the literature: ethnic nationalism and civic nationalism.[63] To put the distinction simply, ethnic nationalism is the more "nationalist" of the pair, what Said would call "filiation," grounding itself in ethnic identity (common language, customs, etc.) as the justification for a set of political arrangements that invariably favor that ethnicity *in perpetuity*. By apparent contrast, civic nationalism, the more "liberal" of the pair, is what Said would call "affiliation," involving a community's shared commitment to a set of political values and institutions freely agreed upon. Ethnic nationalism has been viewed as an insidious form of nationalism grounded in inherited and immutable characteristics and prone to practices like "ethnic cleansing" of small numbers in an anxiety of incompleteness.[64] Civic nationalism, assuming the rational and free choice of modes and orders of government beyond cultural identification, has been lauded as consistent with liberal democratic ideals.

Political philosophers like Bernard Yack and Will Kymlicka, however, have argued persuasively that the dichotomy is a false one. Civic nationalism, Kymlicka shows, like its ethnic cousin, has an undeniable cultural component and so is no more or less immune to the undemocratic chauvinisms with which ethnic nationalism is often saddled.[65] For Yack, civic nationalism is grounded in a well-established liberal fiction. The idea that a political community comes together and chooses to commit itself to a set of political values over and above other commitments seems "a mixture of self-congratulation and wishful thinking."[66] The very distinction between the civic and ethnic forms of nationalism, Yack contends, "parallels a series of other contrasts that should set off alarm bells: not only Western/Eastern, but rational/emotive, voluntary/inherited, good/bad, ours/theirs."[67]

Tamir's conception of *Liberal Nationalism* seeks to address these problems by working in the space between the ethnic and civic forms of nationalism. She makes two rather large but very important assumptions. The first has to do with the relationship of national self-determination to individual identity, and the second has to do with the relationship of national self-determination to self-rule.[68] Of the first, Tamir embraces the importance of what Benedict Anderson calls "imagined communities" for the development of personal identity.[69] She argues that national self-determination is a *cumulative* individual right in which liberal commitments to self-development and expression are tied to the protected existence of a community in which the individual can develop his or her specific identity. For Tamir, membership in a national, that is, cultural or even ethnic, community is a constitutive factor of personal identity, the establishment and preservation of which should be a public policy goal of the nation-state.

The pursuit of a well-developed national identity requires the existence of a shared public space, as in civic nationalism, in which individuals have the opportunity to express and develop those identities. Here she addresses Evan Charney's later criticism of Will Kymlicka's version of liberal nationalism.[70] Charney uses the problem of religious tolerance to argue that Kymlicka's focus on national or cultural community unnecessarily limits the spatial opportunities for identity formation. Tamir seeks to preserve these other sources of identity by tying them to the development of the individual in interaction with similarly situated others. "National self-determination," she writes, "is therefore tied to the aspiration to have a communal domain that is construed not only as an arena of cooperation for the purpose of serving one's individual interests, but also as a space where one's communal identity finds expression."[71] Tamir is aware that preserving a public space for a national community sounds like a group right, but she rejects this reading as counterproductive. As the preservation of this space—including political arrangements and other public institutions reflecting national cultures—is a necessary antecedent to the development of whole individuals with distinct identities (read: good citizens of a liberal polity), the preservation of a space for national self-expression is an individual right, albeit a cumulative one. The task for the larger community is balancing the collective interests of the number of national identities within its borders with the interests of those national entities as sources of individual identity without falling into the trap of suspecting them to be "special interests" or voices of conspiracy or ongoing and irreconcilable dissent.[72]

Tamir's liberal nationalism, she hopes, will simultaneously celebrate the particularity of cultures, albeit limited by a commitment to human rights, while also housing the inevitable tension between cultural embeddedness and personal autonomy. What respecting cultural differences while governing people and allowing for some personal autonomy *means* is the crux of the difficulty Tamir, Kymlicka, and others are attempting to address, and their efforts generated a healthy scholarly discussion.[73] Tamir's work tries to strike the difficult balance between preserving the uniqueness of national experiences and respecting the reality that politics works from a set of established assumptions. The existence of these imagined communities involves recognizing mutual obligations and responsibilities, those of members of the national community to one another and those between the national community and the larger governing entity. Governing a community of diverse populations requires recognizing that we will be partial toward our fellow members but must remain impartial toward all others. Liberalism errs, Tamir writes, by assuming that individuals can have equal affection for *all* others. And this problem of partiality is not solved by John Rawls's suggestion that decisions about how to allocate a community's resources can be based on an objective positionality in which there are no particular others.[74] There must be a space in which we are and should be allowed and encouraged to be "embedded" in Michael Sandel's sense of the term.[75] The objective position merely recreates the problem generated by the presence of particular others. Tamir agrees with Walzer that the necessities of cultural and national life are expressions of the need to commit to particular others. Indeed, the structure of this part of Tamir's argument, that there ought to be autonomous national spheres in which personal identities are safe to develop among similar others, very much resembles the notion developed by Walzer in *Spheres of Justice*.[76] It is the function of good politics to make the spheres cooperate without destroying their particularity. In line with Walzer's suggestion that "good fences make good neighbors," Tamir argues that individuals are better off when they are able to share their lives with some particular others they care about and can see as partners.

Tamir knows that her commitment to public spaces for national identities cannot resolve the difficulty presented by the need for a more comprehensive governing structure, that is, the nation-state. Decolonization and the end of the Cold War necessarily meant the presence of noisy national communities within larger, already established political entities. Her second major assumption derives from this difficulty: a national right to self-determination like the one we have been describing does not necessarily entail a right to self-rule. To assert that each national community warrants its own state is unrealistic. Here, Tamir suggests that we move beyond the assumption that statelessness need be tantamount to homelessness in the following way: stateless communities, properly integrated into the sociopolitical structures of existing states or regional arrangements, are allowed a space in which to make a home. In this way, Tamir tries to depoliticize a cultural home space without removing cultural particularity from the larger political landscape.

Yet we still must deal with the presence of nation-states whose institutional arrangements cannot be, as liberal theory would wish them, neutral. As long as government's chief function is the distribution of resources and the resolution of disputes over those distributions, political decisions will continue to involve the uncomfortable imposition of a certain set of political and cultural values. These values are reflected in the structure of political institutions, in the choice of official language, and in a variety of often subtle but pervasive symbols. Tamir argues that liberal institutions, governing with a minimum of partiality, can create safe spaces, but there will come the need for coercion, which will generate resentment, claims of discrimination, etc. A more reasonable arrangement, according to Tamir, would be a regional "consociational democracy," in which a series of local autonomies were federated under larger regional organizations (the European Union comes to mind).[77] The local autonomy would preserve the sources of its communal identity, its practices, its traditions, its institutions, and its rituals. Larger regional organizations (she eschews the language of the nation-state as it might become a conflicting source of identity) would ensure economic consistency, provide for the military protection of its constituent members, and standardize the region's ecological policies. Though not all of the local autonomies could be made equal in status or power, Tamir argues that the larger members will be limited by self-interest; that is, they will see that it is in their interest to deal with their lesser neighbors fairly.

While she recognizes that her scheme has flaws, Tamir thinks the advantages suggest its possibilities. First, it would allow smaller nations to lead satisfying national lives. Second, such an arrangement would relieve the pressure to assimilate by encouraging cross-cultural cooperation on big regional issues while preserving local cultural autonomy. While the prosperity of the region may require economic standardization, it need not require the cultural standardization of its members. Third, Tamir believes that her scheme makes a "virtue out of necessity" by encouraging the idea that prosperity does not require enclosure and isolation.[78] With her idea of "consociational democracy," Tamir is not wishing away the nation-state, but is attempting to think beyond it.

The convulsions in the nation-state in the early 1990s—the former Yugoslavia, ongoing difficulties in postcolonial Africa, Chechnya, Quebec, the Basques in Spain, and the fierce marginalization of the Palestinians—gave Tamir and scholars like her cause to reconsider its permanence and what the world might look like if the nation-state proved less than resilient. She has acknowledged that asking the modern nation-state to play, in Brian Walker's terminology, "cultural game-warden" is a tall order, but her analysis does offer up possibilities.[79] Like Kymlicka, Tamir finds value in the idea that liberal nation-states should encourage rather than fear national movements. If being a good citizen involves choosing, then the public sphere should be a place in which, as Emily Gill has argued, there are multiple, viable alternatives.[80] Seeing to the preservation of those alternatives rather than preserving a homogeneous image the nation-state has of itself may well be the real calling of the modern liberal polity. Tamir, Kymlicka, Walzer, and MacCormick recognize and appreciate that wishing away the impulse to national identification and national self-determination is even less realistic than wishing away the nation-state itself. Better to recognize and allow for the negotiation of impulses to cultural particularity than attempt to repress them until they blow up.

SAID: THE AMBIGUITIES OF LIBERAL NATIONALISM

Tamir's version of liberal nationalism allows for the expression and perpetuation of national cultures in a two-tiered federal arrangement. Within the nation-state, national cultures get public spaces in which to express themselves as national cultures while participating in the politics of the larger polity. Outside the nation-state is a regional federal organization that sees to the safety and well-being of the national communities in its province. Practices are standardized where necessary, but with a minimum of coercion on the level of culture. The scheme tries to encourage the development of national self-identifications while trying to mute any excessive political ambitions grounded therein. The cultural embeddedness one develops in one's community allows one a sense of mature citizenship in the larger community. Said's vision of the Palestinian movement recognizes that the development of this cultural embeddedness is critical. Being allowed "permission to narrate" the Palestinian story is a prerequisite to overcoming the statelessness of the Palestinian people. His task, then, was twofold: first, to move beyond having to assert the existence of the Palestinians as a people and, second, to suggest a set of arrangements through which Palestinians and Israelis can coexist as interconnected but independent cultures. When Said speaks of a solution, he does so in terms familiar to liberal nationalism.

Said knows that the peaceful coexistence of Israelis and Palestinians demands mutual recognition. To that end, he has renounced the early Palestinian commitment to the destruction of Israel. He has also demanded similar tangible recognition of the Palestinians from the Israelis.[81] In his vision of the future of Israel-Palestine, Said has moved from embracing the idea of one secular democratic state, to the (now impractical) two-state solution, back to "a bi-national state" that, we would argue, has a transitive quality. In doing so, he sounds every bit the liberal nationalist:

I want to preserve for the Palestinians and the Israeli Jews a mechanism or structure that would allow them to express their national identity. I understand that in the case of Palestine-Israel, a bi-national solution would have to address the differences between the two collectives.[82]

A binational solution recognizes the reality of the hybrid transitive space: that Israeli and Palestinian destinies are intimately intertwined. Therefore, dividing up territory and redistributing it among national groups would require positing and enforcing the very kind of purities of essences that Said so distrusts. What makes one a member of a national group and not a member of another? Race? Religion? Hairstyle? In a democratic context, issuing national identity cards cannot overcome the fact that something as simple as intermarriage relegates such distinctions to the realm of folly.[83] Such a stark division works a segregation of populations and their identities that is nearly impossible without either constant use of force or the wisdom of the guardians in Plato's *Republic*. Moreover, the effort seems hardly worth the energy. It furthers the flawed liberal view that identity is legitimated only through the possession of property for the individual, through the command of territory for a national group. The impulse to segregation, Said holds, is fundamentally anti-democratic and, in the case of two populations so interconnected by a shared history of violence and dispossession, works against the interaction among equal citizens that supposedly characterizes liberal democracies.[84]

Said knows, however, that the demographics of the region mean that in a democratic binational state, the Israelis would go from having the political and military power to maintain a Jewish state to consigning themselves to the status of a minority in a Jewish-Palestinian state. Beyond the political impracticality of a powerful group giving up its power to democratic principles, Said is concerned that Jews are a minority in the region anyway. When pressed on their future in the region, he confesses:

I worry about that. The history of minorities in the Middle East has not been as bad as in Europe, but I wonder what would happen.... The question what is going to be the fate of the Jews is very difficult for me.[85]

The history of anti-Semitism and the inevitability of the Jewish minority are the strongest arguments against Israel admitting Palestinians as full and equal citizens in a binational nation-state. The inevitability of a Jewish minority also generates the conditions that Tamir tries to address with her regional federal arrangement, the "consociational democracy." Like his Israeli counterpart, Said knows that Israeli existence is defined by its ongoing, chiefly defensive, response to the surrounding hostile environment. So after arguing that the Israelis would likely have to exist as a regional minority, Said, again sounding the liberal nationalist, suggested:

What I would like is a kind of integration of Jews into the fabric of the larger society, which has an extraordinary staying power despite mutilation by the nation-state. I think it can be done. There is every reason to go for the larger unit. The social organization that would be required is something I haven't really pondered, but it would be easier to organize than the separation Mr. Barak and his advisors dream of. The genius of Arab culture was catholicity. My definition of pan-Arabism would comprise the other communities within an Arab-Islamic framework. Including the Jews.[86]

Without reference to Tamir or the term *liberal nationalism*, Said's "catholic regional pan-Arabism" attempts to recreate the consociational democracy she suggests—and for the same reasons. He seems to be trying to head off a regional conflagration while preserving the possibility of a democratic space in which both Palestinian and Jewish cultures could develop unmolested, along with the appropriate social, political, and educational institutions that American administrations have made the prerequisite to recognizing the Palestinians as an authentic national community.

Said's work on behalf of the Palestinians both in its form and in its content represents a mode of political being that is entirely consistent with that embraced by Tamir's liberal nationalism. In his commitment to the Palestinian cause, Said expresses a faith that, through sheer numbers, Arab culture will or should reassume a dominant position in the region. He attempts to mitigate the force of that blow by embracing a regional organization that looks very much like that posited by Tamir. The geopolitical factors, however, make it very unlikely that the Israelis will be required to submit themselves to the requirements of liberal nationalism, that is, a regional organization or consociational democracy. These actual difficulties reveal the limits of a liberal nationalist response to the Palestinian question. While the requirements of liberal nationalism may be met in pristine conditions, in the real geopolitical circumstances in the Middle East, they become profoundly problematic, and we are left where we started: the stateless, by definition, are at a distinct disadvantage because the official political culture is not likely to reform itself in such a way as to weaken or destroy itself. In the case of Israel-Palestine, the antecedent justification that a Jewish state of Israel is necessary as a cultural sanctuary has been very effective. Demographic shifts may further problematize the existence of an exclusively Jewish state, but the material advantages enjoyed by the Israelis may neutralize those challenges for the foreseeable future.

The politics of the region may well be humanized by the cultural negotiation suggested by liberal nationalism and, in his way, by Said. Liberal nationalism and Said's analysis point to minimizing the role of religious and cultural fundamentalist differences. The desire to minimize these differences is a noble one, but trying to consign them to their appropriate spaces where they are important dimensions of identity-formation and leave the rest to a politics of rational and fair administration of interests is profoundly difficult. When allowed to develop healthy national identities (whether civic or ethnic), people(s) act out of spaces of fundamental self-understandings. To deny those understandings authority beyond their local autonomies for the good of a larger liberal collective seems to work against the development of fully formed identities.[87] Citizenship would presumably turn on one's commitments beyond one's specific identity community or, perhaps, on the way one integrated those commitments into the larger political arrangement. Moreover, as Tamir and others recognize, the larger political arrangement is going to favor one community or culture over others and local autonomy will very much depend upon the self-discipline of the larger, powerful communities and the cooperation and forbearance of the smaller ones. Liberal nationalism, finally, can neither mitigate fundamental cultural differences politically nor can it hope to assuage mutual suspicions through liberal political commitments and processes. What both Tamir and Said hope is that the liberal national form (whether one calls it this or not) will allow and encourage the preservation of cultures in a tolerant multinational political structure.

The impulse to liberal nationalism, however, should not be dismissed simply because there are problems with the pragmatic implementation of its theoretical commitments. Theory suggests direction. Remaking the world is the function of ideology; engaging the world we have from a different perspective is the function of theory. One strength of liberal nationalism as an idea is that it takes seriously important sources of identity and recognizes them as necessary if problematic. Liberal nationalism also takes existing political structures seriously and challenges us to preserve their animating influences while reconfiguring them to meet new demands.

Said's preference for a structure like the Truth and Reconciliation Commission is instructive,[88] as it is a transitive structure. Bishop Tutu and those who put the Commission together wished to avoid the humiliations of show trials and resist the temptation to act as if Apartheid never happened. The issue was how to get the story told, without the feeding frenzy of a Nuremberg-type legal proceeding. The answer was to allow those who perpetrated human rights violations to come forward and explain in detail what they did. In return for full disclosure, an amnesty committee was empowered to recommend absolution from prosecution. Such absolution was not automatic, and the committee could require reparations be made. The shortcomings of the Commission, including its being seen as biased toward white confession, cannot hide its uniqueness. The idea is to have justice as a function of confession, of testimony, which, as Jacques Derrida suggests, implies a community. Therefore, out of an unspoken bond of trust—that one who testifies tells the truth—another community-creation becomes possible. The telling of stories, the revelation of experiences, all without the threat of recriminations beyond the confession and, perhaps, reparations overlaid the traditional model of the trial court with something other, something more productive and less divisive. Such creativity is precisely the kind of governing mindset that liberal nationalism demands and seeks to institutionalize.

The politics of power for its own sake is never devoid of considerations of meaning, even if it uses an asserted meaning only as a justification. Beyond shared language, we suggest that reading Edward Said within the context of liberal nationalism signals the commitment to establishing a context conducive to retaining what meaning there is to be found in politics. The efforts of Tamir and Said transform statelessness into agency through open political structures. The language of liberal nationalism, because it eschews the political relevance of fundamentalisms, is useful to the stateless because it is familiar, even comfortable, to those to whom appeal must be made. Yet its very familiarity speaks of its limitations, for today's language of liberation and normalization was yesterday's language of oppression.

SECTION II

MEDIATIONS OF RELIGION AND POLITICS

CHAPTER 4

SELF-CULTIVATION AND THE PRACTICES OF PEACE: FOUCAULT ON THE STOICS AND PEACEMAKING IN THE MODERN WORLD

In *The Care of the Self*, the third volume of his *History of Sexuality*, Michel Foucault turns to the Roman Stoics and their influence, acknowledged and unacknowledged, on the modern world. His focus is on the emergent notion of the " 'private' aspects of existence" and how they relate to the public: domestic, political, and social frameworks.[1] Foucault's work here continues the postmodern interest in the classical world and its notions of virtue, but also, as he says in "On the Genealogy of Ethics," the interest in where Christian technologies of the self came from and how they have been distorted.[2] In *The Care of the Self*, Foucault, as always, is interested in both power *and* pleasure. He asks how "taking care of oneself," that is, self-cultivation, relates to the larger issues of domestic and political life, specifically issues of control of sexuality and power politics.

In this chapter, we draw on Foucault's insights into the political and ask how self-cultivation can develop practices that lead to peace. Foucault's focus on the self, we argue, points back to Stoic notions of the self as consisting of practices that connect us to others. Simultaneously, his analysis undercuts modern assumptions about the self as a possession or singularity. The self as practice—that is, as an honest, ongoing engagement—is, we suggest, more conducive to peace than the version of self we find in the modern world, that is, as a private possession at once to be displayed and jealously guarded from others.

Our discussion of self-care moves beyond the terms of the classical world and beyond Foucault's own text to the practices of two men of peace, the historical Jesus and the contemporary Buddhist monk Thich Nhat Hanh. In their practices, we find that peace is not possible without living the self among other selves, that is, without the risk and exhilaration of human interactions.

For the Greeks and Romans, we know ourselves through the *agon*—through conflict. The Greek recognition that human life is lived in the *agon* meant that self-knowledge is binary and, as we showed with Hegel's philosophy, contested. Consequently, their attempts to bridge the apparent gap between the psyche/soul and the *polis*—while honoring their independence—were attempts to order, even to domesticate the *agon*. The Delphic Oracle's injunction to "Know Thyself" works its way from Socratic self-examination and Platonic contemplation of the Forms to an Aristotelian conception of happiness as the end of human life, both individually and collectively. The question for the Greeks, then, is not how to rid oneself of the *agon*—for that is impossible—but rather how to live without its adversarial ethos permeating every relationship and action. We will ask a further question: must we live only in the *agon*?[3]

It is perhaps characteristic of Greek philosophy that it did seek a way beyond the *agon* and began to find it in the cultivation of the psyche. While the Socratic *daimon* functions as conscience, guiding Socrates's behavior in the *polis*, Plato recognizes in his master's death the danger of the public practice of that kind of commitment. In the *Republic*, therefore, Plato turns to meditation on the "natural order of things," that is, on the Forms and the acceptance of one's role in the *polis*, in an effort to minimize the *agon* and the risks associated with it. While this leads to an ordering of soul and, in an admittedly remarkable leap, this ordering of soul leads to an ordering of the *polis*, which facilitates individual and collective health, Plato's Socrates is forced to concede that this arrangement, this *polis*, is but a *polis* in speech, that is, in words alone.

In the *Nicomachean Ethics*, Aristotle reworks the Platonic idea, emphasizing the need for practice in the messiness of human existence. In his conception of happiness as a *telos* achieved through a series of practices and in relationship to others, Aristotle turns his back on perfection, embracing instead the hard, imprecise work of attaining and perpetuating balance. Aristotle's vision was not so grand as to posit the impossible need for Platonic philosopher-kings, but he, nonetheless, held fast to the notion of the mentor, the *spoudaios*, who could teach the way to virtuous membership in community and the way to mature friendship with one's others. The *spoudaios* teaches through practice, that is, at least if not exclusively by example. Learning requires relationship, and virtue and human connection are functions of open-ended practice. On this Aristotelian model, one is virtuous only through one's properly directed actions and never finally in this lifetime.

What the Greeks cannot account for is the extension of this set of ideas beyond the *polis*, a limited political community, to the barbarian, to the alien, to the "other." The Romans—through a particular reading of the methods of Aristotle's pupil Alexander the Great— overcome this problem by seeing every "other" as to be either assimilated or eliminated. They absorbed, as Foucault argues, the core of Greek ethics: virility (virile-ity), which involved not purity, but self-domination, and that dictated dissymmetry, the exclusion of the "other."[4] The idea behind the "visible empire" is to put the stamp of Rome on alien places—to translate and transform the other through the *agon* into Latin. Here the *agon* is no longer about balance and reconciliation of the public and private, but about assimilating the other into the self, making the other an extension of the self, that is, Roman, through conquest. This reality affected and still affects practice.

Rome functioned, therefore, as a principle of transitivity as it forced all to undergo the power of empire: all is Rome. All is also not Rome, however. Even as those who were "other" were incorporated into empire, they remained who they were. Pope Benedict XVI calls this process "interculturation,"[5] understanding that as the Roman Catholic Church, through conversion brings "others" into its order, "they" become hybrid: both Roman Catholic and who they are. The Roman Empire functioned in the same way.

Rome also created internal "others" and made "others" related. It is a strange coincidence that, for example, Marcus Aurelius and Seneca, for whom Stoicism was an aristocratic philosophy, were bound in its practice to the ex-slave Epictetus. The philosophy also helped the aristocrat to acknowledge the "otherness" within the self. Marcus Aurelius, for example, preferred philosophy to being an emperor, and his "book records the innermost thoughts of his heart, set down to ease it," to help him "to bear the burden of duty and the countless annoyances of a busy life."[6] From the Stoics on, therefore, attending to the self in meditative practice does not constitute nihilistic self-absorption, but may be seen as an attempt to seek commonality— of self with nature and with other(s)—and to bear the *agon* within. If the *agon* is relocated in the self, it becomes an opportunity for self-development. While Stoic meditative practice does not entail self-absorption, one of its implications in its Roman form is a kind of "other-absorption." In other words, because of its aristocratic character, there is a noted lack of mutuality in Roman practice, if not necessarily in all Stoic doctrine. While the Roman model tends to "otherness" in a particularly aggressive mode, its influence on Christianity generates the possibility of what we want to call a "public asceticism."

Ultimately, for the Roman Stoics, contemplation loses its capacity to change public action. The *pax romana* is order, not peace; it is kept through terror, not meditative practice. Consequently, peace, in our sense, does not enter classical thought, for contemplation is, ultimately, located only in the self who, either as emperor or as slave, has to endure empire. The Stoics, therefore, are where Foucault begins but also, as we will see later in this chapter, where he finds himself trapped.

The search for balance, self with other, learning with practice, and knowledge with action, draws out the inevitable connection of self to "other" that we learn from the Greeks and find at the core of our notions of a lived conception of peace. Peace is not life free from conflict, but is life in right relationship, free from unworthy attachments, and undertaking shared burdens toward a common goal. In this light, we argue that peace involves self-possession, rather than possession of self. The distinction is important. Possession of self is a modern conception of self as a nearly material thing to be owned as one owns a car or even a slave. I own myself—it is not me but a part of me. Of the available modern models, the emphasis has become the Lockean self as "private property" rather than Mill's idea that the self, while ours to develop, must be developed in the context of others.[7] Because it is our property, its protection against others being the *raison d'etre* of human political community, our self can be "lost." To live together in this liberal space is to place our selves in a fearful, defensive mode that generates unrealistic notions about security and an unhealthy aversion to the risk that engaging our others represents.

Foucault's concern with the self is, in part, a rejection of this modern idea of possession of self for he finds it limiting and too intimately connected to structures of power. We find in his work on sexuality a latent notion of what we understand as self-possession. In our conception of self-possession, there is no necessary binary between either self/I or self/other. Indeed, I am not a self without others. Linking self to the world requires confidence and trust, a willingness to be open to challenges, to risk being wrong, and to learn and grow. This self cannot be the product of one's own labor exclusively but lives and is developed when risked in the presence of other selves. From Levinas's conception of "the Face" to Judith Butler's contention that others both make and undo us, peace generated from the self involves knowing and disciplining the self in relation to others in a series of moments and interactions. As such, self is always to be worked at and upon, articulated, and regenerated in the presence of others. Modernity must rediscover that the self is practice, and Foucault finds the beginning of a way back to this understanding of self in the Stoics.

In the Roman Stoics, Foucault argues, the cultivation and care of the self was not for a private purpose as it seems to be in his present. Stoic practice very quickly took on a public dimension. He describes the development:

It . . . took the form of an attitude, a mode of behavior; it became instilled in ways of living; it evolved into procedures, practices, and formulas that people reflected on, developed, perfected, and taught. It thus came to constitute a social practice, giving rise to relationships between individuals, to exchanges and communications, and at times even to institutions. And it gave rise finally, to a certain mode of knowledge and to the elaboration of a science.[8]

Two things are to be noted here. The first is Foucault's appreciation of practice, of work, as the root of Stoicism.[9] These are practices of care, involving care of both the body and the soul. In recognition of this mutual care, body and soul find their relationship through intellectual activity linking commitment to freedom; such activity is, as Epictetus suggests, a "privilege [and] duty, a gift [and] obligation" that "ensures our freedom."[10] In Stoic practice, body, mind, and spirit come under development and care. But there is another dimension at work in Foucault's description, a problem that lurks in his analyses and in our own: the formalization or hardening of these practices.

Initially, there is transitivity to Stoicism when understood as work that the free human being does with bios, utilizing it as material for aesthetics,[11] as material to be developed by individuals in accord with flexible standards and in a variety of circumstances. For Foucault, the subject is constituted in the play of symbols and in real practices.[12] The experimental attitude "cuts across" the multiple symbol systems in which the human being finds the "self" while still using them.[13] Contemplation and action fuse: in each step, the human being is confronting what she is thinking with what she is doing.

As it evolves, however, Stoicism hardens into procedures and formulas, becoming an institution, a reification which, for Foucault, limits freedom. Stoic practice, thereby, runs the risk of hardening into dogma—as it does at Rome. The choice about existence becomes a demand.[14] The difficulty is how to remain in the transitive space: how to facilitate practices without coming to rely upon institutions to do the heavy lifting. As we consider his work on the self, we must bear in mind Foucault's early analyses and suspicions of institutions and how they embody and then distort practices like those of the Stoics.

Foucault's major questions meet in the transitive space where philosophy, religion, and politics either collide or intersect in an interdisciplinary mode. His question of freedom—of how we might live in the way(s) that make(s) us and others most free—recognizes the presence and effects of power, with its "multiple forms of constraint."[15] Power is a network that runs through the whole social body and that "traverses and produces things" like pleasure, knowledge, and discourse.[16] His second question is how we work to attain freedom: "What *techne* do I need to use in order to live as well as I ought?" Both questions are about how to escape the "synthesis" of power.[17] Can we, he wonders, have a "politics" of self[18] that lets us remain free?

Key to and complicating Foucault's understanding of the Stoics is the importance of the public in the care of the self. The activity of caring for the self is not solitary in nature. It naturally leads one to engage with others, and we are reminded of the importance of a mentor or teacher. The body is cared for by health regimens and exercise, and these may be prescribed and/or supervised by a specialist. Using Marcus Aurelius as his example, Foucault argues that effective care of mind, through meditation and intellectual activity, requires a network of others. One is always reading the works of others, educating one's self. One has conversations with friends, with confidants, and, more importantly, with a mentor or "master" figure who acts as spiritual director and guide.[19] In addition, one is engaged in correspondence "in which one reveals the state of one's soul, solicits advice, [and] gives advice to anyone who needs it."[20] These interactions are necessary to effective meditation practice, we argue, as they draw us into reflection of our own internal landscapes and those of our others. Common experiences are drawn from the depths of the psyche out into the world where they must walk—or limp—around in a context beyond the self. Far from an activity that isolates the human being, therefore, self-care becomes a movement toward the world, as Foucault puts it, "a true social practice" and "an intensification of social relations."[21]

Self-care on this model requires an attitude toward self that is transforming rather than punishing. The self is not as one who is imperfect and ignorant, but one who can be diagnosed and treated, developed and changed. Most important, the result of this self-care is that body and soul cease to be alienated from each other. The body and soul come to "communicate with one another and exchange their distresses."[22] The actions of the person that threaten the body also threaten the soul, and so these actions need to be corrected. The goal is self-mastery, conversion to self, and delight in the self.[23]

The mastery of self is not self-indulgence but a training of the self to the minimum, the establishment of a supremacy over the self such that one does not depend on the presence or absence of persons and things.[24] The less we depend upon, the freer we are. The Stoic notion of self-care identified by Foucault, then, marks a bridge from the classical to the modern. The first half of this characterization of Foucault's thought discussed earlier in the text, that the mastery of self is an intrinsic dimension of virtuous action, is right out of Aristotle's *Ethics*. But Aristotle would object to the second part of the statement in a way that a modern might not. The aspiration to be independent of persons (in particular) or things (the *polis*?) is much more a modern conception of self-sufficiency than Aristotle would allow. Indeed, it is one that Aristotle warns us against in the *Politics,* where he cautions that a person so independent as not to need others is either a god or a beast. Foucault also stops well short of embracing the modern ideal of self-sufficiency as self-indulgence. In self-care as self-mastery, we would argue, Aristotle and Foucault have a place to meet, suggesting a way beyond the modern ideal; because, for Foucault, to be free of dependency is to be free for the self and for others.

Self-care, understood as Foucault does, prepares us for struggle, for chance and entanglement:[25] good fortune is precarious, and our lives involve reversal and anxiety;[26] therefore, we must practice detachment from excess in body, mind, and spirit. For Foucault, this is clearly the basis of ascetic practice, the control of pleasure and withdrawal *from* the world, of Christian understanding and Buddhist detachment. But it also, more important for us, suggests the basis for engagement *with and for* the world—a life for the self that is a life for others—that Foucault begins to but does not fully explore here. As we demonstrate later in the chapter, we can find models in peace-builders like Jesus and Thich Nhat Hanh, both of whom are drawn to their practices and to their others.

A theme of the Stoics is that one is "called," to use Calvin's language, to a role in the world by God/Nature/Spirit, and the self is fulfilled in that role. This call is not to be undertaken at the expense of self, Foucault suggests, but in relation to self. Such a life

Is much more concerned to define the principle of a relation to self that will make it possible to set the forms and conditions in which political action, participation in the offices of power, the exercise of a function, will be possible or not possible, acceptable or necessary.[27]

Capable function, therefore, is directly connected to the form into which one shapes the self. We must become fit for our callings. Personal choice is not paramount in Stoic understanding, but, if exercised, is done in context and in commitment. The human being who accepts that action in the world is not an occasional activity but an on-going one in one's social context understands that he or she is involved continually in a multitude of power relations. One is sometimes the ruler and sometimes the ruled, as Foucault puts it in an Aristotelian moment; one sometimes has power and sometimes is the subject of it. But Foucault moves beyond Aristotle's conception of ruler and ruled as roles that we are periodically called upon to play. Instead, he argues, such a position suggests that the self is transitive: a "transition point."[28] Even in transition, however, the self is not a sieve or void; it is a flexible yet stable self that has a "manner of being," that works, through ethics, through practice, out of an *ethos*, an understanding of self and soul established in the activity of self-care.[29] Its stability, along with the capacity to improvise, lets one exercise detachment and compassion, even in the most trying and unstable of circumstances.

Self-care and care of others are intimately connected: "The rationality of government of others," Foucault writes, echoing Plutarch, "is the same as the rationality of the government of oneself."[30] We can find this notion in Aristotle, in the Stoics, and, as we will discuss later in the text, in both Christianity and engaged Buddhism. The challenge for Foucault (and Thich Nhat Hanh, for that matter) is that the idea must be deployed in a transgressive way, in an environment in which the self, for most people, has already been transformed into a private possession.

There is a disconnection between self and other in Foucault's and in our own present. Foucault, like Charles Taylor in *The Ethics of Authenticity*,[31] recognizes that, in the modern world, the cultivation of the self as my personal possession has led to an unhealthy detachment from both political activity and personal responsibility. This development marks an abandonment of the *polis* that is intensified by the fact, Taylor argues, that beginning in the 1960s we embraced what he calls an "expressive individualism" as our ideal.[32] Consumerism is one external manifestation of this phenomenon. What it signals is a focus on private space (and how to fill it)[33] and the pursuit of happiness in that individuated space apart from larger communal concerns.

It emphasizes appearance, what things represent—usually status or some other fatuous identifier—rather than what *we mean*. A focus on youth culture is another manifestation of this tendency. It marks the linking of goods and the need for them with a stage in life in which one is without responsibility and without the need for the self-reflection we find at the heart of Stoic practice and the practices of peace.

Taylor calls this the culture of authenticity.[34] He argues that it begins with the Romantic Movement and comes to its strength in the late twentieth century. It is the notion that

> Each of us has his or her own way of realizing one's own humanity, and that it is important to find and live out one's own, as against surrendering to conformity with a model imposed from the outside, by society, or the previous generation, or religious or political authority.[35]

In the eighteenth and nineteenth centuries, this was the standpoint of a cultural elite, but after World War II, it became the outlook of society in general. "Do your own thing" accompanied therapy and other ways that we have to realize ourselves. We have now seen the response to this mode of being in the manifold fundamentalisms (ideological, religious, etc.) at large in the Western world, but these revanchist movements are inadequate because they are responses in kind; that is, they recreate a false binary. Moreover, they have not stopped—and in some cases they have embraced—the momentum of the globalization of materialist market values. The self either is alone and empty, measured by its purchasing power—the stuff we acquire is who we are—or longs for a mythical past or future where the self is indistinguishable from all others and subject to grand ideological (cum theological) commitments. Either way, as Derrida shows us in "Faith and Knowledge," the modern self is bound to modern "Globa-latini-zation" in that both are dependent on the very global forces that they hate.[36]

The focus on self-actualization brings forward an important new social and religious imagination. Taylor discusses three forms in which people imagine themselves as existing and acting simultaneously: within the economy, within the public sphere, and as a sovereign people. But to these he adds a fourth: the sphere of fashion. Like the others, the sphere of fashion is an area of common action, but it differs from them in the sense that it is an arena of self-display. "I wear my own kind of hat," he writes, "but in doing so I am displaying my style to all of you, and in this I am responding to your self-display even as you are responding to mine."[37] To use Levi-Straussian language, fashion is a space in which we exchange signs and meaning.

It is not an arena of mutual action but rather of mutual display[38] in which, as we are seen by others, we together co-determine meaning. In other words, display says something to others that generates a common mood or tone. For Foucault, this kind of pleasure also generates desire;[39] here, the consumer desires to be able to engage in similar display.

There is, in such public interactions, therefore, an odd combination of loneliness and communication, solitude and togetherness, creating what Taylor calls a "lonely crowd."[40] This, he argues, is a new way of being together in society. One need only consider information technologies and the environs created thereby to see how this notion of fashion has played out. My Facebook status reduces the complexities of my life to a few words that can be multiply translated and understood. In this way, I display that I feel x, where x is an unknown algebraic variable; I am both present and not.

Confusion emerges in such a culture in the fact that there is, yet, both continuity and discontinuity. The notion of a sovereign people, for example, has not been displaced by this notion of the expressive individual. The idea of mutual benefit has not disappeared; on Taylor's argument, it has just taken on a different form: let the individual do his thing. We should not criticize the values of that individual. Everyone has the right to live her life as she wants to and action should be tolerated because of a notion of freedom. In this way, the ethic of authenticity creates what Taylor terms a "soft relativism," without a sense of the commonly held virtues that constitute a good character or good community.[41] The sense is that mutual respect will emerge from the ethic of authentic self-fulfillment.[42] Concomitantly, personal spirituality feels no need to conform. It must conform only to the "harm" principle: it must respect and not criticize others. Intrinsically, however, the spiritual need not relate to the social.[43]

Possession of material things becomes a marker of worth and self-realization, as Max Weber reminded us in *The Protestant Ethic and the Spirit of Capitalism*.[44] But materiality, as Marx's work suggests, only compounds the problem. We no longer concern ourselves with human presence but only with material wealth and power. We will line up to purchase the latest gadget but not to volunteer at a homeless shelter. In political terms, this materiality becomes conquest for resources: a quicker route to India, spices, gold, oil, etc. Our desire justifies exploitation outward, and, as we suggested with the Romans, the inner life becomes something undertaken by particular selves in private and is discontinuous with public action. Similarly, rights that should bind me to all human others instead become "my possession," protecting and distinguishing me from community, rather than connecting me to it. In other words, we do not "sit" in defined communities of tradition and/or choice as our grandmothers and fathers did. This disconnect generates alienation, depression, and religious practice as fetish (from the Crusades to modern fundamentalism; from the desire for Jerusalem to WWJD "stuff" in the marketplace). The political virtue is tolerance, which we suggest is a virtue that implies distance rather than engagement. And, Taylor fears, this dislocation paralyzes us, keeps us from acting together for a common good.

Foucault is trying to move us beyond authenticity, beyond display, and beyond individual genius to some common human activity. He argues that while the notion of a "common humanity" may be an attractive one, it only emerges out of difference engaged in orientation to a common goal. That is to say, what is "common" is our chosen activity toward the good, activity that can be engaged only when we know and cultivate the self in its difference and particularity. Foucault recognizes that this kind of understanding can lead us back to Enlightenment reason as the marker of the human being and to a kind of universal dominant power that is too detached and much too able to manipulate the other. Reason, in the Enlightenment's universal mode, undercuts cultural location and specificity. The Enlightenment was, for Foucault, "a veritable technological take-off in the productivity of power."[45] "From the viewpoint of the relation to the self," Foucault writes, "the social and political identifications do not function as authentic marks of a mode of being; they are extrinsic, artificial, and unfounded signs."[46] For moderns, it seems, only reason can become a term of salvation, institutionalizing "one way," a way not extended to all (e.g., women, people of color, people of other sexual orientations, that is, any who do not fit the "norm"). Arriving here, Foucault's method means that he must turn to institutions—the material form that "reason" takes—and the concomitant abuses of power and pleasure. His preoccupation with power and his emphasis on the ways in which it predates and then utilizes institutional forms speak to modernity's excessive fear of vulnerability. We argue that making peace means dealing with and accepting vulnerability, fear, and pain. It is a different conception of power that helps us to transcend the *agon* by wielding that power for self (and selves). We remain vulnerable because we cannot escape the reality that we are in the *agon*. Jesus, the Greeks before him, and the Buddha all bring us to a similar place: life is suffering and we are charged with "getting on with it."

In addition, Foucault, though he argues for cultivating the self in particularity and difference, is always suspicious of fixed role. Hence, activity is always problematic for him. For Plato and Aristotle, finding or being assigned one's proper role and doing it well do not undercut individual dignity. Indeed, it leads us to the fulfillment of our potential, our nature. Role is not function, that is, mechanical and obligatory. Rather, role is "played" and chosen by one's natural gifts and inclinations. It is another form of self-possession. It is perhaps ironic that we moderns are so suspicious of role when, as Marx told us long ago, we have become mere functionaries in big machines—industry, political parties, mega-churches, for example—with little choice and individual expression, unless we embrace our gifts for making money.

Can we move through and beyond Foucault to suggest an alternative possibility, a way beyond a return to Enlightenment values or a mere revision of them? We want to suggest that the activity of cultivating our particularity may generate our commonality. As with Aristotle, the friendships that Foucault suggests emerge from the duty and obligation of self-cultivation; where this is the case, justice can emerge in the city as well. In self-care, because it is an activity inevitably reliant upon others, we can help create a kind of public space of exchange—of self rather than goods. In this space, we find the possibility of both authenticity and productive kinds of equality and inequality, for it is a space of interdependence in which, to use a Buddhist term, a kind of dependent co-arising is operative. This quest for self-cultivation may be the equalizing force, but one cannot undertake it without depending on the self in a new way and on others in relationships of mastery and giving and of discipleship and need. We all play both roles. In such a configuration, the authentic self is the interdependent and responsible self—a pilgrim, not the alienated and isolated modern individual. As Vaclav Havel writes:

We must divest ourselves of our egotistical anthropocentrism, our habit of seeing ourselves as masters of the universe who can do whatever occurs to us. We must discover a new respect for what transcends us: for the universe, for the earth, for nature, for life, and for reality. Our respect for other people, for other nations, and for other cultures, can only grow from a humble respect for the cosmic order and from an awareness that we are a part of it, that we share in it and that nothing of what we do is lost, but rather becomes part of eternal memory of Being, where it is judged.[47]

Havel's humble and selfless "respect for the cosmic order" demands recognition of our place in it, of the possibilities of our agency in it, and of our utter interconnectedness to it—including our others. We want to turn to two examples of the way in which this interconnectedness can be and has been translated into peaceful practice. The first we find in the person of Jesus himself, who took an aristocratic ethic and made it an option for all human beings—particularly "the least of these"—and through simple practices, a possibility for world, not just self, transformation. Second, we will examine briefly the Engaged Buddhism of Thich Nhat Hanh, whose practices embody the reorientation of the self that we have been suggesting here. Peaceful practice leads us to focused detachment and opens us to the world we inhabit, including our others. For both men, peaceful practices were born of conflict, and each sought to change the terms in which we understand our place in the *agon*.

Let us consider what happens to the *agon*. Let us move through the Greco-Roman, but not to the Judaeo-Christian in its institutional forms. Let us focus on the revolutionary figure of Jesus, recognizing as we do that he is already re-presented in the gospels we draw on. Living on the margins of empire and rethinking Greco-Roman concepts through Jewish ideals, Jesus makes Stoicism the language of the oppressed through love of the self that makes love of others possible. We wish to look at a single moment in Jesus' *agon*, called the Passion. In his *agon* in the Garden of Gethsemane, Jesus prepares himself for the ordeal to come. He asks the selfish thing, "Let this cup pass from me," but, ultimately, commits to act for humanity. Edward Sri connects the Agony in the Garden with the temptations in the desert.[48] In Luke's gospel, he notes, Satan departs from Jesus "until an opportune time."[49] The Garden is that opportune time. The Garden of Gethsemane must make us think of the broken purity of the Garden of Eden, which is redeemed but not fully restored. Jesus warns his disciples, "Pray that you may not enter into temptation,"[50] using, Sri argues, the same word that is used for the temptations that Satan inflicted on Jesus in the desert.[51] In other words, he urges the disciples to resist the desire for power, for glory for the self, and for testing God that we see in Eden as well.

Sri also argues that Jesus is telling his disciples that, though we may be tested, "[we] not 'enter into' those tests in the sense of giving in to them."[52] Pray that, Jesus implores them, we may not yield to the trials we must endure. This sounds odd, but Jesus is suggesting that just as he unites his will to God's, we must unite our wills to a higher calling: whether we call that the will of God or the human good. The *agon* turns inward; it is not the contest with the other, but the contest with the self. Sri explains:

Some scholars have suggested that Luke's description of Jesus being in "agony" recalls the ordeal ancient runners faced as they were about to begin a race. As they approached the starting line, the runners sometimes would become so intense that sweat would break out all over their bodies. This moment was the runner's agony.[53]

We recall Paul's statement that he has "competed well": "I have finished the race; I have kept the faith."[54] This is the struggle for self-cultivation that allows the self to join its bodily strength and its will—not just its reason—to that of a higher power, a higher good. *Agòn* is not between and against but for and toward; it is in the service of the neighbor. The neighbor too experiences his own *agon*, and the *agony* could, potentially, generate a creative tension, but in this tension resides possibility, not necessarily a power over orientation.

Jesus came from a community, a surviving remnant that had known exile—to Egypt and to Babylon—and that, nevertheless, had survived and maintained itself. He came from a part of the world that was a crossroads of empires, given hand to hand in power exchanges. What Jesus insisted upon was twofold: the capacity of law to be flexible enough to meet crisis and, within that, the maintenance of human dignity in the working through of the *agon*. Both were part of his inherited tradition. Law, the discussion of which (midrash) became the core of Talmud, insisted on the human being as important in the creation and maintenance of the world. Every human thought and action, therefore, carries with it the potential for virtue or vice. Jesus, building on this, insists that we are not just *homo sapiens*, but are many things: we play, we work, and we love. All of these activities, not just reason, are necessary for full human happiness, are essential in effective action, and are aspects of world maintenance. Hence, law cannot be mere rules to be obeyed; law is lived, a teaching guideline, and must maintain the flexibility and creativity that characterize the love and mercy that God—the source and standard of behavior—exhibits toward human beings. Along with this, Jesus insists that the community must respect the dignity of and support the weak among them: the homeless wanderer, the widow, and the orphan.

This ethic is realized in Jesus' suffering and is emblematic of Israel's own suffering. He takes on the role of the prophet Isaiah's suffering servant, and he reminds his community and, ultimately the world that suffering with dignity and purpose is a form of freedom—an understanding that Augustine extends to Christian community in *The City of God*. Jesus accepts vulnerability, fear, and pain and transforms them into a kind of power that does not conquer but that transforms the other—not into an image of the self but into human beings in free relation despite social status, work, gender, and other differences. Jesus calls this orientation in the world the Kingdom of God. The Kingdom of God neither is a bounded place, a paradise, for, as Milan Kundera says in an interview, a paradise requires a gulag outside it for those we do not want in;[55] nor does it promise that there will not be conflict. Instead, it suggests a practice of mind—an epistemology—that reframes reality, seeing it in a different way. The Kingdom of God as a mode of being involves nonviolent practice for dealing with conflict, a practice that moves toward justice and peace.

Jesus' way has been taken up by a multitude of nonviolent thinkers, from Leo Tolstoy to Gandhi and Dr. Martin Luther King, Jr., and to, in our day, those nonviolent protestors in Egypt. The latter drew upon Gene Sharp's work, particularly *From Dictatorship to Democracy*, wherein he utilized and expanded King's principles on how to resist nonviolently to practices for undermining dictators.[56]

Thich Nhat Hanh, a Vietnamese Buddhist monk and peace activist, has used the insights of Dr. Martin Luther King, Jr., to highlight, in a deconstructive mode, elements of Buddhist thought and practice, which thereby transform them. A Zen Buddhist and the founder of Socially Engaged Buddhism,[57] Nhat Hanh concentrates on *tiep hien,* or "inter-being," and on the role of the boddhisattva, a being who attains awakening but postpones Nirvana to aid others in their awakening. In his work and thought, inter-being focuses us on the interrelatedness of all things. Inter-being, while maintaining the Buddhist necessity of individual awakening, is simultaneously the basis of a community of (socially) engaged selves.

Zen Buddhism is a transitive Buddhist form. Combining the meditative emphasis of Theravada Buddhism with the mindfulness practices of the Mahayana, Zen Buddhism holds Buddhist forms in tension. Since D. T. Suzuki introduced it in the West, Zen, which Suzuki argued had become a Western form,[58] has appealed particularly to Americans because its emphasis on meditation seems so individual. Thich Nhat Hanh, however, is extending the practices of Zen, getting practitioners off their meditation cushions and into the problematic spaces of society.

The Engaged Buddhist community, one that is global and cellular, in Arjun Appadurai's terms,[59] is founded on a particular orientation of what we have called the self and cuts across geographical boundaries, involving both Eastern and Western Buddhists, and across lay and monastic distinctions. As such, it raises the "ethico-epistemologico-political"[60] that cuts across and problematizes discourse, even that of religious tradition.

We are charged, as Nhat Hanh says, to be "in touch with every-thing that is around us."[61] As the keystone to Engaged Buddhism, inter-being comes as a response (rather than a reaction) to the world as we encounter it. "Our society," he writes, "is founded on a very limited definition of power, namely, wealth, professional success, fame, physical strength, military might and political control."[62] Even were these desirable in and of themselves, Nhat Hanh holds, like Jesus, that these things are all temporary and require an orientation to the world that is against the world, against our others, against, finally, ourselves as formed and understood in these nexuses of power that demand that which does not fit must be conquered and overcome. As our only goals, as the things we believe will make us happy, they distract us from the important work of exploring and facilitating our human-ity. For this we need, he argues, spiritual power. For Nhat Hanh, this kind of power is represented in the bodhisattva, who embodies com-passion and understanding and who understands that awakening is not just a personal attainment, but is a linking to the Buddha nature of all that is. The boddhisattva vows to awaken all to their Buddha nature:

> Beings are numberless; I vow to awaken with them.
> Delusions are inexhaustible; I vow to end them.
> Dharma gates are boundless; I vow to enter them.
> Buddha's way is unsurpassable; I vow to become it.[63]

In Socially Engaged Buddhism, we see, as Sallie B. King writes, "people who are primarily meditation teachers... heavily invested"[64] in activities like prison ministries, working for what we, tradition-ally, call "social justice"—working against the death penalty, for example—but, at the same time, transforming individuals. Inmates, King writes, "make noticeable improvements in developing aware-ness of habitual unwholesome behaviors; taking responsibility for past and present actions in regard to both themselves and oth-ers; maintaining sobriety; avoiding destructive behaviors and rein-carceration; and making constructive contributions to society."[65] King reports that prisoners themselves have started victim awareness programs.[66]

In Nhat Hanh's conception, there are five spiritual powers, and each manifests itself as practice of both meditation and action in the world. The five powers constitute a middle path, one in which one brings along the previous step rather than "moving on." The powers are faith, diligence in practice, mindfulness, concentration, and finally, insight. By faith he means a trust and confidence in one's path, guided by a teacher or mentor, and finding a home in the presence of fellow practitioners. Faith develops when one is diligent in practice, that is, it requires the presence and assistance of others for focus on what is present is of the essence.

By mindfulness, Nhat Hanh means being aware of what is happening in the present moment. As we move around in our lives, we are often "elsewhere," and this inattention takes us out of our selves and our communities. He speaks of "eating our anxieties," in which, as we take nourishment, we are thinking or feeling things that worry us or anger us. Not only is this bad for digestion, but we also cannot then appreciate what we are eating, let alone the fact that we have it to eat, or what kinds of efforts led to our food being available to us. Admittedly, mindfulness is difficult and Nhat Hanh knows this. But the difficulty wanes with the practice of mindfulness, with disciplining the self and doing so with and in the presence of others. These efforts, which never become second nature because of the requirement to be present, generate a kind of public asceticism that may contribute to building communities of peace.

The fourth spiritual power follows from the successful practice of the previous three. Concentration, something exceedingly difficult in this era of distraction, is the capacity and the power to see deeply what is there, what is before one, or who is before one. Finally, concentration facilitates insight. Rather than a clever idea that occurs to one, insight into the nature of what is before us allows us to see and take seriously the impermanence of things. "With impermanence," Nhat Hanh writes, "comes possibility."[67]

The tension in this conception of spiritual power is that focus and attention bring detachment or, better said, non-attachment. The more we look seriously into that which is before us, the more we recognize our connection to all things and the importance of the present moment. "A lot of our suffering," Nhat Hanh writes, "is born from the notion of a separate self."[68] We have seen this in our earlier discussions of Taylor and Foucault. When we look deeply and dwell in the present moment, however, we become aware of what Nhat Hanh calls "nonself." By this term, he "doesn't mean that you don't exist; it simply means that you are not a completely separate entity."[69] A more "un-modern" and "un-Western" notion of the self scarcely could be imagined. If we are separate from others, our vulnerability becomes manifest; it becomes our way of being in the world. But to think in those terms is to think of material rather than spiritual power. For Nhat Hanh, nonself is a function of spiritual power—what Gandhi identified *satyagraha* or King identified in nonviolence—a letting go of the autonomous self while committing to connectedness.

When you are in a power struggle, if you know how to meditate on nonself, you will know what to do. You can stop your own suffering and the suffering of the other people in the struggle. You know that his anger is your anger, his suffering is your suffering, and his happiness is your happiness.[70]

For most of us, just to imagine entering into the pain that we share with others would take an extraordinary effort. It is far too easy to feel anger and let that feeling be the never-ending end of it. This difficulty, however, is precisely why the simultaneous letting go and engagement that nonself suggests must be practiced, with guidance, in a community of other practitioners. Nhat Hanh's engaged Buddhist practice *is* self in community and in service.

Nhat Hanh's handbook called *Interbeing: Fourteen Guidelines for Engaged Buddhism* sets out the parameters of this community of practice. The Order of Inter-being was established by Thich Nhat Hanh in the 1960s, as a way to interject peaceful Buddhist practice into the violent environment of wartime Vietnam. For his efforts, Nhat Hahn was nominated for the Nobel Peace Prize by Martin Luther King, Jr. and exiled from his native Vietnam. Far from a utopian endeavor, the Order of Inter-being sought transformation in the here and now:

Only the present moment is real and available to us. The peace we desire is not in some distant future, but it is something we can realize in the present moment.... The purpose is to have peace for ourselves and others right now, while we are alive and breathing. Means and ends cannot be separated. Bodhisattvas are careful about causes, while ordinary people care more about effects, because bodhisattvas see that cause and effect are one.[71]

The "presence" in this conception must be underscored. Too often, social action puts its object off, into the future. The further away, the more mythical (and dangerous) these objects become. This putting things off also functions as an excuse not to engage in the here and now as Martin Luther King, Jr. reminded his supporters in the "Letter from Birmingham City Jail."[72] Peace, enlightenment, and liberation are not things to be realized in the future, especially in some set of institutional arrangements. Rather, they are ways of being in the world that can and must be practiced in the world now. Here, Nhat Hanh is rejecting the assumption that institutions—whether they are ideo-logical, theological, or philosophical—can do the heavy lifting for us. In inter-being, we take responsibility for our selves and our others, embracing and extending the work of the care of the self freely and openly.

The practices of engaged Buddhism, then, become a tangible way of loving our neighbor as ourselves. Seeing to the practices of peace means taking guidance from a teacher, but also lending support when practicing becomes too difficult. Both guidance and support require others, require community. The way to develop one's self, the way to peace is through practice. Nhat Hanh acknowledged his kinship with Jesus through his encounters with Christians who practiced rather than proselytized, and Martin Luther King, Jr. acknowledged his kinship with Nhat Hanh by nominating him for the Nobel Prize. A cellular network of practice extends and includes, "builds capacity and creates partnership" rather than excluding and making exclusive.[73]

Foucault said that the care of the self is a *epimeleia heautou*: a "working on" that implies both knowledge and technique.[74] How can the I/eye see itself? It has to look into another eye/I: the soul contem-plates itself by looking into another soul.[75] We can love the neighbor as the self, therefore, by following follow Foucault's prescription, but avoiding its end. One engages in a practice of love with the care that one might engage in a practice of power. In such a fluid mode of being, Stoic self-examination, with which Foucault starts, may take many forms, religious, social and political, across cultures. Even as we acknowledge the particular (local and unique) forms, we, neverthe-less, can join the particular forms of practice to the global in alliances for peace.

Forms of self-understanding, like Catholic examination of con-science, for example, or modern Freudian therapy or ruthless self-examination with a true Aristotelian friend can join in larger organiza-tions, like, for example, the United Nations. A fluid orientation to self and society can work towards equality, seek balance with the neigh-bor, not just tolerate the neighbor, and adjust. Change in the self, the care of the self, opens a new relation to the other that is not just a repetition of power over the other. The care of the self accepts change and vulnerability, and both keeps tradition vital and alive and adapts to present conditions, even as it keeps the self vital and alive, giving it a touchstone and center, while letting the self change too. Such "paths" have been spoken of as "middle" ways, in both Buddhism and Christianity and in Aristotelian ethics, but we would call them transitive: not just between, but engaged with both sides. Peace, in a transitive mode, is not a condition (established, done, unchanging) but an on-going imaginative activity, establishing the self as acquired, trained, and formed, not given, and the *polis* as a space, a site in which these selves meet, explore, and join, in difficult work like peacemaking, the varieties of human experience.

CHAPTER 5

"THE BETTER ANGELS OF OUR NATURE" SOPHOCLES' *ANTIGONE* AND THE CRISIS OF UNION

In the Second Inaugural Address, Abraham Lincoln makes a deceptively curious statement, one that draws a critical distinction. "These slaves," he says, "constituted a peculiar and powerful interest. All knew that this interest was, somehow, the cause of the war."[1] Lincoln's reference is to slaves (persons) and not slavery (an institution). He had emphasized the institution in the First Inaugural, and this later statement that these persons, not the institution, are the cause of the war suggests the centrality of black persons to his thought on America and the Union by the time of the Second Inaugural. Indeed, black people marched in Lincoln's second inaugural parade, constituting a significant and, no doubt, unsettling presence. After all, as signifiers these people marked all the contradictions of America: slave/free; human/property; black/white; wealth/poverty. Lincoln's assertion, however, recognizes these black persons as something more than signifiers, however. They are the bodies of living breathing human beings, though yet to be recognized as such; they are the challenge to be met if a deeply flawed community is to move forward together and heal the wounds of civil war.

The issue of black persons, black bodies and what they signify "somehow" parallels the mystery of the body at the core of Sophocles' *Antigone*. Polyneices' dead body "somehow" brings the Theban *polis* to an end. Here we will interrogate the issue of the present/absent body as border, looking at both the play and at Lincoln's inaugural addresses. The conflicts in both *poleis* are deceptively obvious: the political and the civil war. The political, since it operates on the level of the physical body, masks the destruction produced by a civil war in the realm of the spiritual, that is, to the *psyche* or soul. The subtle issues, the deeper wounds, therefore, are spiritual ones. We can understand this more clearly in the American context by reading the *Antigone*, for Sophocles understands from the beginning what Lincoln comes to realize by 1865: that the body becomes a border that represents the impurity at the heart of Union and that creates, by occupying the border, an opening through which the gods enter and work out their will. Lincoln comes to understand that there is opportunity in circumstance. The complexity of body in civil war crosses many boundaries—just as boundaries are crossed in the house of Oedipus. In time of civil war, the suffering of black bodies must be paid for by the bodies of the Union and Confederate dead. When we talk about the War, we talk about bodies and blood. The corpse is a thing—as were the bodies of black persons, especially slaves. Persons are not things, Antigone argues, and must be considered as such, whether living or dead. The transformation of person to corpse is infinitely easier than the transformation of thing to person. Civil war, we contend, is a complex and savage event that transcends our ordinary conceptions of both the human and the political, laying open the spiritual, which, for Sophocles and for Lincoln, always undergirds and underlies transformation and, therefore, the possibility of political community.

Polyneices' body carries the weight of the antinomies that Sophocles sees in the Theban conflict: it is both enemy, one who threatened the *polis*, and brother, beloved because of blood ties.[2] It is part of and claimed by both *oikos* and *polis* but unable to be treated properly by either for to do so would undermine the claims of the other. Further, as the body is dead, it is no longer part of humanity, but it is also left out in the light, unburied and thereby denied due membership of the dead. This body, thus deeply signified, becomes unclean, crossing and unsettling borders and categories of meaning; it is alien, as many translators recognize by using the term.[3] This impurity, this alienation, infects the *polis* and the *oikos* dividing its members. Antigone and Creon take up and articulate the extremes to which the body points.

Antigone stands for the feminine, for youth, and for the claims of the *oikos* and the dead; Creon stands, in contrast, for the masculine, for mature age, and for the claims of the *polis* and the living.[4] Similarly, in the Civil War, black bodies—defined as three-fifths human for the purposes of taxation but as mere things ("property") for the purposes of their owners and the larger political community—were understood as alien and other, even as they occupied the same intimate spaces as white persons. In this space of non- or lesser person, black bodies embody the conflicting stances of North and South even as neither side recognizes their full humanity. The extremes, the completely alien and the overly intimate, become two sides of the same reality. Slaves are defined as alien, and Antigone, Polyneices, and even Creon himself become alien due to Creon's edict. Slaves also occupy overly intimate spaces, and the over-intimacy, particularly sexually, of the Oedipus family is well known. Antigone seeks to transcend the overly intertwined intimacy by seeing herself as one with the dead of the house of Oedipus. Creon too wants to transcend the boundary-crossing intimacy of the *polis* by collapsing his identity into his role. Together, Creon and Antigone, like North and South, become two sides of the same reality; in very real and destructive ways, they are one.

For Sophocles, as for all the Greek tragedians, there is no comfortable separation of these seeming opposites. Masculine and feminine, *oikos* and *polis*, the living and the dead, law and cult are intertwined and interdependent. Keeping them in balance, allotting them due proportion, as Pericles articulates it in the "Funeral Oration," is difficult. Sophocles, like the other tragedians, explores the fragility of human institutions as they struggle to provide that "due proportion." Sophocles' twist is to see the imbalance, symbolized in blood taint, *miasma*, as fated; human beings, no matter how much the "Ode to Man" suggests that they are wonders, cannot easily keep their structures intact. *Miasma*, blood taint, which Polyneices' body represents, externalizes the deeper hidden truth of the *polis*, the secret everyone knows: that the Oedipus *oikos/polis* is overly intimate—father marrying mother and fathering his daughters/sisters and sons/brothers. Therefore, there emerges in Sophocles' Theban cycle a need to recognize that intimacy and speak its truth, if not to honor it. Polyneices must be buried, but the temptation to forget the miasma he represents must be resisted. There will always be the need to maintain distinctions to be able to render sound judgments and to maintain Union. As we will see, Lincoln came to embrace the task that Creon simply could not.

There is a crisis of union in the Theban plays—a perpetual crisis of state, of marriage, and of family, and it falls to the children of the house to articulate that crisis. Ismene, speaking for the concerns of the *oikos*, those of marriage and family, resists Antigone's desire to see the realm of the dead and the tie of blood as the source and site of absolute meaning and judgment—indeed, as the realm of *dike*. Haemon tries to save both the *polis* and his father. Speaking for the concerns of the *polis*, those of the state and its citizens, Haemon resists Creon's demand to find law and his tyrannical stance the sources and sites of absolute meaning. Creon should not, Haemon insists, hold fast to one dimension of mind. Together, Ismene and Haemon speak both for marriage *and* citizenship, that is, the ways (rites/structures) through which the alien becomes intimate, legitimating interaction on the level of *oikos* and of *polis*, while, at the same time, maintaining critical distinctions. We will argue that Lincoln also sought to preserve essential distinctions, but he saw his contemporaries playing the roles of Antigone and Creon, that is, rejecting these structures and, in doing so, cut off the possibility of a future.

Sophocles knew all too well that individual desire and pride can destroy the common good, and with that locus the *Antigone* begins. In *Antigones*, George Steiner notes that Antigone's first speech invokes her sister's head.[5] Antigone invokes her sister's head to stress, not reason, but "sorority, shared destiny, blood-relation, [and] forced 'oneness' "[6] in her plan to bury Polyneices. Ismene refuses, and the grounds of her refusal seem to mark her as a "weak woman" who cannot exercise the kind of courage her sister has. Ismene, first, invokes Creon's edict: "Would you bury him, when it is forbidden by the city? . . . Creon has forbidden it."[7] She then rehearses the history of the house of Oedipus, with its extreme intimacy, to illustrate to her sister that this "oneness" has led only to destruction. Finally, she emphasizes gender and the traditional role of Greek women; we are, she says, "only women/not meant in nature to fight against men."[8]

Urging Antigone to yield to history, state, law, and man, Ismene seems only weak and fearful. Yet, on closer examination, we realize that in collapsing her identity into one with her family—and, therefore, the dead—Antigone begins a double process, of self-assertion and self-erasure, that will parallel Creon's and that will lead to destruction. Antigone embraces death as both identity and goal: "*I* myself will bury him. It will be good/to die, so doing."[9] Ismene, who struggles to maintain distinctions between her self and Antigone's, between family and state, warns Antigone that this conflation is excess: "Extravagant action is not sensible,"[10] she warns; "It is better not to hunt the impossible/at all."[11] At the same time, however, she cannot quite let go of her oneness with Antigone. She urges Antigone to remember that, even in her extreme action, Antigone is not alone. While Ismene will not collapse her will into Antigone's, she will remain her family, her friend, one who, in Aristotelian terms, loves her but is equal to her: "your friends/are right to love you."[12]

Antigone accepts that she is alone and solitary—and Sophocles suggests, anarchical and egotistical.[13] Antigone's excess will lead her to reject the very things she argues that she values most: family and love. When, after Antigone is caught burying Polyneices, Ismene offers her support, asking to share the "common" death.[14] Antigone rejects her: "Life was your choice," she tells Ismene as her sister pleads to share her punishment, "and death was mine."[15]

"Hunting the impossible," so characteristic of Thebes, is both the path to greatness and the path, Ismene and the Chorus warn, to destruction. It de-contextualizes the human being, taking him or her outside the boundaries of self/*oikos*/*polis*/nature through *hubris*. Such a choice sets the human being in conflict with other people, as we see when Antigone rejects her sister, and, more importantly, with the gods, as we see with Creon. Creon's edict puts him in conflict with *polis* (the citizens), *oikos* (his son and wife), and self. He sees his power as one with his masculinity, his identity, just as Antigone sees her choice as her identity. They articulate two valid, but, it seems, irreconcilable positions. In the telling exchange between them, Creon argues for political identities and from political categories, like "enemy," while Antigone argues for personal identities and categories, like "brother."[16] Creon emphasizes the *polis*, Antigone the *oikos*. Creon argues that written law is more important than the "unwritten laws" of custom and the gods and is eternal (a man is his enemy even after death). Antigone argues that the dead have rights of their own, the laws of love, that those are equal for everyone no matter who they were in life, and that those laws are eternal as products of the gods and, therefore, eternal in a profoundly different sense from the way Creon sees things. Finally, Creon is a man only if he can enforce his position, and Antigone unmans him, undertaking a feminine act (burial) in the context of a masculine structure (*polis*).[17] Creon, who embraces the war truths about death—sacrifice of the young and the death penalty—threatens Antigone with the harshest penalty the state can give, but her choice puts her beyond the power of that penalty. He thinks that to kill her is "everything"[18] but she knows that he can do no more than that. He cannot violate her soul.[19]

When Ismene enters, she articulates a middle ground that neither Creon nor Antigone will move to occupy. When Antigone rejects her support, her desire that they die together, Ismene asks, "what can I do to help you still?"[20] She turns to Creon, speaking of Antigone not as a "criminal" to be executed, but, crudely as his son's future wife: she would have been a field to plow, he tells Ismene, but there are others just as fertile.[21]

The lines that follow—"Dear Haemon, how your father dishonors you" and "Will you rob your son of this girl?"—are sometimes attributed to Antigone and the Chorus respectively rather than Ismene.[22] To us, that breaks the sense and power of Ismene's argument. To attribute these lines to Ismene shows her acting, as she said she would, as friend to Antigone, fighting for her sister's life. They also articulate what both Creon, who describes marital love as plowing, that is, only nature and sexuality, an impersonal preparation of ground, and Antigone, who chooses the "Lord of Death"[23] as her husband, reject: the importance of human love, of marriage and the *oikos*. Ismene argues that this rite can bind the levels of being and meaning which are thrown out of sync by both Creon's and Antigone's *hubris*. The marriage rite involves the self, bringing two selves, persons loving "mutually"[24] into one. The rite also involves the *oikos*, joining two families and producing children, who as Plato says in *The Symposium* make the finite human being immortal. The *polis* witnesses as vows are made for and in the state in order to perpetuate it. The rite brings together nature and sexuality, the *polis* and culture, and the transcendent, the gods, tying the human to the eternal as they are the ones in whose presence one is married. In this ritual, in other words, contraries can be brought into relation, making reconciliation and peace possible.

Her argument rejected, Ismene is, from this point on, silent, though, we think, present. She is like her brother, a dead body. Her presence however, like his, represents spheres of being that both Creon and Antigone deny and, in doing so, destroy their own humanity. Creon and Antigone cannot see beyond their own positions; what they lack, though what they claim, and what is always missing in civil wars because they are such deeply intimate conflicts, is love, which Plato describes as the *eros* that is the spirit that binds bodies to structures to ideas, to the good, and to maturity as Aristotle describes it in the *Nicomachean Ethics*.[25] Civil war always reveals the fundamental flaw and resulting dysfunction in the polity itself. Sophocles, as we have shown, lays bare this *miasma* in the Thebes of Antigone. Blood has been tainted; discourse has broken down; and, laws, both written and unwritten, have been either ignored or smashed. Thebes is as far from Aristotle's functional polity, let alone Plato's ideal one, as a polity can be.

The dysfunction of the *polis* is on display when we consider the issue of maturity. There is maturity and wisdom in the Theban *polis* but, for Sophocles, it has been displaced upon the wrong persons: the young and powerless. Ismene and Haemon each try to use persuasion to mediate the conflict, but neither is successful. We are reminded that we are in Thebes, for there is no Athenian sense of order here, at least as it is articulated by Pericles in the "Funeral Oration" and the absence of which is lamented by Plato's Socrates at his trial.[26] Ismene targets the problem of maturity when she offers Antigone not compliance, but friendship. The good *polis* is one in which citizens are capable of mature friendship maintained for the good of the other and the community itself. In Thebes, maturity is silenced or ignored. Nor is maturity and its accompanying wisdom the exclusive province of one of the antinomies in conflict; maturity is neither masculine nor feminine, neither political nor spiritual, neither of this world nor the next. It is always, simply, possible. Aristotle appreciated Sophocles precisely because, for the tragedian, the possibilities of ethical behavior, of membership or belonging, of community and communion are directly related to the presence of maturity and friendship.

We will see that, beyond his immediate military *cum* political problems, Lincoln knows he faces a situation in which maturity, measure, and balance are absent in a polity torn asunder by passion, deadly logic, and blood. In the *Antigone*, maturity is not evident in the leader, for Creon, unlike Lincoln, lacks the self awareness to recognize the need for a measured response to his complex circumstances—namely, the aftermath of civil war and the spiritual crisis embodied in Antigone. In advance of making his edict, Creon suggests that the ruler should be judged, in good Aristotelian, fashion, by how well he takes counsel in acting for the good of the *polis*.[27] But the depth of problems facing him after the civil war obscures this understanding. He very quickly demonstrates the degree to which he lacks understanding by attempting to resolve the conflict laid bare by the civil war through a single, definitive act (his edict) and by trying to control absolutely that over which no human being has control (the divine). Creon, like Oedipus before him and now Antigone, is utterly subject to circumstance. He reacts from a space of fear, a space that, for him, means that political order and stability must be created and preserved at all cost. He sees that order and stability purely as functions of the exercise of his own political power. Consequently, "his" *polis* takes on his shortcomings: it is, at its heart, insecure, fearful and grasping, as we see in Creon's encounter with the guard. The maturity and wisdom necessary for the functional *polis* then, are missing in the leadership in the *Antigone* and are, instead, displaced to the young (Haemon) and the infirm (the Chorus). Maturity and wisdom are also displaced to the dead, the disfigured bodies, who, though they will gain voice through Teiresias, are mute, mutable, and manipulated for much of the play.

The displacement of maturity and wisdom is nowhere more telling than in Creon's wrenching encounter with his son Haemon.[28] The encounter is about duty, obligation, and appearance—the three bases of familial, political, and religious authority. The young Haemon seeks to save his bride, his father, and, thereby, his family and his city. His appearance marks Creon's last real chance to save Thebes from dissolution. Haemon, more than any other character, save Ismene, represents the possibility of a future for Thebes. He is son to Creon the father. He is husband-to-be to Antigone; their marriage would bind together Antigone and Creon and would be an important step in binding the spiritual to the political, as Oedipus does at Colonus, perhaps making Thebes whole again as curse becomes blessing. Finally Haemon is heir to Creon, and he seems to understand his role in the present and future of the *polis*: he would rule and rear his family there. In the figure of Haemon, we want to argue, *everything* is at stake and for the last time (a characteristically Sophoclean move—recreating the environments for/of choice of Creon and Antigone). Creon, predictably by now, refuses to listen to what his son brings forward, turning his back on the future of his family and his city. In the reflective mirror that is his son, Creon's inadequacies are vividly revealed.

When Haemon appears, Creon unconsciously mirroring Antigone who declares her nature is love, not hate,[29] attempts to set the terms of the encounter by rolling familial and political obligations into a single, one-sided and unconditional, conception of love. He asks that Haemon love him, unconditionally, no matter what his decision about Antigone.[30] This unconditional love and support—a grant of license for Creon's whims—is telling, for it is what he asks of both his son and his citizens. Fearful as he is, his is a selfish, immature, and inadequate conception of the love that must characterize both family member-ship and political citizenship. In both the *oikos* and the *polis*, authentic membership demands a love granting forgiveness and taking respon-sibility for the other—a love, in other words, of a much more mature sort than the kind Creon seeks and displays.

Haemon, trying to negotiate an impossible situation, responds, supporting his father's judgment, role as ruler, and father. He says that he will not value a marriage that overrides his father's leadership.[31] Haemon, like Ismene in her encounter with Antigone, demonstrates a subtlety and savvy beyond his tender years. He rejects the uncondi-tional love demanded by his father while appearing to offer support and, therefore, saving face for Creon before the people of Thebes. Like Ismene, he refuses to put an idea of family and community before real flesh and blood obligations. Haemon carefully conditions the obligations owed father and king on "excellent judgment," "the right," and the "goodness of your leadership." But everyone knows that Creon's leadership has been none of these things. Creon, not able to see beyond his own will and ego, fails to understand the point-edness of Haemon's subtle appeal. Hearing only what he wants to hear, Creon takes Haemon's words as words of unconditional sup-port. With the apparent support of his son, Creon launches into his own disquisition on government and on the obligations of ruler and ruled. He argues that a good man is just both in his household and in the *polis*. Creon says that those who break the law or dictate to the ruler, as Antigone has done, will not have his support. A ruler, chosen and given authority by the city, he argues, must be obeyed in great and small things. He concludes: "I am confident such a man of whom I speak/will be a good ruler, and willing to be well ruled."[32]

Haemon's earlier response to his father makes these royal words drip with irony and foreboding. Creon, by his treatment of Antigone, has disregarded the needs of his household by disregarding the wishes of his son. He, similarly, has disregarded the political and spiritual needs of the community through his edict. He is, it turns out, a just governor nowhere. The source of his authority is the power he takes to himself and, as a result, he is to be "obeyed in small things and in just/but also in their *opposites*."

Haemon, pledging his love and support, now tries to save his father and the king from himself. The wise ruler, the just and mature ruler, may find "something useful [in] that some other than you might think."[33] Just as Ismene tries to act as friend to Antigone, Haemon tries to act as friend to Creon. The citizens, Haemon tells his father, fear your face and the city is in mourning for Antigone, whom they think of as heroic and wronged. Young Haemon then reminds Creon how important it is for a just ruler to be generous of spirit and tem-perate of mind. While Haemon affirms that he supports his father and wishes for his success, he urges him not to believe that only his own way is the right way, or he may be seen to be "quite empty." A man, he argues, can learn new things, if he does not hold "too rigidly" to his views.[34]

Creon, already feeling emasculated by the woman Antigone in front of his court, is now lectured by his son regarding the dangers of greatness—of being "unique" and of standing alone, as Antigone does—and regarding the importance of maturity and soundness of mind to the good ruler. Haemon is aware, fully, of what he is doing, but hopes, like Aristotle's just man, that his words and deeds will give his father pause and reason to respond with moderation. He is polite and careful in his response to his father, saying, "If a much younger man, like me, may have/a judgment," that it is good to seek wisdom and to take the advise of other wise people.[35]

Haemon appeals to the gentler side of Creon's nature, a gentler side not evident in the play itself, but an affection that a son and father might share. He also uses Creon's words about the value of good counsel to remind Creon that the wise king knows he should be temperate in his handling of difficult situations. Here, even the Chorus changes; for the first time, buoyed by Haemon's display of courage and wisdom, they encourage Creon to listen, to see that the two men should learn from the other. Creon's humiliation, however, is complete; his inadequacy is laid bare for all to see. Those he ruled or would rule according to his will, Antigone, his family and his citizenry, have recognized and challenged his failings in a most public manner. Efforts to implore him to humility, temperance, and wisdom—"Yield," Haemon tells him as Ismene tells Antigone—necessarily fail.

Creon's response is one of predictable rashness. He equates wisdom with age and posits his own age as the mark of a wisdom superior to that of his son. Haemon speaks for Sophocles and foreshadows Aristotle: "If I am young/do not look at my years but what I do."[36] In a city stricken by civil war, nothing is as it should be; even the proper relationship of maturity to age is turned upon its head. Creon responds to his son as a young boy would: does Haemon really suggest that Creon should have respect for rebels? But the city, Haemon reminds his father, does not see Antigone as a rebel. Creon's telling retort speaks of his unfitness to rule: "Should the city tell me how I am to rule them?"[37] Creon, here, repudiates what he said only a few lines earlier about counsel and the good ruler. Mindful of the turnabout, Haemon asks his father, "Do you see what a young man's words these are of yours?"[38] The encounter disintegrates. Haemon reminds his father that the ruler does not own the city, but Creon refutes that assertion. Haemon, seeing that his father cannot be moved, says, "You would be a fine dictator of a desert."[39]

Creon, hopelessly cornered, childishly resorts to name-calling, saying that his son is a "woman's slave."[40] Haemon recognizes that the conversation is at an end, that no one can tell his father anything. Creon threatens to kill Antigone before Haemon's eyes but Haemon flees, vowing that the father will never look upon his son's face again.

At this point, before the appearance of Teiresias, the state and family have been destroyed. Creon, bent on defending his edict, has lost any sight he ever had of his real task, the task that Lincoln will contemplate so carefully: reconstituting the *polis*. Creon must reconstitute Thebes, mending the rift between the spiritual and the political life of the *polis*. The encounter with his son—more violence perpetuated against children and another violation of intimacy that is civil war—represents the depth of Creon's power. He is completely blind to himself, to the needs of the family, and to the needs of the state. As Antigone earlier turns her back on Ismene, her only living family, so now does Creon turn his back on his family. The situation gets worse as, in the encounter with Teiresias, he will turn his back on the gods. Had Ismene made Antigone consider marriage to Haemon, with what marriage might mean for the city and for the family, those institutions might be saved. Similarly, had Haemon made his father see the true role of the ruler, Creon might have bridged the gap, by endorsing the marriage and allowing burial and mourning, between himself and Antigone, between the political and the spiritual, between human law and natural law, between the *polis* and the *oikos*. Creon, however, like Antigone, has other priorities, and his emerges as the greater flaw.

The *polis* is out of whack; Creon, as one translator has Teiresias put it, has "confused"[41] the categories and spheres of being and meaning. The possibilities of redemption are in the hands of those, who, though reasonable and mature beyond their years, are not yet ready and do not have the power to carry out the task. Ismene and Haemon are young, sensitive, and less ideologically driven than either Antigone or Creon. Those they must persuade, however, are beyond persuasion. The strident voice marks discourse, and the rash action undoes temperance in the time of civil war. Measured, reasoned responses are not heeded because the language in which they are spoken is useless to the combatants. Both sides take possession of discourse—particularly, as Lincoln will say, that of righteousness—and that exclusivity marks the limits of its effectiveness.

Like Haemon and Ismene, Lincoln, though not powerless, found himself betwixt and between the defenders of the Constitution. To his enemies, both the Southerners who wished to preserve "the peculiar institution" no matter what the cost and the Northerners who would eradicate those Southerners without mercy or brotherhood, Lincoln seems to be either like Creon, the thoughtless tyrant, or like Antigone, the committed ideologue. On closer inspection, however, Lincoln is more like Haemon and Ismene than like Creon or Antigone. Lincoln, like Haemon and to a different extent, Ismene, is caught between Creon (those who will become the Radical Republicans) and Antigone (the traditions appealed to by the South).

Lincoln, like Ismene and Haemon, believes he can preserve the polity by saving the marriage between North and South. In the First Inaugural, Lincoln, faced with the secession of Southern states, emphasizes Union. On the issue of slavery, he acknowledges that it is part of the Constitution and therefore a part of Union, but he also suggests that the Constitution is silent in key places: on the surrender of fugitive slaves and on whether slavery can be prohibited and/or protected in the territories. These silences let Lincoln both support the South and control its interests, at once.

What is key for him is the Union, which is greater than its parts. The Union, for Lincoln, is perpetual and eternal. It precedes the Constitution itself; indeed, he argues, the Articles of Confederation of 1778 and the Constitution are descriptions of how "to form a more perfect Union." Union, for Lincoln, is covenantal: a state (part/minority) may protest against it, but even leaving it does not mean that Union (whole/majority) is broken. The *polis*, as the Chorus in the "Ode to Man" suggests, is the proper context for the human being who, no matter how great a wonder he is, needs the laws, the gods, and the hearth, which are the sources of justice[42]; similarly, the Union, for Lincoln, is the source of benefits, hopes, and memories, insuring justice. His conception of Union reflects the Greek sense of the *polis*: a community of relationships across political, spiritual, familial lines. To leave the *polis*, for Sophocles and for Lincoln, invites both the "anarchy" of which Antigone is often accused and the despotism of which Creon is often accused. In other words, it is to invite the extremes that destroy both state and human being.

Like Sophocles, Lincoln uses the metaphors of home and marriage to emphasize the bonds of the Union. In a speech at Indianapolis, Indiana on February 11, 1861, he describes the Union as a "family relation," as a "regular marriage," not a "free-love relationship to be maintained only on passional attraction."[43] In the First Inaugural, in March 1861, he extends that metaphor, arguing that "Physically speaking, we cannot separate," and he compares the North and South to a married couple:

A husband and wife may be divorced, and go out of the presence and beyond the reach of each other; but the different parts of our country cannot do this. They cannot but remain face to face; and intercourse, either amicable or hostile must continue between them.[44]

The metaphor of intercourse, of persuasive discourse and sexual interaction, links state and family, individual and group. Lincoln understands that intercourse cannot be by force: rape is an attack on the person and on intimacy and destabilizes states and families, just as despotism and division undercut Union. Indeed, Lincoln displaces himself as a center, avoiding the trap of greatness of which Sophocles warns; he continually asserts that he is acting without malice and the task of solving the issues is in the hands of the people.

In this context, Lincoln casts himself as mediator. The distinction Sophocles makes between friends and aliens recurs in Lincoln's speeches as he notes that, on the one hand, aliens make treaties, that is, agreements that merely let them coexist for a while. On the other hand, friends make laws: "Can aliens make treaties easier than friends can make laws? Can treaties be more faithfully enforced between aliens than laws among friends?"[45] Lincoln argues that if we cannot rule ourselves together under commonly agreed-upon laws, the persistence of the issues which prevent such an agreement will make it impossible for North and South to make treaties as separate sovereign nations. We cannot fight forever, Lincoln suggests. Rather, we must come to be able to live together in the place, to paraphrase Albert Camus on the Algerian question, where history has placed us.[46] While treaties make an uneasy peace, laws suggest an intimacy, a trust among the governed. We agree to abide by the laws, even if we oppose them. The trust is in the Constitution that provides the means of making the laws. On the other hand, treaties open lines of communication between or among "aliens" that are not natural or obvious and are, therefore, artificial. Lincoln's point, we argue, is that neither laws nor treaties, even if they were appropriate between friends, would be enforceable between those who, by virtue of their initial split, no longer share the mutual trust necessary for their enforcement. Lincoln's invocation of the issue of "intercourse," that is, political, social, and personal intimacy, is one that will have to be addressed, either before conflict or after: "the identical old questions," he writes, will be there either way.[47]

Deliberation and effective discourse, unheeded in the *Antigone*, are what Lincoln urges: "one and all, think calmly and *well*."[48] Friends, in the Aristotelian sense, are those who can do this together, as equals, setting forth arguments and accepting critique; therefore, Lincoln urges friendship upon all: "We are not enemies but friends."[49] Passion, the extremes of feeling, and the shunning of reason, will "break our bonds of affection," and this must not be given licence. He concludes:

The mystic chords of memory, stretching from every battle-field, and patriot grave, to every living heart and hearth-stone, all over this broad land, will yet swell the chorus of Union, when again touched, as surely they will be, by the better angels of our nature.[50]

He uses music as the metaphor for the politically defined but still mysterious bond between us. We are bound by chords, which, in music, consist of three notes sounded simultaneously. This suggests harmonious relations, unity with difference. Lincoln also suggests cords, the idea of ties. Together, we sing a common song; we are a chorus. We are bound, person to person, person to household, household to household, and household to state, by the struggles that made us a Union. The memory of our common inheritance makes us one and can continue to bind us together, when "by the better angels of our nature"—our intelligence, patriotism, and faith in Providence—we face and address our common dilemma.[51]

Like Antigone and Creon, Lincoln, at first, emphasizes the Civil War as a matter of state, forgetting the gods. By 1865, however, when the war is, for all intents and purposes, over, he begins to contemplate that there may be a greater other force at work. He laments the great losses, but he is also thinking in terms of reconstituting the Union and the ultimate inadequacy of the political as a means to that end. The carnage inflicted by and upon both sides transcends the principles asserted as the reason for the conflict.[52] God's will is the name that Lincoln gives for the lessons to be learned, and he begins to try to discern and perhaps to bring his efforts into one with the will of God. The unity of God must be mirrored in the resolution of this conflict through the structure that he understands as the only abiding one: Union.[53] He begins, in the First Inaugural, by saying that he has no desire or right to interfere with slavery. By 1862, however, he has changed his mind, recognizing, in the Second Inaugural, the *miasma* that slavery has put at the heart of America. It is a *miasma* that is worked out, externalized in the war:

Fondly do we hope—fervently do we pray—that this mighty scourge of war may speedily pass away. Yet, if God will that it continue, until all the wealth piled by the bond-man's two hundred and fifty years of unrequited toil shall be sunk, and until every drop of blood drawn with the lash, shall be paid by another drawn with the sword, as was said three thousand years ago, so still it must be said "the judgments of the Lord, are true and righteous altogether."[54]

The mystic chords of memory are in dissonance. What binds us is not only the price paid by those who fought and died for Union, an echo of Pericles' "Funeral Oration," but also the suffering of those who made the wealth of a nation possible. For this blood curse, for the suffering of those under the lash, Lincoln realizes, others are to die by the sword.

Teiresias articulates this principle in the *Antigone*. Civil war, as we have argued confuses categories. Polyneices' body—a dead body of a young man, a brother and nephew, that has become the symbol of rebellion and that lies in the light of day—and Antigone's and Haemon's bodies—young, living bodies in a tomb that marry, "dead upon the dead"[55] with no issue except more death—like those of the slaves and of Northern and Southern dead, signify the city's sickness and the violation of the laws of God. Creon's edict intensifies the pollution, and his act costs him everything—even, finally, the life he knew. Antigone's stance, though not wholly right, emerges as the more powerful one: rites must be done and words spoken to reunite, to honor and heal. Teiresias supports her, saying that he divines by the birds and that he heard "an unwonted voice among them."[56] He refers to the moment the fearful and self-interested guard spotted her as a goddess in the whirlwind, sprinkling dust over the body of her brother and crying like an "embittered" bird "[t]hat sees its nest robbed of its nestlings/and the bed empty."[57] Earth and sky, chthonic gods and Olympian gods, mix in the whirlwind, meet at this moment of burial, approving Antigone's act.

For Lincoln, Union remains, as burial does for Antigone, the site/rite of memory and of healing. Only in this unified, yet simultaneously transitive, structure, in the context of this covenant, he believes, can the wounds of the nation be bound and can the proper care be given those who survive. Union is, to use Toni Morrison's words in speaking of her novel *Beloved*, the altar, the fixing place, where the "unspeakable things unspoken," acted on black bodies and paid for by white bodies, can be spoken, brought to light and healed.[58]

The body—Polyneices' body which is at the heart of the conflict in *Antigone* and the black bodies which are at the heart of the Civil War—is the symbol of the spiritual and political conflicts that are brought into sharp relief in a civil war. Body and state, Elaine Scarry argues in *The Body in Pain* are inextricably interwoven.[59] On the body of the citizen-soldier, the true issues of conflict manifest, and, there, the "unanchored issues" of war are settled, confirming one cultural reality over another.[60] In a civil war, the issue of contest and winning—we killed more bodies than you did and, therefore, we win—are complex. As Judith Butler among others has noted, the non-combatant bodies count in the final tally, too and, finally, there is no winner.[61] In civil war, in which both sides are bound in one cultural reality despite their disagreements, the body is a container of meaning, like the body politic itself. Despite giving the illusion that it is solid and stable, and, perhaps, eternal and perpetual, the body politic is ultimately incapable of either devising or housing a resolution to the spiritual-political conflict. The body and its significations get lost in discourses of right interpretation, just as Polyneices is "forgotten" in the conflict between Antigone and Creon and slaves are "forgotten" in debates about issues like states' rights. The claims of the forgotten, of those who cannot speak, Sophocles and Lincoln argue, are upheld by the gods and can surge to the fore in terrible ways. To deny them is to deny the holy, the gods themselves, and to deny the significance of holy in our relations with each other.

Creon confuses categories; so, too, does slavery as it denies within the black community the distinctions of family and, instead, seeks to make a faceless mass, a large unit of energy. Moreover, it denies intimate blood relations and ties between slaves and their masters. To right that confusion takes the true visionary and healer, whose word is, in Teiresias' case, too late, and in Lincoln's unheeded. In civil war, Teiresias emerges, as does Lincoln we think, as the figure who shows us the balance necessary for healing. As a blind seer, Teiresias embodies a transitivity that can mediate: When proper rites are done to honor the body, conflicts can be mediated, if not wholly healed. Tierisias, leaning on his young companion, who guides Teiresias as Teiresias guides others,[62] shows us how wisdom is a combination of the capacities for decision and discernment that come with the experience of old age and the openness to possibility of the heart and mind of a child. To see all possibilities and to be able to choose among them, to make critical distinctions, is true wisdom. There is no accident, therefore, that children are central symbols in the Theban plays. The *Oedipus the King* begins with Oedipus surrounded by children; Oedipus' children lead him and betray him; Creon and Antigone reject children; and, finally, it is the "true born child of Zeus," Dionysus, whose ecstasy destroys in order to purify, who closes the play.[63]

Aristotle is drawn to Sophocles because Sophocles understands the difficulty and the importance of the mean. One should not want to be great, like Antigone and Creon, for greatness—to stand alone and unique—is too extreme, too self- interested and much too reckless. Neither does one want to be too small, like the guard; this figure is too small to be anything other than self-interested and fearful. The extremes become the same; they meet at the site of the desecrated body and destroy all that is. The "Ode to Man" warns us of the need to be in context, and Lincoln knows this. He eschews uniqueness and seeks structures—legal ones, primarily: laws, citizenship, Union—that can mediate the extremes.

The mean, which we call transitivity, gives both sides the power to *be*, to exist in balance and in creative tension. Children, who are so central to these plays and who are central and problematic to the nation are both sign of and signification on this balance. As hope, they are past and future, *oikos* and *polis*, a sign of finitude and a hope for immortality. They are also signification: the conflict, both in America and Thebes, holds all the signs of balance but that possibility remains problematic, particularly when the children are the children of mothers and their sons; of masters and their slaves. Teiresias and Lincoln, the mature visionaries, know that hope and *miasma*, the future and what Lincoln would call "original sin," are inseparable. Rites, like marriage and burial, within structures, like *polis* and union, are sites at which what is unspoken can be said, what is hidden—Lincoln's "somehow"—can be brought to light, what is confused can be and, momentarily, righted. In the ordinary, social religion of the *polis* and the extraordinary religion of the cult, opposites can meet, and we are one, if only momentarily. A true self accepts and seeks this meeting, this belonging, involving friendship, mutuality, and maturity, judgment and wisdom. In this resides the mediated will of the divine. Without it, character, with which Sophocles is so concerned, stands alone, disconnected and ruined—and, finally, broken by the gods.

CHAPTER 6

OEDIPUS AT COLONUS AND THE GOSPEL AT COLONUS: AFRICAN AMERICAN EXPERIENCE AND THE CLASSICAL TEXT

At the core of *Oedipus at Colonus* and of *The Gospel at Colonus* is the working out of divine justice in one human character.[1] The "lonely I" of the *Oedipus the King*, the accursed object, in Sophocles's last play, written at the end of Sophocles's life and set in the place of his birth, is transformed into a blessing for Athens. He is changed through suffering and choice and by a rite that lets him do the most simple yet most difficult of acts: tell his story. So too, in a subtle way, Lee Breuer, in his African American Holiness-Pentecostal rendering of Sophocles's Oedipus at Colonus, *The Gospel at Colonus*, tells a tale of African American life in America. The consequences in the rite done and the story told mark the differences between the settings and ultimate meanings of these plays, one Greek and tragic and the other, finally, Christian and transformed by joy. As Oedipus confronts us, he points to the complexity of the human being—in short to us: to "those strange, unthought-of connections—sex and death, lust and violence, desire and degradation—[that lie] deep in even a good heart's chambers"[2] and to, to borrow Abraham Lincoln's phrase, spoken at the beginning of the American Civil War, "the better angels of our natures."

We can enter Sophocles's play, *Oedipus at Colonus,* through the African American experience. In the haunting opening of *The Gospel at Colonus*, the Preacher speaks an epigraph:

> Think no longer that you are in command here,
> But rather think how, when you were,
> You served your own destruction.[3]

This is a call to surrender—but to what? It is a call that demands a response—but how and in what voice? This epigraph prefaces the Preacher's first narration of the "Book of Oedipus"[4]—the story is told numerous times—and is followed by an equally haunting song:

> Live where you can
> Be happy as you can
> Happier than God has made your father.[5]

This is Oedipus's prayer, we are told, for his daughters, who are also sisters and grandchildren, all caught in the "Net of incest, mingling wives, sisters, mothers/With fathers, sons, brothers."[6]

The song and Oedipus's prayer, we suggest, point to key elements of the African American experience in America. Positively, they suggest movement and empowerment: African American life involves an aggressive and audacious living forward toward freedom, the hope by African American fathers and mothers that their children will live happier than they are. But they also point to a second darker thing that is the problem for Oedipus: blood. America, we might argue, is defined by two things: by race worked out in place, on the one hand, and by space, the frontier, on the other. Lest this sound simply cute, let us explain. American identity is defined by the frontier—that imagined opening to unlimited possibility that unsettles the fixed. It is also defined, however, by the arrangements, acknowledgments, and denials, social and personal, that we make to live with each other at home. These have been, as Alan Tate put it in *The Fathers*, the agreement slowly arrived at to leave the abyss alone.[7] The blood is the sign of the abyss. Oedipus is the abyss, the accursed object, and the sign of *miasma*. Miasma is contagious. The family of Oedipus, entangled, entwined, and inseparable in blood, in story, and in identity, carries and extends this *miasma*.

Miasma is what slavery generated. Slavery was the attempt to create units of labor out of human beings. Slavery, therefore, meant the erasure of kin, clan, and family so that one does not know one's sisters and mothers, sons and brothers, and can be caught in a net of incest. It meant the mingling of Euro-American and African blood that is always a secret and that means that we are related by blood. And it meant the blood of sacrifice: the dead, black and white, but also the blood of Christ that bound black and white together. All that blood knowledge unacknowledged marks a part of American becoming. Blood is the source and sign of both intimacy and distance, of both terror and love. It is, as Abraham Lincoln mused in his second inaugural, our original sin. No wonder the Preacher warns that being in command has led to destruction and the call for surrender. But to what and how?

These inseparable conjunctions, the warring binaries of the historic and the mythic in American experience, send one either to passivity or total madness or to Toni Morrison. In an interview about her novel *Beloved*, Morrison, at one point, muses that, as America faces the consequences of slavery, there must be "For purposes of exorcism [and] celebratory rites of passage.... Things must be made, some fixing ceremony, some memorial, some thing, some altar somewhere."[8] What will happen there? The "unspeakable things unspoken"[9] will be spoken so that they can be acknowledged—not in the secret and haunted way they are in *Beloved*, but openly. When the home is the place of speaking, it is altered and cannot be a place of safety. Indeed, in the black church experience depicted in Breuer's play, the surrender to the spirit is in the safe space of the church. Church as "sanctuary," as Oedipus calls it in the play, reminds us that post-Reconstruction America—we can say from the 1880s when the Holiness movements began—to pre-Harlem Renaissance when the Pentecostal movements began, was a place of terror (lynching, for example), disenfranchisement, movement, and struggle for black Americans—a time when life must have seemed, at times, "Without Sanctuary." The church as sanctuary echoes Morrison's hope that there will be some "other" place that transforms the altered space of suffering, the postcolonial, post-slavery place, into an "altar-ed" place of healing.

The altared place is Colonus, and the fixing ceremony is a rite done and a story told. Colonus is a place of shade trees, and of nightingales, ivy, narcissus, crocus, rivers, olive groves, horses, and the sea. All these indicate that in Colonus, opposites exist harmoniously. The ivy reminds us of Dionysus, the god of Thebes and of the theater. The ivy crowns the "twin goddesses," Demeter and Persephone, who represent the cycle of death and resurrection, the city of Athens and the pilgrimage site of the mysteries of Eleusis. The waters are associated with Aphrodite and the muses. The olive is Athene's gift to Athens.

Horses are the gift of Poseidon, god of the sea. This beauty is offset by sadness. The nightingale is the bird of mourning, and the narcissus and crocus are associated with Demeter and Persephone.[10] This nexus of opposites, this place of life, of fecundity and beauty, and of death, of passage and of transformation, is Oedipus's resting place.

The action of the rite is the same in both plays and carries a similar double meaning. In *Oedipus at Colonus*, the Chorus of old men describes the rite that Oedipus directs his daughter, Ismene, who is the principal agent of movement, to do for him. In the *Gospel at Colonus*, Antigone, the Evangelist, directs Oedipus, who does the rite himself. To these differences we will turn in a moment. The rite involves a libation of pure spring water brought by unsullied hands. The offering bowls should be topped with wool shorn from a ewe lamb.[11] The libation should be poured toward the rising sun in three streams, the last emptying the bowl. The third bowl should be filled with honey and water. Finally, when the last libation is poured, the offering should be covered with nine sprigs of olive. Then Oedipus should pray— in Sophocles's play, silently "As we call these the Kindly Ones, with kindly/hearts may they welcome this suppliant for his saving."[12]

The symbols of the rite indicate its purpose. The lamb, from which the wool comes, is the symbol of resurrection. The Christian connection is clear: Jesus as the lamb or carrying a lamb is an important symbol, particularly in the early church, and Breuer connects Christianity and African traditional religion through the pouring of libation. In Greek mythology, the image is connected to Hermes, the shepherd of souls to the underworld. Honey is a desired food and a preservative. It is associated with both Aphrodite and Demeter, the feminine potency of nature and the goddess of reincarnation and resurrection. The olive is beloved of Athene, the goddess of Athens, and it is self-regenerating. Water is the symbol of purity, and it is the mother element, associated as well with Aphrodite and the Muses. Ismene, who does the ritual for her father in Sophocles's play, acts, we assume, as Oedipus speaks. In the *Gospel*, Oedipus does the act and then speaks. In both, Oedipus confesses; he tells his story.

In the Sophocles play, Oedipus and the Chorus, who are old men like Oedipus, engage in a *stychomythia*, a call and response, concerning his act and its justice. Though Oedipus has asserted that he will not be moved from Colonus, this confession puts him in a difficult spot. Oedipus is an object of potential punishment, of retributive justice for the murder of his father. His arguments that he is innocent of the murder may strike the reader as strained. Oedipus argues that he has suffered into truth: "for deeds—/ . . . done without knowledge./ In all of this there was nothing of conscious choice."[13] He acknowledges that he did kill his father, in innocence and ignorance, but that, however this death came about, his father, thereby, had "Something of justice" from him.[14]

What is Oedipus arguing? Oedipus is not in the same position as Orestes in Aeschylus' *Oresteia*. Orestes acts with full knowledge of what he is doing and of its consequences and, thereby, becomes what Camus calls "an innocent murderer."[15] Oedipus, in contrast, does only that what he thinks is good in the situation—a situation in which he is caught between two "bads"—death or murder. He, therefore, has to be purified of the actions. This purification is accomplished in his wandering and in his blindness: in short, in his suffering. He does not have to be purified of guilt or, more accurately, of shame.[16] Further punishment cannot resolve his complex moral position. The rite, therefore, is not just about expiation for the murder/death of his father.

Then for whom is it? For his mother, Jocasta. The Kindly Ones, the Eumenides, we should remember, are the Furies: those chthonic goddesses of darkness who punish matricide. Oedipus, therefore, is in the same position as Orestes: he participates in the death of his mother. The last thing Oedipus sees before his blinding is his mother. She has hanged herself, and he takes the brooches of her robe, which falls away, confronting him with the truth of his existence: the body from which he issues and with which he made life. Oedipus's rite, done by his daughter and full of feminine images, is for the mother, and his story, which is the confession not only of the murder but also of the incest, positions Oedipus properly in relationship to the *oikos* and the chthonic gods.

The ritual does not wipe out the past. It reframes the past: it opens the possibility that the unspeakable can be spoken. The rite allows the old men of the polis of Athens to see Oedipus in the proper perspective and opens the way for him to be granted "resting place" through the citizenship granted to him by Theseus. Citizenship is the final reconstitution of the relationship with the father—with the *polis* and the Olympian gods.

The movement of bodies—the focusing of tensions on the dead body—is a key theme in Sophocles's Theban trilogy. The *agon* is central for Sophocles; the battleground is the psyche, and the symbol of the battle is the dead or dying human body. In *Oedipus the King*, the dead bodies of mother and father lead to exile and suffering. In *Antigone*, the dead body of Polyneices leads to the destruction of family and *polis*. Likewise, Oedipus's body is central to *Oedipus at Colonus*. The rite also restores self: Oedipus's right to make the choice of what will happen to it. Oedipus's body becomes the object of justice and power. He is envisioned as property in both plays. He is a thing, a commodity, to be owned, stripping him of spirit, as African Americans in slavery are owned. Polyneices and Creon believe that Oedipus bene-fits the *polis* only as object. Both intend to keep him a prisoner, on the boundaries of Thebes, to leave him forever suspended. They under-stand justice as the advantage of the stronger, won through owning Oedipus as a commodity. Justice is a goal to be achieved, if necessary, through violence.

Oedipus's control of his own body, because he has citizenship given by Theseus, is his claim on humanity and nobility and on the "resting place." His stubborn insistence that he will not move places Oedipus in the position to make a conscious choice. His inability to be per-suaded had been a serious flaw in the young Oedipus. Now, in the old Oedipus, the dirty, pitiful beggar, it is a positive virtue. Oedipus does not change and, in consequence, becomes more and more himself. He stands at another crossroads, but this time, he knows the significance of his choice. It leads to his death, but what kind?

As Oedipus sits at the edge of the sacred precinct of Colonus, on the edge of death, he moves in transitive, ritual space, reviewing his life, which comes to him in the persons of Ismene, Creon, and Polyneices. This receiving of persons echoes the structure of *Oedipus the King*, and again Oedipus is, indeed, in command. What these inter-actions in transitive space indicate is the nature of Oedipus's choice. Oedipus's choice is between two places. He can turn back to Thebes, a city founded on violence, a house divided against itself, that is the city of Dionysus, the god that destroys in order to purify or move forward to a connection with Athens, a symbol of rationality, democ-racy, and order, beloved of Athene, goddess of wisdom. Colonus, as a transitive space, is both passage and contact zone. It connects and, with Oedipus's body there, perhaps reconciles these. It is home, for example, to the Eumenides and to the Olympians as well. Upper and lower worlds join here. It is a place of death and life, a site of sacri-fice. In a sense, Oedipus stands between these. He is, paradoxically, Giorgio Agamben's "bare life" *and* sovereign. He is the exception, as Agamben argues, and, therefore double: the exception is "what can-not be included in the whole of which it is a member and cannot be a member of the whole in which it is always already included."[17] But he is also in a tripling, a sovereign who determines his status, the terms of his own membership. The sovereign, Agamben argues, is the other exception. Sacredness, Agamben argues, does not exist polit-ically, except in the purview, the domain, of sovereign power. The sacred is the exception. Oedipus, as sacred, is transitivity itself, poised for and as decision: as a strange symbol of reconciliation.

Decision, the human act, is at the core of Sophocles's notions of justice. Zeus's thunder sounds in Colonus, and Sophocles seems to echo Aeschylus' assertion that human beings suffer into truth. Conflict and human choice open a space for the god to enter, either to destroy or to bless. We are, Sophocles indicates, responsible for the consequences of our own actions. Victimization, while a fact of existence, is not an excuse for individual actions or for inaction. There is a conflict between freedom and necessity, but true freedom recognizes necessity; embraces the truth of *hamartia*, missing the mark; and suggests that we should act as well as we can. Death, as the unknowable and inevitable limit of existence, is the challenge.

The challenge is to accept the inevitability of death and to make choices anyway—and, more importantly, to take responsibility for those choices. Death, in the play, is a gift for Oedipus. He can choose the place of his burial, and choosing the final resting place of his body, he blesses his friends, Theseus and Colonus, and punishes his enemies, Creon and Polyneices. His burial in a secret/sacred place reconciles the public and private tensions in both the play and in the man. His death and burial, rather than his incest and patricide, become what he is remembered for. His death is the moment that he stands alone, in the most positive sense. He is not the "lonely I" he was in *Oedipus the King* and as Antigone remains. He is unique but in relation: he is again noble and again a hero. He corrects the mistake of his youth and in so doing he exercises justice; that is, he exercises the capacity for judgment that restores balance to what is out of order.

We can see the movement of the character of Sophocles's Oedipus as an analogue to the way Breuer uses the myth. In the Theban trilogy, as we have seen, Sophocles's Oedipus is displaced, but that displacement leads him back to himself. Breuer's work suggests we see myth in a similar fashion. As with Sophocles's character, to displace a myth to an-other location is not to forget its original location; it is to create a signifying relation between the original and the new location. There are many reasons Breuer turns to Oedipus. This play has been one that, in translation and in the criticism, has been overlaid with a Judeo-Christian ideology. Indeed, Robert Fitzgerald's translation of the play, which Breuer uses, identifies Oedipus with Christ and as savior.[18] And the final "resting place" of Oedipus as secret identifies him with Moses. Breuer builds on the fact that, in slave theology, Moses and Christ are identified with each other, signifying liberation, resurrection, and life and connected with freedom from slavery in the Exodus.[19]

Breuer uses the Pentecostal/Holiness structure of testimony, its styles of repetition, and of call and response, and has them intersect with similar structures in the Greek text, namely, the *stichomythia*, and in doing so manages to give them new meaning. At the center of his play is the testimony of Oedipus and how it moves in the church. Jon Michael Spenser, in *Protest and Praise*, argues that testimony shapes and rejuvenates the common consciousness of the church.[20] The individual speaking energizes the whole. In a movement between extradependence, the "reversal to connexion (*sic*)," "the recognition of the Centre and the act of turning again to it," and intradependence, the expansion of the individual into his or her own being,[21] a self is formed that is a self for and with others and that, simultaneously, can face and negotiate an often difficult world alone. Testimony, Spenser argues, is a kind of regression, a deep movement into the self that, through the connection others make with that self, brings about transformation for the whole. "If sacrifice is at the heart of rite," he concludes, "then perhaps testimony is also sacrificial."[22]

In the regressive movement of the testimony, a creative energy is released,[23] a spirit that moves in the congregation. The infectious power of *miasma* is rewritten as the infectious power of the Spirit. This is signaled in *The Gospel* by the multiplicity of voices that are Oedipus. The preacher speaks Oedipus' sins, in tongues, connecting with the spirit of Oedipus. As Creon comes to take Antigone and Ismene, Oedipus becomes a combination of himself, the preacher, and a quintet. This multiplicity of voices, an African American literary motif of multiple narration, signals the movement of the Spirit in the Colonus congregation, drawing what has been "audience" into a participant role. Oedipus, in this Christian reading, is Everyman. Oedipus is the symbol of sin. The movement of the Spirit, generated by his confession, signals the presence of God's grace, forgiving that sin. What Theseus grants Oedipus, therefore, in exchange for the "advantage" he brings to Colonus, is not citizenship, but grace.[24] The evidence of grace is clear as the Spirit moves through the congregation. Oedipus, in this play, does not become more and more himself; everyone in the congregation becomes more and more Oedipus, acknowledging that his sin is theirs and joining him in his acts—in, for example, rebuking Polyneices as he testifies and in participating in the curse Oedipus places on him. Finally, however, they join him in his transformation: they, and we, join Oedipus as he is saved, descending and taking all sin with him.

The movement from terror to love is the movement of both plays, but the sense in which Oedipus becomes guide to all of us is different.

In the Greek play, Oedipus's nobility marks him as the exemplary man. In *The Gospel*, Oedipus becomes prophet, Moses and perhaps, Elijah, and savior, Christ. In the latter, the sound of Zeus' thunder is not just a sound of imminent death and of justice but also of salvation. The Preacher and Chorus confirm: "My soul is salvation bound."[25] Oedipus as savior figure asks in a Christ-like way, "Remember me."[26] He also pronounces, in a prophetic way, that God's justice is inevitable: "Put off God and turn to madness. Fear not./God attends to these things slowly; but he attends."[27] This is the promise to an African American community in distress; it was also Abraham Lincoln's, to end where we began, understanding of the price of slavery—an *agon* of the national soul, continuing until God wills the end. It was his hope for a war-torn nation, his hope for peace, within the United States itself and with other nations. In the opening call, the Preacher calls for surrender, and Oedipus responds. The church, becoming more and more Oedipus, and Oedipus taken together are the Suffering Servant, signaling that one must surrender to God, and through Oedipus' suffering, He will attend.

This power is confirmed as Oedipus not only dies but is also resurrected. While both plays call for the weeping to cease, in *The Gospel at Colonus*, Oedipus returns, as the church cries, "Lift him up in a blaze of glory," and echoing "Amazing Grace," "I was blind and now I see . . . I was blind! He made me see!"[28] And Oedipus is present to hear the summary of his life, the judgment, and is restored to life in the church.

Both plays end with an end to lamentation. In *Oedipus at Colonus*, however, the peace is momentary; more tragedy awaits. Antigone, who demands and is refused the knowledge of her father's resting place, is on her way to Thebes to try to stop her brothers.[29] *The Gospel at Colonus* ends in unity and in peace, a momentary earthly peace that is the promise, the foreshadowing, of eternal peace:

> Now let the weeping cease.
> Let no one mourn again.
> The love of God will bring you peace.
> There is no end.[30]

CONCLUSIONS

"There is no end."

Some of the first words we learn as children are "Once upon a time." Some of the first words we learn, as spiritual children in the

West, are "In the beginning was the Word." Story forms our minds and souls and shapes our identities. In our innocence, we know that the story of the other is our own, but as we grow, we resist and then forget. Then the Preacher must call us back: "Think no longer that you are in command here,/But rather think how, when you were,/You served your own destruction."[31] Restoring that memory—and an accompanying sense of wholeness—is the work of both religion and politics, in their different but complementary ways, and the final point we take from both *Oedipus at Colonus* and *The Gospel at Colonus*.

Toni Morrison called for a memorial, a "fixing place," somewhere. Morrison's language of "somewhere" suggests transitivity: a space in which wounded human beings can gather in an-other form of community, testify, be acknowledged, and begin to heal. For her, that altared space is the story. Robert Detweiler said two things that illuminate the ethical and moral implications of the idea of a community of readers. And we will use his remarks to conclude. He said, first, "there are only moments."[32] He also reminds us that, second, story is erotic: For Detweiler, the beauty of story is that participating in telling it means that I may come to be unable to think my story without thinking yours.[33] In that relation is a new community. We would add—irrelevantly, really—that the erotic nature of story is that it moves us toward the good, the true, and the just. In the *logos* (the story, the Spirit, the Word, etc.) may be found the truth and reconciliation that lead to reconstruction and reconstitution of self and society. This meeting, as we would call it, is the transitive moment. For Detweiler, it may last only a moment and pass into memory—but it happened. The moment of epiphany, of meeting, for him, is enough.

This moment of meeting is, potentially, full of terror and love, as the Oedipus story illustrates. The erotic moment may mean participating in the pain of, the being of, others we never imagined we might know. Every black person, we would venture to assert, knows what it feels like to be bare life, the accursed object. What *The Gospel at Colonus* does, using a foundational myth of Western culture, is to extend that knowledge to those who might never have felt it.

In simple terms, it makes us identify with the "other"; in Sophocles's construction, Theseus has been in exile and the citizens of Colonus are old; they, too, share in Oedipus's being, each in his way, and that makes them hear his story with sympathy and give him a home. His Athenian audience, facing the end of democracy, should have felt such sympathy. In less simple terms, such identification in the moment may change us forever. In Breuer's play, Oedipus speaks, finally, out of every voice. The Preacher is Oedipus;

the Chorus is Oedipus; and in the death and resurrection, the church is Oedipus—and so, we would bet the playwright hopes, is the audience. Elaine Scarry, in the *Body in Pain*, argues that when pain speaks, it silences everything around it.[34] So too does Oedipus's pain, but the silence after speaking—the deep breath that is the relief from the Spirit—signals communal silence, communal guilt, and communal expiation.

Sophocles wants to suggest—and Breuer's play extends this suggestion—a sense of justice that, we would argue, comes only from the rite performed and the story told and heard. A notion of justice rooted in ritual and story causes a reexamination of matters of social and political justice. That transitive space of the ritual or story is one that invites us to move, not *from* the political *to* the religious space, *from* the institution *to* the rite, *from* the law *to* the story or myth— back and forth *across* borders and *through* the *limen*—but to move *in* the space between these, in a more unclear, a potentially contentious, but also creative space. Such a process is dynamic, based on the values of the *polis* but constantly evolving, as the alien enters and upsets the balance as he or she acts, and speaks. In short, such a dynamic process requires the active imagination. Perhaps, developing—and we fear we are losing the capacity to do so—and engaging such a faculty, we can begin to imagine a just and compassionate world and, perhaps, since the grace we can have, as Toni Morrison's Baby Suggs puts it, is the grace we can imagine,[35] we are never obliged never to stop imagining.

> Now let the weeping cease.
> Let no one mourn again.
> The love of God will bring you peace.
> There is no end.[36]

CHAPTER 7

THE POWER OF HORROR:
VARIATIONS AND RE-FRAMINGS
OF *THE BACCHAE*

Postmodernism has argued against a fixed sense of identity and has therefore questioned notions of essence. To essentialize is to reduce, to type, and to confine. For those who are among the colonized, however, ideas of identity and essence are not so simply resolved. Cherokee writer and activist Marilou Awiakata, in *Selu: Seeking the Corn Mother's Wisdom*, argues that essence does not mean static, reduced, completely defined, and finished.[1] Instead, essence indicates a stable point, a balancing point from which to take off, a taproot from which to draw nourishment, and a spirit that creates. "You adapt your form," Awiakata writes, but "never, never your essence. Your spirit sustains the balance."[2] The sense that there is "someone there" who is and is inviolable sustains those who have been defined as "other." If essence is *esse*—to be, soul, identity, deep self—what do we lose by saying it is not?

The late Robert Detweiler, in his scholarship, addressed this question. Here, we look at two of Detweiler's essays, "From Chaos to Legion to Chance: The Double Play of Apocalyptic and Mimesis" and "Torn by Desire: *Sparagmos* in Greek Tragedy and Recent Fiction," in relationship to the work of Euripides in *The Bacchae*; Toni Morrison in, primarily, *Beloved*; and Wole Soyinka's *The Bacchae of Euripides: A Communion Rite*.[3] We intend here to be naïve and speculative and, therefore, perhaps contentious as we explore the dark side of myth, dismemberment, apocalypse, and death, and the doubleness in myth, represented by Dionysus in Euripides's *The Bacchae*.[4] Finally, we want

to think about the journey through the "dark night" of dismemberment and into something else, an altered/altared space made, as Toni
Morrison insists, in narrative.

In "From Chaos to Legion to Change," Robert Detweiler writes:

[Frank] Kermode in the midst of an argument about the "as-if" nature of
fiction compares the "consciously false apocalypse of King Lear to that of the
Third Reich: "If *King Lear* is an image of the promised end, so is Buchenwald;
and both stand under the accusation of being horrible, rootless fantasies, the
one no more true than the other." It is a jolting comparison, one that compels
us to recognize our present-day reality of apocalyptic and mimesis intertwined
and that was presaged by Shakespeare: the apocalyptic, mediated by the ordering mimeticism of the Nazis—their compulsion for total order provoked by
the terror of chaos—has happened in our day. Moreover, it continues to happen via other forces, always fundamentalist in their need for absolute control,
but it is an apocalypse that has lost its myth and thus coincides with sheer
accident. Is this not the other side of chaos?[5]

Detweiler, who worked to process refugees after World War II, speaks
from the standpoint of both witness and critic. He speculates at the
end of this essay about the significance of the "dark" side of myth,
arguing that we must recognize the ambiguity in the notion of the
daemonic, that the imagination can work for good and for evil, and
that the job of the critic is "to tell the difference that may help to make
the difference."[6] I believe, Detweiler writes,

That we can plot narratives of survival, minister to this critical moment in
history, to engage the social I to persevere in existence by changing the use
of literature in the cause of belief—as if we finally, on some level, ever did
anything else with our literary texts.[7]

Instead of using our stories to command and destroy/de-story the
other, we can use them to survive "as intact communities that nurture
dignity and affection. Writing and living that faith may be our last
chance against chaos."[8]

Detweiler sees in myth not only an attempt to explain but also
a sign of what cannot be explained. The doubleness in our stories means that the Nazis, for example, and their inheritors do not
create an apocalypse without myth, but are the actors within a
myth—of Western culture's supremacy, of whiteness, etc.—taken to
its extreme implications. What they desire, they create through the
always present, grotesque elements of myth. What they desire, in
acting in this extreme, is reshape the world. The technological and

myth-making/narrative power of the crematoria, for example, is the attempt to leave "no remains": to eliminate the other such that there is nothing to witness and nothing to remember. Alan Tate in *The Fathers* argues that "civilization is the agreement, slowly arrived at, to let the abyss alone."[9] Yet the dark side of myth takes us to the edges of the abyss. We play along those borders and sometimes, as the Nazis illustrate, cross over—joyfully, with *hubris*, narcissistically, and unrepentantly.

Ashis Nandy, as we saw in Chapter 2, reminds us in *The Intimate Enemy* that underlying every culture that "goes rabid" is its undoing, usually coming, we would argue, from the same mythic source.[10] That doubletime, the double power of myth, is its capacity to put self and other side-by-side and reveal not only their differences but also their relatedness, as Pentheus and Dionysus are positioned in Euripides's *The Bacchae*. Sometimes that relation can be revealed only by blood, that which is let in apocalypse and *sparagmos*. Detweiler argues that the failure to see the self as/in the other and the other as/in the self— what we would call the inability to face ambiguity and to live with faith—brings about the blood-letting, the violent destruction either actually or in the psyche.

In the *Powers of Horror: An Essay on Abjection*, Julia Kristeva speaks of what the Nazis wrought for the modern:

In the dark halls of the museum that is now what remains of Auschwitz, I see a heap of children's shoes or something like that, something I have already seen elsewhere, under a Christmas tree, for instance, dolls I believe. The abjection of the Nazi crime reaches its apex when death, which, in any case, kills me, interferes with what, in my living universe, is supposed to save me from death: childhood, science, among other things.[11]

This provocatively worded statement points to trauma. Is it shoes or dolls? To be unable to speak, to be unable to identify what remains, blocks the sharing of memory, interpretation, and healing. No language, as Jenny Edkins reminded us,[12] functions to speak the truth of the event, a truth that is neither the simple innocence of the child nor the complex knowledge of science. This is the power of horror: it breaks apart meaning. We remain in the abject.

Kristeva indicates that the abject exists on the borders of our structures and institutions. We create boundaries there and set specialists along those borders, to manage the power of horror, to mask the realities that underlie our lives. To function, we must keep them out and us in. Language plays a role, as it masks reality: "collateral damage," for example, masks the death of innocents. Those borders are sites of attraction and repulsion, intimacy and revulsion. Crossing them, we release our unarticulated *jouissance* at transgression at breaking boundaries and taboos. "One does not know it, one does not desire it," Kristeva writes, "one joys in it, violently and painfully. A passion."[13]

The abject encroaches on all our borders, particularly in institutions and structures that have been set up to mask. Sometimes, therefore, our institutions are portals through which darkness enters: slavery and sweatshops, concentration camps and colonial stations. Kurtz, the most effective of the "company men" in *The Heart of Darkness*, recognizes this horror in himself and in the capitalist structure in which he participates. "The horror! The horror!" is not only his own self but his efficiency in creating a structure, participating in a mode of being, that gives free reign to his desires, to his ultimate desire to be god.[14] It is the movement towards frontiers, across ambiguous and dangerous spaces that we, in our frailty, create in our own images as we attempt to be at home.

For Kristeva, the abject is the experience of terror itself and the product of terror. It is the intimate that is, simultaneously, wholly other. Perhaps there was or is somewhere a community or society in which individuals, in a pure Durkheimian way, thought the same thoughts as they make the same gestures to the totem.[15] Once modes of being either travel into colonial spaces or are moved into, by immigrants, those gestures and thoughts are signified upon, take on different valances. In masking, in denial of relationality, we may be plunged, like Pentheus, into the darkness where we wrestle with ourselves and in which we either suffer the dark night of the soul or turn away from the horror that is us. Postmodernism, in its extremely nihilistic forms, may be an attempt to turn away from what we have made; thus, essence is too painful to face.

Let us use African Americans as an example. Toni Morrison explores this refusal in *Playing in the Dark: Whiteness and the Literary Imagination*. She argues that the problem of the enslaved is at the heart of the democratic experiment:[16] "Nothing highlighted freedom—if it did not in fact create it—like slavery."[17] America, she argues, offered immigrants the possibility to be "new white men,"[18] taking on a new sense of authority and autonomy that came from absolute control over the lives of others as they settled property in what they perceived to be a half-savage world. The positive qualities in the American psyche, therefore, have their shadow sides. Autonomy, the sign of freedom, becomes an isolating individualism. Newness becomes clinging to a false innocence. Distinctiveness becomes an unbridgeable difference. And authority and absolute power become a "conquering heroism, virility and wielding power over the lives of others."[19]

The shadow is projected onto blackness, such that blackness carries all the contradictory features of the white self. It is, simultaneously, evil and protective, rebellious and forgiving, fearful and desirable.[20] All this, Morrison points out, has deep ideological utility in the operation of the American democracy, modes of usefulness we find it hard to face. To face it is to tell a true story in which one is implicated. Detweiler writes in *Breaking the Fall*:

> Above all, narrative theology and its relationship to irony is key to the irony of death. I exist and yet I do not. I exist as ironic. That is why we tell our stories.
>
> Narrative fiction, not all that secular to many, explores this relationship. Story is redemptive by nature, hoping against hope that we will be saved by and through the telling.[21]

In the double vision of Dionysus, Euripides presents the postmodern doubletime and double consciousness. We may see in his suffering the possibility of redemption, but we cannot have it until we suffer it. As Charles Long puts it, we must crawl back through history on our hands and knees—not strolling, as through a museum—to face what we have done. That suffering may tear us apart, and with that we turn to *sparagmos*, to dismemberment.

Sparagmos is apocalyptic in the sense that it is a ritual destruction out of which a world is created. Detweiler points out that the intellectualizing of the myth of Dionysus masks its true action: the "outrageous treatment," the "scandalizing" of the body. To that we will return. Let us say, first, that the ecstasy of Dionysus is grisly, violent, but, because it is those, it reveals something about who we are.

Dionysus in Euripides's *The Bacchae* dismembers not only Pentheus but also the Athenians' assumptions about who they are as a city-state. He takes the virtues of holiness, peace, wisdom, sanity, and honor—that is, the virtues of Apollo that Athens claims—to the border, revealing their dark sides. He asks, "What do these really mean in the service of empire?" Wisdom, *sophia*, is, in the person of Dionysus, cleverness and shrewdness. It is sophistic. Self-control, *sophrosyne*, becomes the capacity to wait until the right moment to execute a plan. The sense that human beings should live in nature reveals the tendency of human beings to act on rational impulses, that is, to follow the herd, like the Bacchants. Are human beings most like ourselves when we are like the animals? Perhaps, but animals have no memory. The beauty and frustration of this play is in its capacity to give us double vision. It confuses and dismembers our vision, making it impossible to carry out the Platonic imperative to see clearly and, therefore, to know well. With our vision doubled, we are forced to rely on something or someone other to make sense of the world, as the power-hungry and religiously skeptical Pentheus relies on Dionysus, who is his intimate, a family member.

The power of Dionysus is the power of intoxication and the intoxication of power. It is that "something other." To see double may be to become confused, but it may also mean to go beyond our own categories, own sense of what is reasonable, and our fixed selves to become a self with others. That too is part of *esse*, spirit: spirit requires an-other. One does not just possess spirit because one is, but because spirit is recognized in one by others and because one recognizes being in others. To deny this is to objectify, and the only end of that is death: the actual dismemberment of the body or the soul that is the core of atrocity. Perhaps symbolic dismemberment, undergoing the removal of masks and looking critically at our understandings, is, as the tragedians show us, our only hope.

Pentheus suffers a *sparagmos* of both vision and body. When Pentheus falls into the hands of his mother, the most intimate other, he loses his old vision and sees his origins and his ends, just as Oedipus does before he blinds himself in *Oedipus the King*. In that moment, he becomes most himself:

> . . . snatching off his wig and snood
> so she would recognize his face, he touched her cheeks,
> her face screaming. "No, no, Mother! I am Pentheus,
> your own son, the child you bore to Echion!
> Pity me, spare me, Mother! I have done a wrong,
> but do not kill me, your own son, for my offense."[22]

Removing the mask that hides him, he is seen by the other; he also sees the other for what she is, both mother and murderer, and faces the otherness in himself: "I am" and "I am part of you."

As for Agave, his mother, the victory she carries home is grief. As she is brought to remember the work done by the "white/and delicate hands of women,"[23] an image of supreme horror, Cadmus is re-membering the torn and dismembered body of Pentheus that she was forced to reassemble because it "lay, scattered in sheds, dismembered, / . . . no two pieces in a single place."[24]

Wole Soyinka, in his reworking of Euripides's work in *The Bacchae of Euripides: A Communion Rite*, adds another touch of horror, to make apparent the insights of Euripides's play for the postcolonial world. His title, "a communion rite," suggests both the Eucharist, holy communion, which is the body and blood of Christ, and the community formed out of that consumption. In Soyinka's play, as Agave begins to see clearly, in the middle stage of her vision, she does not see her son but a slave.

KADMOS.
You must look. Look closely and carefully.
She brings herself to obey.
AGAVE.
Oh. Another slave? But why did I nail it
Right over the entrance?[25]

Agave's "Oh. Another slave?" points to the routine violence of life: dismemberment of slaves is normal. In Soyinka's play, however, it is the slave leader who is one with Dionysus, who cooperates with transformation and change. In both Euripides's and Soyinka's plays, to remember her son and herself, Agave must "mourn each piece of Pentheus' body separately as she places it on the bier," remembering it into human shape, re-being.

The horror of the modern is that there may be "no remains" to re-member into human shape. The ashes of Holocaust victims, Toni Morrison's controversial "60 Million and More" to whom *Beloved* is dedicated, the unnamed in mass graves in so many places around the world, often cannot be remembered. Is it shoes or dolls? Yours or mine? You or me? That confusion is what Euripides points to: the abject on the borders of our existences. What is on the other side? Perhaps darkness and horror and also—not or—perhaps paradoxically, a way home.

For Detweiler and Morrison, story is the site of memory, of "rememory," as Morrison calls it, even without remains. The artist re-members out of traces—irreducible absences[26]—the marks that must be remarked at the site of rupture. In such instances, story may be all that *can* witness and give some form of justice. Desire may be our undoing, but it also may remake us as we enter into the intimacy of the relationship between the teller and the listener, the analyst and the patient, the witness and the world, through the mediating power of the tale. A rememory, therefore, is not just a representation or copy. It is the novelist's making the space for us to step into and to experience the past—to remember—in our present plane of existence, which adds another layer of multiplicity. The scar from the injury remains, as Karla F. C. Holloway reminds us, but the site becomes transparent, lucid for a moment in our joining.[27]

Narrative, Morrison said in her 1993 Nobel Lecture, "has never been merely entertainment for me. It is, I believe, one of the principal ways in which we absorb knowledge."[28] Narrative, as Morrison defines it, is not static or finished. She speaks of the gaps that she leaves in her texts, gaps into which the reader enters and, thereby, participates in the text. This absence invites presence. The interaction of minds—"the dance of an open mind when it engages another equally open one"—is, for Morrison, the production of peace.[29] In the gaps, a meeting takes place, an interaction between writer and other writers, canonical and not, and between writers and readers, and, as her fiction deepens, between those and something sacred. Morrison's hope is that a further action between that contingent, fragile community, and world follows. Detweiler shares this hope. In these fragile communities, we can produce something that Morrison leaves purposely unnamed except to call it "lovely," "together."[30] The art of fiction, Morrison suggests, therefore, gives us clues for how to make a world. The artist is, in that sense, a rebel.

In myth, in story, deep intimacies that can smother and intimate differences that seem to be eternally destructive can be acknowledged and brought into balance. In all tragedy, there is too much intimacy, over-relation. That deep relatedness is a symbol of who we truly are and of what we fear. Julia Kristeva, in *Tales of Love*, asks us to look into the abject so that we can love.

All love discourses have dealt with narcissism and have set themselves up as codes of positive, ideal values. Theologies and literatures beyond sin and fiendish characters, invite us to carve out our own territory within love, establish ourselves as *particular*, outdo ourselves in a sublime Other—metaphor and metonymy of the sovereign *Good*. Because today we lack being *particular*, covered as we are with so much abjection, because the guideposts that assured our ancients toward the good have been proven questionable, we have crises of love. Let's admit it: lacks of love.[31]

Kristeva knows that what she asks, the restoration of love, is not without cost and dangers. In love, which Kristeva defines as self-overcoming, one never ceases "to be mistaken as to reality."[32] Our narcissistic tendencies are to be preoccupied with the self and to objectify the "other." Nonetheless, we must, she argues, be willing to engage the fantastic for the sake of creative existence. Neither is this work finished in a short time. The artist—the analyst, for Kristeva—mediates resurrection and reconnection: "What is at stake is turning the crisis into a *work in progress*."[33] Kristeva calls for the unleashing of creative chaos, which Dionysus represents.

Crossing the borders we have agreed to leave alone may save or destroy us, lead us to isolation or to community. Toni Morrison makes this emblematic as Sethe in *Beloved* speaks: "You are Beloved and you are mine."[34] That line is the most terrible and tender, the most terrifying and the most intimate, and the most self-defining and self-dissolving line in the novel—perhaps in modern literature. Desire is our curse and undoing when we cannot express the existence of separate selves—as Sethe's "thick love" cannot do.[35] And, yet, to make the claim is a step toward freedom. It becomes a sign of hope when, as Detweiler puts it, our narratives so intertwine that I cannot think my own story without thinking yours.[36] That opens us to larger notions of self and community, the capacity to engage in more complex or whole relationships.

Detweiler, in "From Chaos to Legion to Chance," reminds us, in this statement, of the classical meaning of the demonic, the daemonic:

In Classical Greece, as *daimon*, it had positive denotation and meant a guiding or protective spirit. J. Bruce Long says that "In the late Greco-Roman period, the term *daimon* . . . like the Latin *genius*, was commonly employed in reference to lesser spirits or demigods, especially patron or guardian spirits. Still later, the word *daimonium* (transliterated into Latin as *daemonium*) was assigned to evil spirits . . ."[37]

Detweiler wants to recover the ambiguity of the term and charge us with the responsibility of "telling the difference" in particular moments.[38] *Esse* or self, as Kristeva might argue, is internality, the essential element of the human being. What we must learn is how to relate externality, the other, rightly to the *esse* or self. Self, in this regard, has stability and a capacity to change, to relate in the senses of tell and join.

Toni Morrison does not accept that there are no remains. In Beloved, Sethe tells her daughter Denver that her "rememory" is material.[39] One can step into the memory of another:

"Someday you be walking down the road and you hear something or see something going on. So clear. And you think it's you thinking it up. A thought picture. But no. It's when you bump into a rememory that belongs to somebody else."

. . .

Denver picked at her fingernails. "if it's still there, waiting, that must mean that nothing ever dies."

Sethe looked right in Denver's face. "Nothing ever does," she said.[40]

Detweiler said in a presentation once, "There are only moments."[41] That provocative statement becomes clear as we look at it in relation to Toni Morrison's statement. It is not an existential statement about disconnection, but a statement about an apocalyptic moment that begins something new by immersing us in the past. The moment itself is an event and an end: no remains. But it *does* remain: in memory. As Morrison suggests, time is not linear and spaces are not separate but fluid. We can and are called to rememory not only our own lives but also the lives of others. We step into an intersection of self with other, dark with light, ancestors with the present, and memory with history. It is in that in-between—in the interstitial space, as Homi Bhabha reminded us in Chapter 1, on the border—that myth is made and story is written. What is torn is not reconstructed, whole, but reconstituted, a term we will explore further later in this volume.

Alice Walker in one of her recent memoir/short story collections, *Everything We Love Can Be Saved*, speculates on the state of the soul of America:

We have reached a place of deepest emptiness and sorrow. We look at the destruction around us and perceive our collective poverty. We see that everything that is truly needed by the world is too large for individuals to give. We find we have only ourselves. Our experience. Our dreams. Our simple art. Our memories of better ways. Our knowledge that the world cannot be healed in the abstract. That healing begins where the wound was made.[42]

Returning to a site of one of our American woundings, slavery, Toni Morrison in an early interview concerning *Beloved* pauses and muses that there must be

For purposes of exorcism . . . celebratory rites of passage . . .
Things must be *made*, some fixing ceremony . . . some
memorial . . . some thing, some altar . . . somewhere.[43]

One site at which the *altered* space of diaspora becomes *altar-ed* space of healing is, in the postcolonial/postmodern world, in the art of fiction itself. "I send you my sorrow," writes Alice Walker. "And my art."[44] The *work* of art—the making, the process—suggests one model for remaking a world. The work of art—the product—is a site at which we stand to imagine another possibility. It is a site at which we can imagine justice—not as distributive or retributive but as *epieikeia*: the restoration of order and balance that corrects, as Alasdair MacIntyre puts it, "that justice which would consist in the application of already laid down rules"[45] and that issues from the contemplative self in relation to others.

The work of art, the process, suggests ongoing action. Tying narrative to justice reveals its complexity, as Morrison does in her term rememory. For Morrison, the novel is such a space (in Michel de Certeau's sense of that term) of engagement that turns our gaze always back to the site of fracture. Art, in this way, is, as Karla F. C. Holloway describes it, a "recursive structure" that is both emblematic of a culture and interpretative of that culture at the same time.[46] Morrison's are, therefore, multiplied or layered texts, with characters positioned at the nexus of multiple planes: between what has been defined for them and potential spiritual wholeness, between the physical and the spiritual world, and between history and memory. The writer calls the reader into the complex reality and danger of that orientation, as we are positioned between culture and text. This positioning invites us into a "clearing," as Baby Suggs does in *Beloved*,[47] another, altared space of being and knowing in which we can embrace the other and love.

There, we participate in what is significant: freedom. In Soyinka's *Bacchae*, slaves talk about life and freedom, as they dress Pentheus to send him to his mother, to his fate:

OLD SLAVE.
What does it mean, life? Dare one
Hope for better than merely warring, seeking
Chance, seeking the better life? Can we
Control what threatens before the eruption?
Defeat what oppresses by anticipation? Can we?
Dare we surrender to what comes after, embrace
The ambiguous face of the future? It is enough
To concede awareness of the inexplicable, to wait
And watch the unfolding.
SLAVE.
For there are forces not ruled by us
And we obey them
Trust them. Though they travel inch by inch
They arrive.
OLD SLAVE.
Dionysos? or—Nothing.
Not even a word for these forces.

> They lack a name. We call them
> Spirits,
> Gods
> SLAVE.
> Principles,
> Elements,
> ANOTHER.
> Currents,
> Laws, Eternal Causes.
> ANOTHER.
> But they are born in the blood
> Unarguable, observed and preserved before time . . .
> SLAVE LEADER.
> As freedom. No teaching implants it
> No divine revelation at the altar.
> It is knotted in the blood, a covenant from birth.[48]

The slaves speculate on life, freedom, and what makes a human being who he or she is. They decide that freedom is in the blood, in a covenant in which we share when we embrace what we can control, our humanity, and what we cannot, "the inexplicable," and move toward truth, as Pentheus and his family are about to do.

At the end of Morrison's *Paradise*, the final volume of Morrison's trilogy, two women—the mother and daughter reunited—sit on a beach. The mother sings. But this is not the usual beach, the paradise envisioned by those who came to the New World. It is an Old World—and a New New World. The beach is littered; a lot of "someones" have been here already. Coming ashore to this already altered space in which love, nevertheless, has begun is a ship. "Another ship, perhaps, but different, heading to port, crew and passengers lost and saved, atremble, for they have been disconsolate for some time."[49] We are these scared people who must acknowledge that this place has been inhabited already and needs reparation, needs work. Paradise is where we—together, in an altered place where love can begin again in acknowledgment of what has been before—"shoulder the endless work we were created to do"—"appropriately and well."[50] That process of making exercised between our New World and the New New World is our part in the fixing ceremony—and the altar, this world come of age, is not out there, in the future, but is at hand—"down here" and right now.

Charles H. Long, in "Du Bois, Race, and the Nature of Civil Religion in the United States," a paper given in the *God Talk with Black Thinkers* interdisciplinary course, at Drew University Seminary,

argued, with American pragmatist Charles Sanders Pierce, that reason
has to be rendered, torn, to make it functional.[51] Only when reason
is rendered can it be a gift, because only then are we vulnerable to
one another. Those who have experienced *sparagmos*, and this is all of
us in the postmodern and postcolonial worlds, and moved, through
hybridity and adaptation, reconstitution of self and world have much
to teach. Affirming that, we close with Alice Walker's message about
the moment in her letter to her young husband in *The Way Forward
Is with a Broken Heart*. Healing, Walker asserts, begins where the
wound was made.

Maybe there is no promised land for us. Just look at this poor country, like the
orphan of the Universe. But even this fails to frighten me anymore. I believe
that the only moment we are in is promised, and that it, whatever it is, should
always be "the future" we want . . . Why should the killers of the world be "the
future" and not us?[52]

SECTION III

THE POSSIBILITY OF PEACE
AND THE BELOVED COMMUNITY

THE TRANSITIVE "IN-BETWEEN": CULTURE, MEANING, AND THE POLITICAL IN VOEGELIN AND BHABHA

INTRODUCTION

Political questions force us to explore the directionality of the transitive space. Here, we will examine the work of two thinkers: Eric Voegelin, a political philosopher, and Homi K. Bhabha, a political sociologist. Voegelin argues that the transitive—the "in-between," as he calls it—is most efficacious as a vertical space: one that seeks truth while remaining anchored in the "ground of being" that undergirds all reality. He turns towards theology—namely, that of Paul Tillich[1]— as does Giorgio Agamben in his own way, in the current generation of thinkers. Despite Voegelin's insistence to the contrary, the "transcendence" of this ground of being does suggest marked territory, a territory anchored in symbols. Bhabha, in contrast, argues that the transitive is most effectively understood as a horizontal space. He turns to the anthropological model of Michel De Certeau and the "practice of everyday life."[2] The "practice" of everyday life is a way to redefine political language, as well as other binding structures, through the creativity of the active human being. In a sense, we argue, Voegelin and Bhabha cross, and at that crossroads, we locate transitivity, which, for us, involves the contact zone, the space in which the colonial overcomes the "other." But it also suggests more: the reality that, in that space, as Ashis Nandy showed us, symbols are both in tension and

merging into new forms.[3] Could we but harness this power, our reading of Voegelin and Bhabha suggests, we would have a fertile ground,
though not one without tensions, for rethinking identity, community,
and political form in the (post) modern world.

Contrary to criticisms, we argue that the emergence of "posts" in
political philosophy and in religion (postmodern; postcolonial) in the
last quarter of the last century does not suggest a willful attempt to
supplant elder ancient (e.g., virtue) and modern (e.g., property, self-
governance) categories. Rather, this development suggests that those
elder categories have hardened and no longer serve as comprehensive conceptions of matters political and religious. Under the weight
of the "post" critiques, the assumed hegemony of western symbolizations has been destabilized and forced to rethink itself.[4] The more
perceptive of the "post" thinkers realize that the elder categories have
not disappeared. In fact, postcolonial scholars like Homi K. Bhabha
suggest that coming to grips with the reality that prevailing symbols now work in transitive spaces may well be the real challenge
for contemporary political theory.[5] Politics as a rough-and-tumble
competition of symbol manipulation, in which the acquisition and
maintenance of power are the twin objects, is even more problematic when multiple cultural understandings meet in contact zones and
utilize symbols in their particular ways. In discussing politics, Homi
Bhabha's postmodern thought bears a curious similarity to that of
the more conservative Voegelin. The latter argues that reinterpreting
symbols can be a check on a Machiavellian conception of politics as it
indicates the multiple modes of a search for meaning.[6] This search, one
that is always seeking, demands we take seriously symbols that are possessed by multiple peoples in a political unity and that, therefore, move
between and among divergent traditions and circumstances in a shared
space. This makes the symbol transitive: "in-between" and "open."

This chapter interrogates the function of symbols in the work of
these two, apparently divergent, voices: the very reluctant modernist,
Eric Voegelin, who relies on ancient texts for his analyses, and
the postcolonialist and postmodernist, Homi K. Bhabha. Voegelin's
general thesis in *Order and History* (1956-1987) is that human
participation in reality has to be understood in terms of "leaps
in being" that signify the authentic search for truth.[7] Remaining
open to the divine ground of being, as Paul Tillich also put it,
anchors us in the knowledge of our locations in the Platonic *metaxy*: a
space in-between the tensions of human existence expressed symbol-
ically as tensions between life/death, order/disorder, truth/untruth,
time/timelessness, et cetera. Voegelin's commitment to the symbol

"in-between," we are arguing, suggests not only an ontological and philosophical position, but also a space for necessary political exchange, a suggestion reinforced by the idea of "openness."

This desire for a space of exchange also guides the impulse of postcolonial theorist Homi K. Bhabha. Attending to the margins of cultural discourse, Bhabha preserves the power of symbol even as he rethinks the categories of the modern Western discourse on which Voegelin's analyses rely.[8] Bhabha witnesses the ongoing struggle for meaning, not in terms of the dangerous simplifications of ideologies, but in the power of discourse(s), particularly at the point of their interactions. Bhabha draws on the critical distinction between symbols and signs to show how cultural symbols are changed from the margins inward, making political space transitive space.

Symbols, for both Bhabha and Voegelin, point to values transcending a particular culture. Bhabha's postcolonial analysis works from the argument that most of what we universalize into symbols are signs, that is, they are not universals but are rather culturally-referential marks of value. Signs are valuable as conduits of understanding, but they are also limited, static representations not easily communicable across cultures. Bhabha demonstrates that many Western symbols are, in fact, signs of cultural preferences. He does not mean, thereby, to dismiss them, but, rather, to contextualize them, to draw them into conversation with those of other symbolic systems.

This tension between symbols and signs is critical to both thinkers because signs mark the values, the preferences, and the development of cultures through, among other things, text and language. The contemporary willingness to engage literature and literary theory as political and philosophical documents—and both Voegelin and Bhabha share this willingness—suggests the importance of cultural symbols to political discourse. The value of symbols may be found in the ways that they provide continuity in time and help justify specific forms of managing space—in short, they meld the temporal and spatial dimensions of human political existence.

For Voegelin, time is the essential element. We can see the development of cultural symbols by attending to cultural movement and change over time. Voegelin, however, does not want to surrender to the idea that change is what defines us. Instead, he posits the source of our political being out of time, concerning himself with the *philosophical* or *religious* verticality of human existence, one anchored in the divine ground of being.

In contrast, Bhabha embraces space. He accepts a fluid conception of time and reintroduces a more overtly *political* concern with the spatial dimension of politics—that is, with the horizontal relationships between and among cultures. Signs as symbols are the coin of these relationships. His is a pluralistic view wherein the impulse towards hybridity governs cultural contact, transforming, mixing in new forms, cultures, and their symbols. Both Bhabha and Voegelin argue that it is the accommodating complexity of the symbol *in-between* that is key. The symbol as transitive, as in-between, for example, allows Bhabha to write of things political in terms of cultural encounters and hybridity: "Minority discourse sets the act of emergence in the antagonistic *in-between* of image and sign, the accumulative and the adjunct, presence and proxy."[9]

VOEGELIN: THE VERTICALITY AND OPENNESS OF THE IN-BETWEEN

Writing at the precise moment that the Western symbol system was beginning to collapse under the weight of its own philosophical, technological, and colonial adventures,[10] Eric Voegelin works from within the canonical tradition in an effort to save it from itself. He seeks a productive, creative synthesis that will salvage the meaning of Western symbols without turning them into the fetish objects of ideology. Voegelin uses the term "equivalence" in his discussion of symbols to signify a cross-contextual sameness in symbol-making. This concern with a unifying sameness that occurs across cultures, we argue, links his analysis to that of someone like Homi Bhabha.

In "Equivalences of Experience and Symbolization in History," Voegelin's philosophy of history posits a series of equivalences, which, as an ever-expanding intelligible whole, tell the tale of man's representative participation in "the divine drama of truth becoming luminous."[11] Philosophers are inheritors of a "field of experiences and symbols." The symbol is "neither an object to be observed from the outside, nor does it present the same appearance to everybody."[12] The philosopher's understanding of these symbols is either determined by his "openness toward reality" or "deformed by his uncritical acceptance of beliefs which obscure the reality of immediate experience."[13] The modern philosopher's vantage point has been skewed by the fundamentalism of the latter approach: "The doctrinaire theology and metaphysics of the eighteenth century were succeeded by the doctrinaire ideologies of the nineteenth and twentieth centuries; an older type of fundamentalist doctrine was followed by a new fundamentalism."[14] As fundamentalism confronted fundamentalism, we slipped, Voegelin asserts, into the "age" of modern wars of dogma vs. dogma. Consequently, the contemporary philosopher must resist succumbing to the pressure of his "age" as determined as it is by the emergence of ideologies.[15] The very proclamation of an "age" (of Reason, of Revolution, etc.) demonstrates, Voegelin suggests, the hubristic tendency of modern political philosophers to substitute systems for the authentic search for order.

The loss of consciousness and intellect symptomatic of this "age" is the direct result of our inattention to the transitive quality of our existence. The critical loss occurs when we, Voegelin writes, "hypostatize the poles of the tension [of our in-between existence] as independent entities" and thus "destroy the reality of existence as it has been experienced by the creators of the tensional symbolisms."[16] When the extremes—yes/no—are simplified for philosophical or political expediency, we have ceased attending to the depth of the questions, that is, to the tensions endemic to our experiences as human beings. Our symbols are hardened into tools, resume their status as mere signs and history becomes, if we may manipulate Voltaire, "tricks we play upon the [experiences] of the dead." Avoiding this hypostasy requires that human beings remain mindful of time: of their participation and place in the on-going process of reality. Voegelin argues that the

Cognition of participation, as it is not directed toward an object of the external world, becomes a luminosity in reality itself and consequently, the knower and the known move into the position of tensional poles in a consciousness that we call luminous as far as it engenders the symbols which express the experience of its own structure.[17]

For Voegelin, the symbols generated in this moment of consciousness endure and make up man's philosophical inheritance. They suffice until they no longer adequately express man's experience of the process of reality. Consequently, the process of cognition in time is a profoundly self-reflective one. We must resist the temptation to think that the "new" symbol discerned through this self-reflective process renders older ones unnecessary; the elder symbolizations of experience merely become part of the inherited historical field, that is, of tradition.

The philosopher's on-going "openness" to this process of reality, his acceptance of his own transitivity, constitutes his discipline. The philosopher can allow neither the symbolizations nor the experiences they engender to harden into hypostases, for this will lead to the formation of a system. Voegelin defines "openness" as a modality of consciousness that reveals the depth of both the psyche and what he describes as the primordial field of reality. The descent into the depth of the psyche occurs in a kind of "Dark Night" of culture which, Voegelin writes, "will be indicated when the light of truth has dimmed and its symbols are losing their credibility; when the night is sinking on the symbols that they have had their day, one must return to the night of the depth that is luminous with truth to the man who is willing to seek for it."[18] At the same time, there may not appear to be but there is a "primordial field of reality" made up of the community of God and man, world and society. Each movement forward simultaneously reveals an awareness of a depth: the psyche below consciousness and the Cosmos below the primordial field. The psyche of the human being, linked "in trust" with the depth of the Cosmos, reveals that there is "neither an autonomous conscious[ness] nor an autonomous depth, but only a consciousness in continuity with its own depth."[19]

Equivalence emerges as the "new" symbol that is revealed in the thinking process. It encounters and, perhaps, sets itself off against the "older" symbol(s) of a culture—symbols that have emerged from the same depth. Voegelin's insight into the sameness represented by this consciousness existent in "continuity with its own depth" has implications for history, or more specifically, for our historical perspective. History, for Voegelin in a Hegelian moment, emerges as itself a symbolization process: as the symbol of these confrontations in the presence of the process of reality. The philosopher stands, in temporal terms, in a present between past and future and must work to remain open to presence of the eternal.

Voegelin can afford such assertions because his faith in a unity of being that the tradition has explored undergirds his own work and, he believes, our very existence: "The trust in the Cosmos and its depth is the source of the premises that we accept as the context of meaning for our concrete engagement in the search of truth."[20] At the same time, there is something radical in his acknowledgment that symbols have their day and that when their light dims, we must return to the night of the depth[21] because it suggests the very possibility of that which Bhabha embraces in his own work. To argue that an "emergent truth" will posit itself as equivalent but superior to an older one is, at least, to leave open the possibility that the newer truth might emerge from outside the currently accepted (e.g., Western) field of symbolizations. In fact, opening oneself up to the depth may well mean having to quiet the, often distracting, noise of accepted truths. The danger inherent in this radical movement is that the carrier of the newer truth, by his or her discovery, opens the search to hypostatization—that is, to the vagaries of politics as power: "Behind every equivalent symbol in the historical field stands the man who has engendered it in the course of his search as representative of a truth that is more than equivalent."[22]

History, therefore, becomes a series of equivalences in which truths differentiate themselves from elder concretized others. What cannot be lost in the philosophical search, however, is that this differentiation is likely to be deeply political. In the political arena, truths—differentiated or not—are reinforced by cultural and other more martial technologies. Sometimes, the newer truth is the one most differentiated, but this is not necessarily the case. For the other side of Voegelin's methodological coin is that history is also the story of *failed* challenges to older truths in which those challenges are revealed as hypostases. The failure of a truth, however, does not mark the extent or limit of its influence, for that philosophical failure may well be masked by access to technological or other resources. Voegelin knows that the intervention of politics into the search for order closes us off from both the relative depth of our own experiences and from experiential insights engendered by different cultures through different methodologies, like religion. The everyday urgencies of politics may demand a philosophical closure which is utterly at odds with the openness of the transitive. Voegelin tries to insulate the search from politics, but can only do so by resorting to a faith: "The search that renders no more than equivalent truth rests ultimately on the faith that, by engaging in it, man participates representatively in the divine drama of truth becoming luminous."[23]

Voegelin, through his philosophy of history, is concerned primarily with cultural symbols across time. His political philosopher seeks the presence of an "openness" to the divine ground of being in the symbolic articulations of others' experiences in order to make connections (and judgments) across time. We stand in a present moment unfolding in the presence of eternity. The absence of these presences marks the philosophical crisis of Voegelin's time, and this diagnosis forces his use of the category "gnostic." A politics that claims truth for itself in some final or complete sense, Voegelin argues in *The New Science of Politics* and elsewhere, is ideological, gnostic,[24] or a function of sorcery[25]— as he describes both Hegel and Marx. His vertical conception of the in-between (e.g., between the presence of the divine and the ugliness of politics) brings with it a corresponding obligation to attend to the past to discern equivalences of experience and distinguish among their articulations.

Yet when confronting the modern impulse to construct systems, Voegelin is drawn out of the tension and into the bipolar political landscape of his present. Ideologues, laying claim to the truth, force their opponents to deny them rather than negotiate with them. This denial necessarily takes the form of a negation, the ideological practice *par excellence*. While Voegelin has not constructed an ideology, he has been dragged into ideological struggles that, it seems, he can escape only by either embracing the methodology of ideology—like using a philosophical term "gnosticism" to negate rather than negotiate—or turning his back on politics altogether.

In other moments, Voegelin avoids this trap. Through his use of the symbol of the in-between, Voegelin seeks a third way, suggesting a value in his work beyond the press of his immediate philosophical and political circumstances. The symbol of the in-between, suggesting persistence, negotiation, and movement in the realm of the political—in short, the transitive—makes valuable methodological demands of the political philosopher. The in-between signifies that fluid, necessarily incomplete understandings should be discerned and understood to play off of and inform one another. Each holds part of the other's truth. Voegelin's emphasis on the vertical dimension of the in-between (*metaxy*) suggests that discerning authentic from inauthentic experiences is a dangerous game. We must, as he proposes to do in *Order and History*, take experiences as they are and feel obligated to understand them to the degree we are able—which is to say, never finally. The corollary, symbol "openness," requires the presence of a philosophical discipline that comes from a sense of one's own strength. A functional politics, our concern is *political* philosophy after all, requires an openness not only to the "divine ground of being" but also to cultural experiences of which we have no experience. Voegelin's caution against "deformations" is well-intended, but, as we will see from Bhabha's analysis, the cultural and political power embodied in our symbols means culpability in generating the "deformed" experiences of others. Voegelin's unfortunate deployment of the philosophical sledgehammer "gnosticism" reminds us that the temptation to forget that our symbols are signs is great. If we forget that our own symbols are limited by their nature, that is, that they reflect equivalences—rarely neither more nor less than those of others—we cease tending to the very tension that needs to be preserved if we are to avoid acquiescence in injustice. Demonizing one's other is the surest way to hypostasize our own "truths."

HOMI K. BHABHA: THE HORIZONTALITY OF THE TRANSITIVE SPACE

Voegelin targets mostly Western ideological constructs and their assumptions about their universality. Homi K. Bhabha, from his postcolonial perspective takes seriously emergent non-Western responses to these apparently hegemonic conceptions. His work marks, he argues, "a shift of attention from the political as pedagogical, ideological practice to politics as the stressed necessity of everyday life."[26] The stressed necessities of everyday life put to the lie the relevance and universal applicability of ideologies.[27] No longer willing to accept the universal application of Western ideologies, Bhabha also will not take the confrontation between ideologies as the most interesting problem in political philosophy. Ideological claims to universality, his analysis suggests, have been displaced by the confrontations with and interactions between cultures formerly alien, colonized or colonizing. These interactions are not the zero-sum conflicts of ideological clashes, but rather an opportunity, as Leela Gandhi puts it, to "re-member" the colonial past to make it more approachable.[28] The data for that re-membering are the experiences articulated in our symbolic systems. When these meet, when the *hegemon* is confronted by that over which it no longer rules, cultural differences emerge which must be articulated and negotiated.[29] Assumptions about the relevance, about the authority of particular symbols must now be negotiated where cultural meanings overlap, that is, where neither holds sway. "The contribution of negotiation," Bhabha writes, "is to display the 'in-between.' "[30]

Time and the appeal to tradition as a strategy of power and authority are critical to Bhabha's analysis. The unity that Voegelin seeks (and to his credit never finds for long) is the intellectual attempt to tame the fluidity of human political existence using stable generalities and symbols. Colonialism was the physical imposition of a Western unity that, for all its strength and subtlety, could not eradicate and, indeed, finally helped generate the sources of resistance that eventually emerged as hybrid cultures. But postcolonial claims of new, pure national identities (ala Fanon, etc.) failed to recognize the permanent effect of the Western presence on both the colonized and the colonizer. Bhabha, therefore, recognizes the need for theory of a different order.

Theory, Bhabha contends, must resist explaining everything using cultural signs as universal symbols with settled understandings. Instead, theory must confront politics and, functioning as critique, open up a space of translation between competing cultural meanings.

The challenge lies in conceiving of the time of political action and understanding as opening up a space that can accept and regulate the differential structure of the moment of intervention *without rushing to produce a unity of the social antagonism or contradiction. This is a sign that history is happening*—within the pages of theory, within the systems and structures we construct to figure the passage of the historical.[31]

Our cultural symbols suggest unity—a functioning politics seems to demand it—but that unity breaks down on borders (physical, philosophical, and religious, etc.) where it is confronted with the unity of the Other's symbols: "The problem of cultural interaction emerges only at the significatory boundaries of cultures," Bhabha writes, "where meanings and values are misread or signs are misappropriated."[32] The colonial order violated the signs of the Other, either by translating them into the categories of Western ideological systems or by obliterating them. There is, however, a double consciousness to these misappropriations and mis-readings in that the important signposts of both self and other are being transformed by their forced interaction. Hegemonic conceptions defend themselves in terms of the past, assuming an authority that has been de-legitimated by the countering claims of postcoloniality. These claims out of time, however, undermine themselves in what Bhabha calls their transparency: their self-justifications reveal that "the action of the distribution and arrangement of differential spaces, positions, knowledges, in relation to each other, [are] relative to a discriminatory, not inherent sense of order."[33]

In the wake of the breakdown of the colonial order, and, one might add the "simple" Cold War dualism that emerged alongside it, the number and sources of important cultural symbols has multiplied. The problem in sorting out the differences among cultural symbols, Bhabha argues, is "how, in signifying the present, something comes to be repeated, relocated and translated in the name of tradition, in the guise of a pastness that is not necessarily a faithful sign of historical memory but a strategy of representing authority in terms of the artifice of the archaic."[34] Like Voegelin, Bhabha takes cultural symbols seriously, but he also recognizes that bringing the categories and authority of the past into the present means substantiating, and trying to instantiate, power relationships which are no longer enforceable as legitimate. Interpreting transformed relationships among culturally diverse symbols requires an extraordinary willingness on all sides to let go of their authority.

The pact of interpretation is never simply an act of communication between the I and the You designated in the statement. The production of meaning requires that these two places be mobilized in the passage through a

Third Space, which represents both the general conditions of language and the specific implication of the utterance in a performative and institutional strategy of which it cannot "in itself" be conscious.[35]

Bhabha describes this Third Space—the "in-between" manifest—as a discursive space of demystification in which "the meaning and symbols of culture have no primordial unity or fixity" and in which "even the same signs can be appropriated, translated, rehistoricized and read anew."[36] While cultural symbols stabilize a political environment, locating us in our world, any adventure of cultural confrontation (e.g., colonialism) puts the certainty and universality of cultural symbols at risk. Even as the adventurer finds ways to create and to assume authority by undermining then supplanting native symbolic systems, otherness persists as a double presence—of both colonizer and colonized—as "a pressure, and a presence that acts constantly, if unevenly, along the entire boundary of authorization."[37] The persistent, inevitable doubleness Bhabha identifies suggests what Ashis Nandy describes as the violent intimacy of any colonial situation. Once cultures engage each other, a co-dependence develops that alters both permanently and that links them together in ways not easily undone.

The cultural encounter, then, is not simply a question of the imposition of one set of cultural meanings on territory formerly home to another set. The act of imposition, through military action, economic influence, education, et cetera. requires translation, that is, a hardening of those symbols into representations, into tools which can be used in overcoming the native culture and governing the population that culture formerly held together. The hardening of symbols, as Voegelin puts it, becomes part of what it means to govern according to our symbols—and is the danger of any politics to truth. In any concrete political situation, cultural symbols are given meanings that are subsumed in political exigency. To the degree that this is so, Bhabha recognizes politics as involving an inevitable double displacement of symbolic meanings. The displacement is two-fold through what he calls *hybridity* which is "the revaluation of the assumption of colonial identity through the repetition of discriminatory identity effects . . . that turn(s) the gaze of the discriminated back upon the eye of power."[38] Colonial values come to be seen as coequal with the violence that imposes them and, as the native's cultural symbols are transformed, so too are the colonizer's symbols. For instance, "Liberty, Equality, and Fraternity" mean one thing for the French and quite another for Algerian Arabs. Once symbols are imposed by force in order that the colonizer may govern, their value as symbols asserted as universals is revealed as a simple but powerful set of local/alien discernments, preferences, and "discriminations" binding only when enforced by some kind of coercion (physical, cultural, etc.). Once identified with the coercive needs of "orderly" politics, symbols and the truths they claim to represent generate their own resistance as we demonstrated in our reflections on postcolonial and post-slavery readings of Greek tragedy.

Political use of symbols shuts off discussions of meaning, re-creating them as what Bhabha calls "empty presences of strategic devices."[39] In other words, the process empties the symbols of any meaning beyond their status as masks for coercive political action. Bhabha, however, wishes to reconceive of the postcolonial cultural encounter as a space of negotiation—a reframing of political conflict in recognition that common or historical understandings have been undermined by the cultural encounter and that which they symbolized must be—and, whether acknowledged or not—is recreated in new, negotiated and negotiable terms. To this end, we must understand that it is not, he argues, that cultural differences as such are the source of conflict. The conflict is, rather, the "*effect* of discriminatory practices—the production of cultural *differentiation* as signs of authority."[40]

The emergence of hybridity[41] signals a resistance to the unity of the colonial presence, altering it instead into what Bhabha calls a "metonymy of presence," in which the hybrid object "retains the actual semblance of the authoritative symbol but revalues its presence by resisting it as the signifier" of the unity.[42] The meaning of the symbol is transformed or appropriated by the "native" presence until it is forced to govern that which it can no longer represent. In other words, in the colonial situation, symbols are invariably destabilized by the force of hybridity:

Such a reading of the hybridity of colonial authority profoundly unsettles the demand that figures at the centre of the originary myth of colonialist power. It is the demand [of colonial authority] that the space it occupies be unbounded, its reality *coincident* with the emergence of an imperialist narrative and history, its discourse *non-dialogic*, its enunciation *unitary*, unmarked by the trace of difference. It is a demand that is recognizable in a range of justificatory Western "civil" discourses.[43]

What Bhabha seeks is a recognition that hybridity is a *tendency* in the confrontation of cultures and not a conscious *strategy*. Indeed, his work suggests that, as we negotiate with those who work from different ontologies, epistemologies, and mythologies, as Ashis Nandy argued, that prior or present contact generates its own conditions which have ceased to be—if they ever really were—articulable by a single set of symbols. The fluidity of the hybrid "is finally uncontainable because it breaks down the symmetry of the binary of self/other, inside/outside."[44] In Bhabha's work, therefore, we are in-between our selves and the other, but—as in Voegelin's work—this is an intensely creative but profoundly difficult place to be. We are not paralyzed by our in-betweenness, but we are checked in our certainties and the power they have given us, and we are then forced to negotiate our symbols, rather than impose our signs as universals. Negotiation *sans* final authority becomes the basis for cultural interactions and cross-cultural understandings.

Bhabha takes seriously—in a way the Voegelin of *Order and History* seems to—extra-Western experiences and positionalities. He writes with a keen sensibility, like that of Michel Foucault, that the understandings that Voegelin properly values bring with them assumptions of power. Bhabha argues that we should confront the power dimensions of our symbolic language honestly in order to communicate in a fruitful dialogic way. Writing as a postcolonial (and post-Cold War) thinker, Bhabha must be concerned with cultures across space and is, therefore, more overtly concerned with the politics of the transitive. Spinning our symbolic language works internally—where signs may be taken as symbols—but where cultures meet and interact, cultural differences must be respected, and we should abandon the impulse to universalize diverse cultural meanings into sameness. Bhabha's analysis demonstrates that the attempt to take cultural symbols in their own terms requires that we recognize that *any act of cultural translation is an act of power and bound to meet resistance* and will, therefore, require negotiation on the level of cultural meanings. These overtly political concerns make Bhabha's a decidedly horizontal conception of the in-between.

The Intervention of Politics

Bhabha's work addresses itself to some of the same issues as Voegelin's, and we think it would be a mistake—indeed this is what we are arguing—to see their analyses as mutually exclusive. Bhabha is thinking in categories that Voegelin cannot afford to indulge, even were he so motivated. By the late twentieth and early twenty-first century, Bhabha recognizes that the tensions in political reality are no longer exclusively Western and, therefore, they are not so starkly polar. While conceding symbolic sovereignty over interiors (itself increasingly problematic), Bhabha shifts the discussion to an interstitial space, a transitive space, where meanings are much less authoritative. To produce fruitful outcomes, these meanings and their symbols must be negotiated at the multiple points of contact between diverse cultures. They can no longer be "resolved" through action based on the elder colonial model, that is, by asserting—via whatever means—the superiority (e.g., the "differentiated" character) of one set of symbols or experiences over another. We can no longer afford to ignore the doubleness—and we might argue for the term "multiplicity" given the technological web-linked world—in our signs/symbols: first, that they are what we say they signify and second, that we articulate ourselves in space and in time by identifying and asserting the meaning of the symbol.

Voegelin's commitment to philosophical openness, it seems, allows for the recognition of this doubleness which is the very essence of what it means to be in the *metaxy*, that is, "in-between." Bhabha suggests that the consciousness of this doubleness must be present at the point of cultural interactions and constitutes the very stuff of negotiation. Naming what we cannot know is an act of power—Voegelin identifies ideologies as a function of this hubristic tendency—but the effect, Bhabha shows us, is reciprocal and results in the generation of false binaries, that is, hybrids over which we have little or no control. Bhabha recognizes the critical roles hybrids play in the outcomes of cultural negotiations. But what negotiable symbols lack in certainties regarding eternal permanence, they can add to politics by forcing a constant dialogue on their meaning and a resistance to their hypostatization in the name of political expediency.

"The philosopher's way is the way up toward the light," Voegelin writes, "not the way down into the cave."[45] Voegelin knows, however, and his Plato-Socrates and knows full well that the way of the *political* philosopher takes him back down into the cave where he teaches, learns, and finally dies in and for truth. While Voegelin focuses on the verticality of the in-between, on our position between the temporal and the eternal, his philosophical commitment to an "openness" to equivalent experiences across time easily translates into a concern with such equivalences across space. Correspondingly, Bhabha's emphasis on the horizontal and spatial dimension of the in-between, on the contact between symbol systems across space and in time, suggests the practice of philosophical openness has a place in political discussions between cultures and suggests one way of making that philosophical openness politically viable. The task is to communicate the insights of philosophy in such a way that they may be made to inform politics, that is, to bring the vertical to bear on the horizontal and to take neither as the sum total of human political existence, if we are, finally, to take the political seriously.

CHAPTER 9

NEGOTIATING SPACE(S):
REFRAMING POLITICAL CONFLICT
IN WALZER AND LYOTARD

INTRODUCTION

Contemporary theoretical conceptions of political justice, because politics involves the interaction of self-interested human beings on the level of stuff and power, equate justice with the distribution of "goods." The assumption that there are goods to be distributed "justly," brings a corollary assumption about the environment in which those goods are distributed. Postmodern, postcolonial, feminist, and other critiques, however, suggest that taking the contents of the political environment for granted, works against our grasping the complexities of establishing and maintaining a just social order. There is, in other words, a need for a careful consideration of the space(s) in which this distribution occurs.

To the degree that politics is about governing, as Max Weber reminds us, it is about acquiring and exercising authority over a given area or space. The exercise of political power in its many forms, that is, establishing rules, setting up institutions, defining the requirements of membership, determining the language in which these matters are discussed, would seem to require the assumption of a relatively stable space which the power itself defines. Well-established valences of power, in personal and institutional relationships, in discourse, etc., define political space in a certain way. In consequence, political action, from the most basic or subtle speech acts to agitating for the most profound political reform, would seem to depend upon the ability to alter the contents of that space. Renewing justice (if that is the appropriate way to put it) depends on access to the physical and/or discursive means required to alter that space. If we are on the right track, then, the way we conceive justice is intimately bound up in the way we fashion space.

This chapter explores questions of the content of space, the contest for the means of naming political space, and the problems of equating justice with the results of those conflicts in the work of Michael Walzer and Jean-Francois Lyotard. From their apparently divergent perspectives, Walzer in *Spheres of Justice* and Lyotard in *Just Gaming* both theorize political space by questioning the implications and possibilities of the very project of creating just and useful political spaces.[1] Walzer reclaims the otherwise familiar categories of classical liberalism in an effort to break down structures of political domination. He does so metaphorically by conceiving political space in terms of more or less stable "spheres" wherein social and political goods are distributed according to "complex equality." Lyotard's postmodern approach works through that discourse to destabilize established political spaces, reducing their interaction to "games" and suggesting that any political order tends toward grand or meta-narratives which subsume diversity in the name of convergence and, therefore, works against human freedom. Yet Lyotard's "games" suggest the same set of difficulties as Walzer's "spheres," and each arrives at a different response to the problem of theorizing about politics. If the discourse on which Walzer relies and to which Lyotard refers is corrupt, then whatever the character of the space we occupy together, we may well be left with Rousseau's political order of "chains."

The difficulty of theorizing about politics stems precisely from the fact that it is a rough-and-tumble and all-too-human activity in which interests are identified, clash, and are made to (appear to) balance. The healthy polity, it has been suggested, requires both the stability of established rules, institutions, and languages as well as destabilizing presences, art and questioning, resistance and claims against political power exercised. Politics, that is, requires order and creativity, contest and compromise, certainty and a place for uncertainty. Emphasizing the "what" of politics, our analyses often assume the "where" and, therefore, miss the key questions.

Decolonization and the apparent breakdown of the Western intellectual hegemony suggested by postmodernism, feminism, etc., require that we question those initial assumptions before we attempt to piece together politics and find justice in political processes. The corresponding interest in space, particularly in what happens (the

realm of the "just") in spaces beyond those set by political conditions (including discourse), then, becomes critical to identifying the
conditions necessary before we can speak of justice. The metaphorical
use of space in discussions of politics is complicated by the fact that
politics is necessarily about "spaces," for example, the elements of a
territory over which someone claims sovereignty. Do the less tangible
elements of that sovereignty (especially discourse—the language we
use to contextualize and justify our social and political environments—
lend themselves to the spatial metaphor without being implicated in
the assumptions that go along with sovereignty over territories? Is justice simply concerned with the appropriate management of space or
does the problem of discursive space render conceptions of justice as
distributive as problematic in and of themselves? Far from answering
these questions, this essay proposes an approach to addressing these
issues and hopefully raises more questions than it answers.

MICHAEL WALZER: POLITICAL SPACE AND THE SOCIAL MEANING OF JUSTICE

The context for Michael Walzer's *Spheres of Justice* is the basic tension
in contemporary theories of justice between equality and freedom.
In general, theories that emphasize equality concern themselves with
processes, with the distribution of a society's resources ("goods"). The
influential formulations of John Rawls, Ronald Dworkin, and Walzer
are excellent examples of this. Each concerns himself with ethics, but
each relies heavily on "equality" rather than the exercise and management of freedom and, therefore, concentrates on how the goods
of society are distributed in order to assure justice. Rawls emphasizes
"basic liberties" which make up an environment of nondiscrimination. This nondiscrimination can only be guaranteed, however, in
a system in which "primary goods" are distributed equally, that is,
via the "difference principle" according to which the individual with
the fewest primary goods is considered as occupying the maximal
position.[2] Dworkin relies on an equal sharing of resources or primary
goods of both the human and the material sort. The difficulty is that
while arranging for the sharing of material resources is complicated,
providing for the equal sharing of personal capacities is nearly impossible. A just distribution will still require the voluntary cooperation of
those possessed of a more than equal share of both kinds of primary
goods.[3] Walzer's conceptualization of "spheres of justice" acknowledges that comprehensive justice is an unrealistic goal without first
trying to provide for it in particular interest areas of the community.

Freedom is a key element in thinking about justice. Communitarians like Michael Sandel argue that the community provides the context in which individuals may explore their freedom, but in which they, simultaneously, are responsible for the consequences of that exercise.[4] Lyotard's postmodern approach also emphasizes freedom, though in a necessarily less settled social context, and his analysis therefore would seem to suggest a counterpoint to Walzer's work. In both cases as we will see, the distribution of the material things of society assumes the defined or definable presence of a community, a space in which those goods are identified and distributed.

Walzer's chief interlocutor might be Rawls. Walzer engages the social contract model seriously but does not indulge in the temptation to trace social relationships, existent or imagined, back to an "original position." Rawls' social contract model seeks to find us as we would be with a minimum of interests, behind a "veil of ignorance," from where we could choose what we value and how (and to whom) those values are to be distributed. The idea is that justice entails the maintenance of a substantive, if minimum, level of sustenance for each member of the community.

Rawls's scheme is careful not to hamstring those possessing the resources to augment the community's development. Among the difficulties with this approach is that human beings, especially as *zoon politikon*, are incapable of detaching from their own interests for any substantial period of time. Machiavelli, for instance, knew well that politics, though we may wish it otherwise, values cleverness and the manipulation of the resources that make up the political environment.[5] Usually, this manipulation comes in the service of preserving the primacy of a particular set of values, with requisite institutions and relationships. Walzer seems to work out of the Rawlsian impulse to make justice a question of distribution, but he also seeks to avoid the temptation to domination(s) or social tyranny. Walzer wants us to have control over our interests, "to check them at the door" when engaged in a different or only tangentially-related interest or value "sphere." At the same time, by invoking the spatial metaphor, Walzer's analysis (and Lyotard's too, for that matter) proceeds from the assumption that these values, institutions, and relationships all make up political space. The struggle either to maintain or supplant that primacy, the struggle over the content of political space, is the very stuff of politics.

Walzer grounds his vision of political space in local understandings of social good and their articulations, both material and discursive. "All the goods with which distributive justice is concerned," he

begins, "are social goods."[6] As such, these goods have shared meanings among the members of a given society and, therefore, cannot be
denied. We attach meaning to objects and must recognize them as
the community's media of social and political intercourse. As social
and political beings, men and women derive their identities from the
way they create, possess, and exchange these goods. Walzer wishes to
avoid universalizing a given set of goods because he wants to respect
communal decisions made over time about the relative worth of those
goods. "There is no single set of primary or basic goods," he writes,
"conceivable across all moral and material worlds." There is a corresponding concern with theoretical coherence: were there to be such
a list, the conception of the goods would have to be so abstract that
"they would be of little use in thinking about particular distribution."[7]
So Walzer tries to keep his abstractions grounded by using the spatial
metaphor. Spheres, as he calls these material and discursive spaces that
comprise a given political space, are, like polities themselves, manage-
able because they are bounded, enclosed, defined. Walzer is mindful,
however, that social meanings can and do change over time, thus
his respect for local meanings determined by communities over time.
Enclosing territory is one thing; carefully defining non-material elements of the community (like ideas or issue areas) is problematic. Such
an enclosing of the elements of discourse, as some of his critics have
noted, is an opening for the very kind of tyranny Walzer wishes to
avoid.

The social goods Walzer values are things, tangible resources, but
they also include less physically tangible commitments like elements of
discourse. These commitments are critical precisely because goods, to
have social meaning, require communication and reinforcement. The
justification for the way goods are distributed (to whom and how)
depends upon how the social goods are understood in themselves and
how those understandings are articulated. Therefore, the character of
the discourse that derives from and substantiates the social meaning
of these goods is decisive. How we describe, talk about, and criticize political (that is for Walzer, distributive) activities and actors are
as important as the activities themselves. But, and Walzer's predilec-
tion for democracy invites this, attending to the many voices that
should or do make up discussions about social meaning may tend
to chaos if not properly monitored and regulated. Walzer, to resist
the potential tyranny of having governing bodies monitor public discourse, grounds his vision in the presence of a responsible democratic
citizenry. He hopes, in other words, that the voices will be self-
monitoring. "Justice," he writes, "begins with persons,"[8] but these

persons should remember their locations when they speak, and it is in this requirement that we encounter the metaphor of the "spheres."

When meanings are distinct, distributions must be autonomous. Every social good or set of goods constitutes, as it were, a distributive sphere within which only certain criteria and arrangements are appropriate.... In no society, of course, are social meanings entirely distinct. What happens in one distributive sphere affects what happens in the others; we can look, at most, for relative autonomy.[9]

Preserving the integrity of a structured public discourse is at the center of Walzer's vision. As such, it is the invasion or the corruption of these semi-autonomous spheres that characterizes the domination(s) that he opposes. Preventing or policing these incursions, Walzer argues, that is, conversions of power in one sphere (usually, the economic) into power in another (chiefly, the political), should be the function of democratic institutions and individuals concerned with justice. In Walzer's conception, social (*cum* political) space is made up of these spheres, each providing a context for discussion about a social good. Minding them, keeping them grounded in their relative sovereignties, is the very point of all democratic governing activity. The distribution of specific social goods, in their appropriate spheres, Walzer writes, "is what social conflict is all about."[10] That there are different rules governing the distribution of these different goods in their appropriate spheres is what Walzer means by the "complex equality" that characterizes just communities.

The spatial as metaphor, though appropriate to discussions of politics, is nonetheless problematic. Even when the subject matter invites its use, Walzer is caught up in its complexity. In his discussion of "membership," Walzer understands the degree to which politics is driven by, often determined by, spatial concerns. If justice consists in the distribution of social goods, then it presumes "a bound world within which distributions take place" called "political community."[11] This world is a physical place, but membership decisions entail making more subtle distinctions about the content of that space, particularly its human content.

The first decision a political community makes in reference to its legitimate self is "who is a member?" Political being, Walzer writes, requires a state, a home space, as it were. By contrast, the implications of "statelessness" are far-reaching. When we are stateless, he argues, we are in "a condition of infinite danger."[12] One of the first privileges of membership, therefore, is having a role in determining whether

strangers shall have membership (and to what degree) or whether they
will be consigned to statelessness. This is an enormous responsibility, requiring that we juggle our preferred vision of the content of
our space(s) and our sense of commitment to the stranger as human
being. It is a virtue of Walzer's analysis that he will not let us avoid this
choice, for, much as we saw in *Oedipus at Colonus* and *The Gospel at
Colonus*, it reaches to the very core of what we conceive ourselves to
be. The distinctiveness of cultures depends, he says, on "closure" and
the willingness to say where or when that closure will be drawn. Political maturity depends upon getting comfortable with the fact that some
must be turned away at some times: on whether the culture encour-
ages or limits transitivity. The painfulness of closure, its human cost
to chooser and to those not chosen, is key to the self-determination
Walzer seems to find essential to political justice. Access to democratic
processes, Walzer concludes, depends first on living within the territory (being a member) and second on how one treats strangers. How
we handle our immigration and naturalization decisions, the discussion of membership suggests, speaks not only to the actual content of
political space, but how well or poorly that space is managed.

Membership is only the first of the social goods that must be distributed in their spheres. Because the physical space that membership
requires is literal, that discussion does not, strictly speaking, involve
the use of the spatial metaphor. Walzer's discussion of the physical
space involved in discussions of membership, however, encompasses
each of the social goods that he proceeds to discuss. All distributions of
social goods will occur in the context of this bound territory, though
membership decisions (like discussions of the other such goods) are
reserved to their own sphere. Walzer's discussion does not distinguish the literal from the figural use of space he uses in the rest of
his analysis. The image is translated into the management of non-
physical spaces. His discussion about managing physical space offers a
blueprint for the way we should handle distributions of non-material
social goods in non-material spaces. Without boundaries in physical
space, he argues, communities of character do not get the chance to
develop and grow. Inhabitants do not get the chance to commit to one
another in a way they are not committed to others ("strangers"). The
(en)closure that Walzer insists is necessary for the development and
preservation of a community's culture, he finds equally essential to
preserving public discourse, that is, to preserving the integrity of and
appropriate balance among the spheres of the various social goods.
A just community makes itself comfortable with carefully demarcated
boundaries in both physical and discursive space. Walzer underlines his

commitment to boundaries by making his notion of "complex equality" require defense of those boundaries and the preservation of a differentiation among the spheres. Drawing figural or metaphorical boundaries around discussions about the distribution of potentially competing or complementary values, however, is of a different order than drawing literal boundaries around physical space.

The boundaries suggested by Walzer's spheres are less easily defined and much less easily safeguarded than Walzer's discussion seems to assume. He relies, perhaps overconfidently, on the integrity of those boundaries, that is, on citizens' abilities to keep various communal and individual interests segregated. In his discussion of the function of recognition, for example, Walzer understands that the exercise of that kind of self-control and self-awareness requires a difficult to acquire sense of self-possession. But this is the responsibility of citizenship, of membership. "What is necessary," he writes, "is that the idea of citizenship be shared among some group of people who recognize one another's title and provide some social space within which the title can be acted out."[13] If one has the appropriate understanding of the importance of recognition, then, when one speaks, one does so from a space asserted by self, but also recognized by others. A comfort in one's place, a comfort with the dimensions of social recognition, is part of what it means to be a wholly integrated self. It is the responsibility of the community to distribute social goods in such a way as to make this development in character possible. "The problem that justice poses," he suggests, "is precisely to distribute goods to a host of Xs in ways that are responsive to their concrete, integrated selves."[14] For Walzer, then, recognizing hierarchies is essential to ordering social space, to the just ordering of the democratic community, in the same way as recognizing hierarchies in various abilities is necessary to preserving other balances in the make-up of the community.

Walzer contends that the hierarchies found in the different spheres, including the sphere of recognition are not automatically converted into hierarchies in the exercise of political or other kinds of power. This assertion of non-convertibility, while appealing, is the most difficult of dimension of Walzer's argument. Predictably enough, the difficulty with non-convertibility reaches critical mass in Walzer's discussion of the convertibility of economic into political power:

I am concerned now to sustain the integrity of the other distributive spheres—by depriving powerful entrepreneurs, for example, of the means of capturing political power or bending public officials to their will. When money carries with it control, not of things only, but of people too, it ceases to be a private resource.[15]

In other words, when money can be used to buy things it should not be able to buy thereby violating the integrity of the spheres of both money and political power, "if we can't block the purchase, then we have to socialize the money, which is only to recognize that it has taken on a political character."[16] We must, Walzer contends, change society's recognition of the relationship of money (and other forms of property) to the political sphere. The verb "socialize" suggests political action which for Walzer means the power of the citizenry, but the assertion of that power neglects the problem of a broader social understanding of currency. How quickly or effectively can the understanding of currency be converted from an economic to a political one? Is the very idea not a violation of the integrity of the spheres involved? Even if the integrity of the political has been preserved, its limits reached in various redistributions,[17] what of the integrity of the spheres of money and commodities? Transitivity, then, becomes internal economic exchange, generating different forms of "currency." The questions this raises are not adequately answered because the maintenance of boundaries is left to the political sphere.

Walzer's discussion of the sphere of political power leaves these questions undetermined until the political public has the chance to act. Political sovereignty itself is the authority and responsibility, assumed by those who engage in politics, of guarding the boundaries within which every social good is distributed.[18] Politics is a sovereign sphere among other sovereign spheres, but, because it is charged with guarding the boundaries of the other spheres, it would seem to be not so disengaged from activities within the other spheres. Walzer claims that citizens engaged in politics, when they are, should only be engaged in politics. They should possess the capacity and respect the requirement to check their other interests at the door, barring interstitial spaces like the ones we saw in Homi Bhabha's theory. While Walzer suggests that each of us wear many hats, it is not clear whether our place in the hierarchy within a given sphere automatically excludes us from participating in the decision-making discussions that go on in reference to that sphere in the realm of the political. Democratic citizens are informed, persuasive speakers willing to make themselves vulnerable in the public space that is politics. These are the gifts that are rewarded in the political sphere. The political sphere, therefore, is based on the possession of these skills rather than power or authority derived from power exercised in a sphere like the economic. "What democracy requires," Walzer writes, "is that property should have no political currency, that it shouldn't convert into anything like sovereignty, authoritative command, sustained control over men and women."[19] Democratic politics is the monopoly, he contends, of politicians and every citizen "is a potential participant, a potential politician."[20]

Checking our interests at the door of the political sphere and allowing the political to regulate the other spheres to which we belong and in which we may even have power or standing are ideas difficult to reconcile in the *zoon politikon*. "Democratic politics," he argues, "once we have overthrown every wrongful dominance, is a standing invitation to act in public and to know oneself as a citizen, capable of choosing destinations and accepting risks for oneself and others, and capable, too, of patrolling the distributive boundaries and sustaining a just society."[21] Here is where the use of the spatial metaphor to discuss and regulate non-physical or discursive spaces reaches its limit. The required segregation of our public political selves from the other interests which make us fully integrated selves is unresolved. The likely impossible resolution is made even less likely by the employment of the spatial metaphor because we are, at the very least, the sum total of our interests. We would not concern ourselves with conflicts over social goods were we not interested in them in some way. Walzer's democratic citizens simply must be congeries of competing and contradictory interests. It is the competition among interests and their reconciliation or, and this often amounts to the same thing, our learning to live with those contradictory interests that Walzer properly leaves within the sphere of the political. The problem is how we resolve or even talk about those disputes in the arena of political discourse without bringing in the vested interests we hold as a result of our membership/participation in different spheres? As informed citizens, we also must have knowledge of the nature of spheres involved in disputes to arrive at useful, just decisions regarding their governance.

Walzer knows that the complexity of political processes outstrips his metaphor.[22] The metaphor itself is vulnerable to setting up a politics of exclusion (justice is "relative to social meanings"; "good fences make just societies," etc.). The need to regulate the potential tyranny involved in boundary-crossing can and has functioned as a way of shutting down the very discussion Walzer argues is at the heart of democratic political activity. Walzer's (en)closure argument is good news if you had a part in building the fences or constructing the story. "A community's culture," he writes, "is the story its members tell so as to make sense."[23] But it may be that Walzer over-commits to the stability of those fences. Moving or changing them requires going through the political sphere, but in such a way that "your interest" does not get in the way. The question is "how" one carries this off when addressing the nature of "your interest" is the political question to be settled. Walzer's use of space as a metaphor for how political discourse can be engaged in and how it is to be limited requires a discussion of discourse *as discourse* and this is the province of a postmodern like Jean-Francois Lyotard.

JEAN-FRANCOIS LYOTARD: (UN)NAMING POLITICAL SPACE

Lyotard approaches politics from a concern with the way political spaces are articulated and justified. He assumes the importance of political discourse because it involves representations to consciousness that are made in order to communicate a set of values or ideas through a rational order or structure of concepts.[24] Political power, especially in the democratic context suggested by Walzer, demands a due consideration of the symbolic importance of our language. Political power, inasmuch as it involves the use and mastery of such representations, implies winning the contest over the control of the discourse. Lyotard begins, therefore, very sensitive to the reality that what Walzer calls social goods are functions of those who claim they are goods or have the capacity to name them as such. Walzer assumes, within different communities, of course, the existence of an authority (legitimate or not) charged with naming or representing those social goods. In consequence, it is precisely the case that we take those social goods argued for and distributed by the powerful for *the* social goods.

Lyotard's analysis interrogates the discourse which speaks of those goods and their importance and validates and authorizes the relationships among those terms. Those who set or control the terms of the discourse claim the authority to define those terms and, whatever universalizing claims the discourse may or may not make for itself, it is *only* within that discourse that those terms and conditions may properly be said to function. Lyotard introduces a transitive principle: every discourse is made up of innumerable and, ultimately, incommensurable "language games," a Wittgensteinian term Lyotard uses to connote the singularity of every "language-act." The acts of language that make up the social and political environment each come with expressed and implied rules about how the components of the act relate to each other and to the acts which both preceded and are to follow them. Each act, then, necessarily reflects the rules which control it. Each is also reflective of the rules that govern the larger discursive/political space in which they are contained. But for Lyotard, all is not determinism. There is, in each act, the latent possibility of creatively stretching those rules thereby adding dimension to the game or rewriting the discourse.

The implications of this view of the importance of discourse in our present context are two-fold. First, there is a creative potential in recognizing our presence in and the corresponding limits embodied in the rules of "language games." Second, there is a "terror" implied and expressed in acts which assume the power of naming social or political space. When a series of these acts are used, across boundaries of language games, to consolidate understanding and therefore power, discourse as "grand" or "metanarrative" becomes at once both a locus and a source of enormous political and cultural power. The appeal of metanarratives in political discourse is their apparent explanatory power. As they set the terms in which a problem is expressed, the problem can be explained using that same set of terms. A metanarrative functions much as an individual game, except that it claims authority over and explanatory power for every language game. By so doing, metanarratives obscure the very real content of social and political space, conflicts Lyotard describes as *differends*.[25] In *The Differend: Phrases in Dispute*, Lyotard distinguishes a differend from a more familiar way of resolving social and political disputes in the West:

As distinguished from a litigation, a differend would be a case of conflict, between (at least) two parties, that cannot be equitably resolved for lack of a rule of judgment applicable to both arguments. One side's legitimacy does not imply the other's lack of legitimacy. However, applying a single rule of judgment to both in order to settle their differend as though it were merely a litigation would wrong (at least) one of them (and both of them if neither side admits this rule).[26]

Resolving a differend in terms of one of the disputants puts the loser in the untenable position of lacking legitimacy or standing in the dispute. Rather than admit so fundamental a shortcoming as the inability to resolve a dispute, political expediency demands the resort to the metanarrative which by definition translates *every* differend into terms established and accepted by the meta-narrative.[27] The metanarrative, that is, co-opts the differend, defines it in its own terms and in so doing sacrifices the singularity of the language-act ("event") that the silenced side(s) of the differend represent(s): it "translates" hybridities into the singularity of the metanarrative. We would describe this process in Lyotard's literary critical language in the following way: the metanarrative seizes control of the rules by which phrases may be linked, shutting off linkages that it cannot accommodate and, therefore, shutting off the possibility of the creative growth of the language game by concretizing its rules. Lyotard's analysis, in its political dimension, reveals the subtlety of the process and seeks "[b]y showing that the linking of one phrase onto another is problematic and that this problem is the problem of politics, to set up a philosophical politics apart from the politics of intellectuals [which he calls 'academic discourse'] and of politicians [bound up as they are in concerns about 'exchange' and 'capital']."[28]

In *Just Gaming*, Lyotard, in dialogue with a young philosopher named Jean-Loup Thebaud, suggests that politics is principally the realm of the ruse, the means by which the grand narrative weaves all the ideas and institutions we assume as goods (including "justice") into a seeming "self-evidence," that is, into a viable and given relationship.[29] What characterizes our "postmodern condition" is that we no longer accept ontological justifications for the primacy of what Walzer calls the social goods. Naming or burying the differend in a metanarrative has been unmasked as an exercise of cultural and political power that obligates us to what Lyotard calls "witnessing." What we are witness to is a recognition of the groundless ground underlying what we have called modernity. What we must witness is the degree to which this is so, and we do this by telling "little stories" back to the ruling metanarrative.[30] The struggles in political space are not exclusively, as Walzer would have it, contests among social goods. They are much more fruitfully considered contests over the discourse in which we talk about social meanings themselves. Disputes in terms established by metanarratives, however, turn these contests into events that obscure the fact that terms we use to discuss politics and political goals are used without precision, that is, they move too freely between and among language games. When language is used across language games, the authentic human aspirations the language can represent and the meanings formed in contact become vulnerable to manipulation, like being re-constructed in terms already established in the meta-narrative. Language, in other words, codifies and reinforces social assumptions (just or otherwise).

Language games in Lyotard's analysis, including and especially the game of "justice," come to look like Walzer's spheres in that each has its own discursive space and, therefore, its own rules of play. Taking the differend seriously, Lyotard suggests, requires breaking some bad habits, particularly in the realm of political philosophy. The fingerprints of what he calls the *classical* view can be found all over the way we talk about the management of political space. In this older view, a writer "justifies, defends, what he has done in the name of a system of values that are the values held by this public."[31] In terms of the problem of justice, classicism allows the Platonic practice of deciding upon just criteria, usually extrapolated from an essentialist picture of human nature (being), and then judging. Here, the internal human landscape is tied to a set of eternal verities and then re-transcribed into the concrete world of the political. The implication is the association of justice with distribution, for that is what institutions do. There is also acceptance of a corresponding creation of a kind of (potentially, iron) circle: "The distribution of all that circulates in a given society is just if it conforms to something defined in Plato as justice itself."[32] Justice, then, is defined in terms established by the utterer. However, justice is not simply what we say it is, but also because we can justify it from a set of ontological truths derived from our picture of human being. Then it is a simple matter to give social and political form to that vision. "Plato believes," Lyotard says, "that if one has a 'just' (that is, true) view of being, then one can re-transcribe this view into social organization, with intermediate instances, to be sure (such as the *psyche*), but nonetheless the model remains that of the very distribution of being."[33]

For Lyotard, the chief problem with the Platonic or classical view of justice is that it requires passing directly from the true (*descriptive* "is" statements about the nature and content of the soul) to the just (*prescriptive* "ought" statements about the analogous relationship of the structure of the soul to that of the polis). One cannot have an idealized vision of the properly-ordered polis without measuring prevailing political orders by that vision:

When one says politics, one always means that there is something to institute. There is no politics if there is not at the very center of society, at least a center that is not a center but everywhere in the society, a questioning of existing institutions, a project to improve them, to make them more just. This means all politics implies the prescription of doing something else than what is, is prescription itself: it is the essence of a prescription to be statement such that it induces in its recipient an activity that will transform reality, that is, the situational context, the context of the speech act. I cannot see then that, when one speaks of politics in the West, one can think of this word without bringing the prescriptive into the picture.[34]

But for Lyotard, there is incommensurability between statements that narrate or describe something and statements that prescribe something. "One describes a model of strategy, of society, of economy," Lyotard observes, "and then, when one passes to prescriptions, one has jumped into another language game."[35] Lyotard argues that Aristotle is the first to suggest the modern or *pagan* recognition that politics is a realm in which we must act and must choose—that is, that it is primarily a prescriptive activity. The mean, however, is not pre-determined. We must choose from case-to-case. We prescribe without criteria, that is, without those ontological assumptions that the Platonic conception relies upon. Because it is of the order of the prescriptive, the just is a matter of dialectics, of the constant interaction of the speech act with its environment, making each act a hybrid. Ethics becomes transitive movement in the contact zone. The movement is between the judge's encounter with the conflict and his/her resolution of the conflict. Justice is not to be found by an externalizing of the human soul or via an indescribable ideal not to be realized. Rather, justice is found in the judge's act(s) of judging.

It is Aristotle's insight, argues Lyotard, that the mean cannot be determined outside the situation. Judging, the chief political skill is *techne*; the art of judging is a technical knowledge. Consequently, it is technical rather than, he suggests, abstract philosophical knowledge that is required of Aristotle's political actor. Politics occurs in the order of opinion and not truth. This *pagan* view recognizes that the judge cannot put himself outside of that which s/he judges. S/he is inevitably *of* that which s/he judges. The political implication of the idea of the pagan is that judgment, and therefore political activity itself, is prescriptive and of the realm of opinion rather than truth. Never, Lyotard argues of the pagan, will we say a judge is always just. The struggle over political space, Lyotard suggests, has taken the form of a struggle over which of the claimed (not to say real) criteria should be the ground of judging when, in fact (and this is what the postmodern is willing to admit), none of them is. If we accept the pagan view, then political space, and justice therein, is what we (the community) say it is, and we accept that there are no acceptable criteria upon which to base, once and for all, our choices. The pagan view is and has been a recipe for terror, but it can also free judgment and all human political activity from the chains of ontological assumptions and prejudice. For the latter reason, Lyotard, while recognizing that the pagan is inadequate, builds on it rather than abandoning it.

Like the classical view, the pagan is vulnerable to the emergence of a metanarrative and the resultant silencing of one or all of the discursive elements of the differend. Unlike the classical view, and thus its appeal to Lyotard, the pagan view accepts that there is no ontological justification for its judgments. The refusal to cloak itself in these justifications makes the pagan a potential source of terror but also a potential source of enormous creativity. Judgment depends on the judge's recognition and interpretation of the rules of the language game in which s/he is judging. Lyotard is still concerned, however, that the terror of the metanarrative is easier than the rule-shaping challenges of a more creative approach to games. He still seeks some kind of justification out of which the political actor can challenge while respecting established rules. He seeks a standard but it must not be one that simply creates a metanarrative. Rather than assert a standard external to the human, Lyotard suggests the development of a "properly reflective" orientation to judging, what he calls a "faculty." He finds this political faculty in his reading of Kant who, he finds, proffers the Idea of the suprasensible nature of human being. Kant's imperative "*so that*," Lyotard suggests to Thebaud,

marks the properly reflective use of judgment. It says: Do whatever, not on condition that, but *in such a way as* that which you do, the maxim of what you do, can always be valid as, et cetera. We are not dealing here with a determinant synthesis, but with an Idea of human society.... Which means...that this use ultimately *leaves* the conduct to be adopted *un*determined. Suprasensible nature *does not* determine *what* I have to do. It regulates me, but without telling me *what* I have to do. It regulates me without telling me *what* there is to be done.[36]

Sensitive to the fact that this finding of a suprasensible nature in Kant creates a totality and, potentially, a meta-narrative of its own, Lyotard suggests that this suprasensible nature points to the presence of a faculty of judging which should be exercised, not against a horizon of totality, but only "against the horizon of a multiplicity or of a diversity."[37] In this construction, the judging faculty chooses not according to the will—that is, we are not dealing with a willful choice to preserve a meta-narrative—but rather one chooses in reference to preserving that multiplicity or diversity of language games (or discourses) that makes up the social and cultural environment. As idea, this faculty of political judgment itself regulates the political arena; it is "the faculty of the social bond."[38]

The complexity of political space re-enters the discussion at the precise point that Lyotard suggests the need for this faculty and its exercise against a horizon of multiplicity and diversity. Now Lyotard must deal with the polyvalent character of political space. The task is to order without privileging the contingent elements (the "games") that make up a given political space, but to do so in a way that does not inhibit the creative development of the human content of that space. If "one has the viewpoint of a multiplicity of language games, if one has the hypothesis that the social bond is not made up of a single kind of statement" but that it is "made up of several kinds of these games" then we must admit that we participate in many of these games.[39] This "multiple belonging" belies any essential or, especially, static identity for community or individual. It also denies that the claims of majoritarian "democratic" politics can be anything but the assertion of a metanarrative. It is to our status as members of various minorities that we should attend: "Basically, social minorities are not social ensembles; they are *territories* of language," he argues. "Every one of us belongs to several minorities, and what is very important, none of them prevails."[40] Just governance "prohibits that the question of the just and the unjust be, and remain, raised."[41] Justice requires maintaining the borders of these territories, that is, maintaining the plurality of language games thus making "it impossible for anyone to establish her- or himself in a field and proceed to produce its laws in a sort of universal language or generalized metalanguage, and then go on to extend these laws to all the fields of language."[42] The rules of each language game apply to it alone, like laws to physical territories. Once one accepts this limitation, Lyotard argues, the language of one game will not come to dominate or terrorize the others. Maintaining plurality, assuring the integrity of the language games, works against the emergence of majorities and against the emergence of meta-narratives that take in more than the single appropriate game.

Recognizing and protecting the integrity of language games, Lyotard concludes, does not suffice for there to be justice. Healthy, just games are not static, unyielding entities. Nor is a static political space just. A self-reflective conceptualization of the just must have space for both order and creativity, so Lyotard suggests two dimensions of justice. First, there is the *multiplicity of justices*, "each one of them defined in relation to the rules specific to each game."[43] The prescriptive rules in each game are seen or received as "good" inasmuch as they reflect the minimum criteria each game establishes for itself. But, in the context of these known criteria and rules, justice preserves the opportunity for creativity, for growth, for re-describing what it means to be in the game itself (or move beyond it). "Justice here," Lyotard contends, "does not consist merely in the observance of the rules; as in all the games, it consists in working at the limits of what the rules permit, in order to invent new moves, perhaps new rules and therefore new games."[44] Within the multiplicity of games, there is variation and diversity of understanding of what membership, participation, and justice itself all mean. The possibilities within the

multiplicities of justice, however, are preserved in the context of the
justice of multiplicity:

> It prescribes the observance of the singular justice of each game such as it
> has just been situated: formalism of the rules and imagination in the moves.
> It authorizes the "violence" that accompanies the work of the imagination.
> It prohibits terror, that is, the blackmail of death toward one's partners.[45]

Here the formalism of the rules and imagination involved in play ("the
moves") are seen as two parts to be preserved by a functioning political
faculty of the social bond. Balancing the space from which one speaks
with the diversity of the space(s) or games in which one is situated is
the singular challenge of justice, of acting justly, and the possibility of
authentic political life in Lyotard. For Lyotard, political space necessarily entails the presence of both order and creativity, but neither can
derive its possibility from terror. While politics may imply violence,
justice can have nothing to do with terror.

CONCLUSION: "BOUNDARIES" AND THE POSSIBILITY OF JUSTICE

Theoretical discussions of politics lend themselves quite easily to the
metaphor of space. Political communities define themselves externally
by the extent of their territories. Historically, international pres-
tige ("empire") has depended upon territorial expansion into distant
spaces, usually spaces rich in natural resources but otherwise, until
colonized, alien—a transitivity that is translated into sameness: space
becomes place.[46] Defining this kind of political space very much relies
on drawing and defending borders, but inasmuch as political space
denotes the physical, space is not a metaphor, but rather simply
another name for territorial expanse. The metaphor is much more
useful, but also correspondingly problematic, in discussions about
social and political meaning. "Space" there suggests the extent of
the appeal of elements (discursive and otherwise) of a given political culture, so it is that Walzer and Lyotard use the spatial metaphor
in their conceptions of "spheres" and "games" respectively. Relationships among meanings are rarely as easily demarcated as those between
physical territories. Border disputes between nations, for instance,
are very rarely about the territory, but more often about the symbolic meaning of that territory. The physically small territory called
"Jerusalem," for example, is possessed of meaning transcending the
few square miles that it occupies. What it *means* is really the sticking

point between Israelis and Palestinians (and Christians). Articulating meaning requires discourse, but we reach the limits of the effectiveness of language in a situation like that involving Jerusalem. It is a differend: it has supreme religious significance for the parties involved and therefore conceding any part or all of it would be to give over a significant part of what it means to be, especially, Jewish or Palestinian. Resolving the dispute by carving up the territory has been difficult precisely because this kind of fundamental meaning does not lend itself to being carved up.

Not all political disputes are or should be seen as differends. The disputes that result in blood or fundamental transformations of accepted communal meanings, however, usually are these kinds of questions. In politics, material elements and their contingent value are expressed through language, that is, discourse. Lyotard's analysis attends more to the complexities of discursive space than Walzer though both men appreciate that political actions are justified, when they are in fact explained at all, with well-established language. When Lyotard speaks of choosing "without criteria," he does not mean that political choices are made without reference to any criteria whatsoever. Rather he demonstrates that, on this side of the Nietzshean critique, political action is justified using criteria established or embraced by the actor/utterer. Political action can only be justified in its own terms—which is no justification at all. Both analyses assume politics is a matter of bound social and political value spaces. Governance, just or otherwise, is a question of negotiating differences within those spaces and minimizing conflicts (boundary violations) among those spaces. Both men equate injustice with the violation of value or discursive borders that must be respected in the orderly political space. Political spaces are fluid yet bound and the integrity of the boundaries separating both Walzer's spheres and Lyotard's games must be maintained in order for justice to attain in the larger societal space.

Political structures, from procedures to discourse, evolve out of a dominant culture's self-understanding. Discourse is implicated to the degree that it is utilized to explain prevailing arrangements and assumptions. Even Walzer concedes that the story of a community must be told in such a way as to have the form of the community and its decisions make sense. But justice, to the degree that it may require resisting established orders, also has to do with what happens outside of ordinary political processes contained within the spheres and games, as Homi Bhabha, Charles Long, and Ashis Nandy showed us. Walzer's regard for established structures, the integrity of the spheres, does not seem to allow for the kind of recognition outside the political process sometimes required of an effective critique. Lyotard, with his emphasis on play, his commitment to an admittedly difficult to define horizon of diversity and multiplicity, and in his recognition of the possibility of creating new games and new rules for the old games allows the opportunity for resistance. In Lyotard as in Walzer, however, it seems that this critique, this resistance must come from within the prevailing narrative. Lyotard does observe that boundaries between the games are not borders, that is, they are somewhat porous and, therefore, potentially creative or regenerative—transitive—spaces.

Lacking a distinction between settled and established space and something outside the norms implied by the term political space (or spheres or language games), it is hard to argue that either Walzer or Lyotard appreciates the power of a critique that positions itself outside of the order out of which it is born. Walzer might say that this is the critique encouraged by democratic discussion, but checking the interests that define our public selves works against this idea. For his part, Lyotard likely would argue that being born in a particular order limits one's ability to be "outside," and this is correct as far as it goes. Inasmuch as such a critique is prescriptive, however, being "outside" must be an imaginative possibility. Beyond borders (physical and discursive), there might be the possibility of (there almost certainly will be a need for) an "external" critique. This was the justification and *modus operandi* behind post-colonial theory which, in the words of Edward Said, posits a "talking back" to the tradition—in Lyotard's terms, the telling of "little stories" which may be undetermined or, at least, less determined by the grand ruling meta-narrative. Creative space(s) in which unconventional social and political forms of action are encouraged are doubtless still partially determined by communal understandings, but they may offer the chance for disenfranchised minorities to compare notes and produce strategies. Whether or not we can clearly draw and then defend boundaries around territories of social and political discourse, the use of the spatial metaphor suggests a presence that cannot be bound and offers the possibility, as in Vaclav Havel's account of resistance activity in late communist Czechoslovakia, to create an other or "second" culture—alongside the first—out of which the first is challenged to grow and adapt.[47]

CHAPTER 10

ALICE WALKER: SUFFERING
AND THE TASK OF THE
REVOLUTIONARY ARTIST

Alice Walker's *In Search of Our Mother's Gardens* was, on its publication in 1983, a revolutionary work in two ways.[1] It offered, first, an alternative to or African American extension of feminism and even black feminism with its definition of a "womanist," and it signaled the first in many volumes of the exploration of this black woman's life and consciousness. Walker, along with Maya Angelou, has been one of our most fearless autobiographers, engaging, in the tradition of the slave narrative, in self-revelation in the public eye. Doing so, she is a symbol of transitivity—particularly of the transitivity without violence that Emmanuel Levinas seeks. Walker has extended her self-examination into an on-going examination of self and society.

Most scholars, and we include ourselves here, tend to work with *In Search of Our Mothers' Gardens* and Walker's other autobiographical pieces as collections of essays and in a fragmentary way, mining their many gems without considering each alone and all together as a whole: the story of a woman's life, a practice of nonviolence, and a search for peace. Keeping the principle of transitivity in mind, we want to focus on *Mother's Gardens* and to argue that Walker's work constitutes a "spiritual autobiography." Its postmodern style bridges and connects the slave narrative's critique of nineteenth century America and the postcolonial critique of modernity, as it explores the identifiers of being black, female, Southern, and a writer—in short, being what Alice Walker calls a revolutionary artist. These identifiers come together in the narrative around two *loci* of meaning: the civil rights movement, which Walker extends and expands in her Buddhist practice, and motherhood.

We begin with the two discursive areas *Mother's Gardens* bridges: the slave narrative and the postcolonial critique. Kimberly R. Connor, in *Imagining Grace: Liberating Theologies in the Slave Narrative Tradition*, reminds us that the needs that the slave narrative addressed— the establishment of identity as a strategy for liberation of self and freedom for the race—were not satisfied by the legal end of slavery and, therefore, are on-going in the African American tradition.[2] Suggesting this, Connor reminds us, along with thinkers like Paul Gilroy, that strategies for liberation, actions that simultaneously define one's situation and change it, are embedded in seemingly secular arts. Connor suggests, through Mark Ledbetter, that narrative is one of those arts. Narrative, Ledbetter writes, "is itself a process not only revealing hidden meanings but also establishing meaning within and by its very structure."[3] Therefore, secular works, like Walker's, may "be more random and discursive [than, say, a theological text], but nonetheless are equally cogent for liberation."[4] Connor suggests that contemporary artists create "on the level of religious consciousness and produc[e] new cultural forms by which to reveal the transformative potential of the creative process."[5] These creations are authentic testimonies, and they remind us that suffering and oppression for African American peoples is ongoing, as well as offering strategies for overcoming that suffering.

Walker's work can and must be considered in the light of the epigraph to *In Search of Our Mother's Gardens*. The work is dedicated to her daughter Rebecca, who, looking at Walker's right eye, which was blinded when Walker was eight years old,

> Saw . . .
> what I considered a scar
> And redefined it
> as
> a world.[6]

Making wounds into worlds is at the core of what Walker does and writes about. Her most famous work, *The Color Purple*, for example, lets us watch a troubled black family—really, a group of psychically isolated individuals—who begin to put together their lives after Reconstruction and who become a whole and vital community.[7] The modern Civil Rights Movement was, for Walker, a movement that did the same for the African American community and, as such, it shapes and defines Walker's work. Walker says, her life found "its beginnings and purpose at the precise moment" that she heard Dr. King speak, and that purpose continued even after his death, as a "debt" that she felt she owed to his memory and work.[8] The writer's continuation of that work is to be "the voice of the people" and, in many ways to be "The People"[9]—that is, to express the situation and consciousness of black people and to suffer, in intimacy, with them. We will return to the latter issue. The first issue is to be a voice for freedom, which is, for Walker, the deep gift and responsibility that the Civil Rights Movement gives the black writer.

The movement, she says, was a call to life and a call to intimacy with self and other, giving the African American community "each other forever."[10] Most important, Dr. King and the movement returned, to African Americans, continuity of place and a sense of home in which community can be.[11] Continuity of place forms and informs the voice of the writer as she reconstructs the consciousness of those who live in that place.[12] Indeed, Walker argues that the black Southern writer's inheritance is a sense of community that must be rendered in all its complexity.[13]

This responsibility requires a particular attitude towards the self and towards history, one that is honest and that, thereby, can reconstruct the black situation and consciousness that Walker depicts in, for example, *The Color Purple*. Describing situation and conscsiousness, she quotes Albert Camus. The Southern writer, she says, "having been placed . . . 'halfway between misery and the sun' . . . knows that 'though all is not well under the sun, history is not everything.' "[14] Walker, in a postmodern and postcolonial mode, argues that history is not the only way to construct meaning: there are unauthorized ways of knowing and being, other modes of and for understanding human lives.

Walker came to this understanding, in the 1960's, in activist work. As a Civil Rights worker, she was supremely aware of the importance of the moment, but when she was asked to teach black history to a group of women in Mississippi, she was confronted with women who knew no history, as it is academically defined. She writes that these women, at the same time, were crippled by history, having been taught that their slave past was shameful. Her desire to help the women recover a pride in having prevailed "should have been as simple as handing them each a mirror,"[15] but it was not.

In a bold theoretical move, parallel to that of Edward Said, whose work *The World, The Text, and the Critic*,[16] appeared at almost the same time, Walker expands the notion of history to embrace memory, including in history "the faith and grace of a people under continuous pressures"[17] and the strategies that helped black people to stay in "a beloved but brutal place" without "losing the love."[18]

Linking memory and history, Walker enters the postmodern and postcolonial landscape, with all its issues. In "The Politics of Memory: Remembering History in Alice Walker and Joy Kogawa," David Palumbo-Liu argues that memory is problematic. While memory can "inscribe significance where none was allowed," he writes, memory "has yet to find a stable alternative site on which to found its memory and which can move memory to the point of history."[19] In other words, memory has no homeland. Walker wants to argue that the homeland of memory and history are one and the same, that they occupy the same epistemological territory, and that they inform, enhance, and nuance not replace, each other.

Womanist thought occupies and defines this paradoxical space. Black woman's identity and spirituality and participation in historical, social, and political reality are the twin poles of womanist thought. A womanist is a black feminist or feminist of color, one who is, as a self, "outrageous, audacious, courageous, capable, and willful."[20] She is "Responsible. In charge. *Serious*."[21] She is also socially and politically committed to growth of not just her self, but of the community. She is "committed to survival and wholeness of entire people, male *and* female,"[22] to recognizing and celebrating the diversity of peoples—and to their freedom:

"Mama, I'm walking to Canada and I'm taking you and a bunch of other slaves with me." Reply: "It wouldn't be the first time."[23]

As this section of Walker's definition suggests, this mode of identity and its commitment are born in and shaped by the sufferings of slavery and its aftermath, as well as hope for the future, represented by Canada. Womanist intensity—"Womanist is to feminist as purple is to lavender"[24]—is forged in suffering, but so is womanist joy. Womanist joy, most of all, is an unconditional and boundless love that embraces all that is and that moves with and in the creation under all conditions of being: *Regardless*.[25]

Walker's personal movement from scar to world, therefore—her courageous and on-going reconstitution of the self, reminding us that theory, as Edward Said argues, is, at first, local, at the site of the original wound—connects Walker with larger issues of African American existence—which she knew well growing up poor in rural Georgia. She, as a writer, makes this public, in an ontological and epistemological re-mapping of familiar terrain, claiming it as her own and as shared space. Walker explores how we, in location, in place, with all the complications of being there, choose to stay, an option that Dr. King highlighted, and to live out identity even in the most problematic places we call home.

This conversation about the local and its intersections and tensions with the universal, localized the postmodern project described in Jean-Francois Lyotard's *The Postmodern Condition,* taking it in a postcolonial direction. Lyotard emphasizes how the local story or the small narrative should and could stand as witness before the metanarrative. We have argued that for Lyotard, we cannot throw out or wish away metanarrative. We can express incredulity towards it—for example, we tell little stories back to it as a form of resistance—but to speak back to it indicates that it exists. The recognition of this tension—a feature of the counter-classical (which we would call the postmodern)—remains a constitutive of human existence and points to the creation of meaning in the transitive, in the interstices. Walker's work plays in the interstices: between the slave narrative and the postmodern, the personal and the social, and private art and political action. These coalesce under her womanist identification as a "revolutionary artist."

The structure of the autobiography, its collection of fragments—pieces of Walker's life in her various essays—suggests the problem of history in African American, or in any postcolonial reconstruction. Walker, however, is meticulous in locating herself as a Black, Southern, Woman Writer whose task is to gain a new world by reclaiming an old one.[26] She addresses the metanarrative directly when she asks, early in the narrative "What is my place or role in the great story?"—both in terms of history and culture.[27] Walker's work and voice are postcolonial in reconstruction. Hers is not a singular voice, but one that emerges from and within a collection of voices: from those of the women she teaches black history in Mississippi to her mother's to her students'. Self is relationally defined. The discernment and descriptive process of the revolutionary artist presents these voices as authentic witness and is an aid in the revelation of how black people have told their story. It suggests an identity that is choral. In speaking with others, Walker defines self.

Being in place and in community define the black, southern, womanist revolutionary artist. Continuity permits a reconstruction of community, which is the black Southern writer's "natural right"[28] and, most important inheritance, allows that writer to render its truth in its complexity, both in its authorized form (history) and its discredited ones (memory).

The revolutionary artist's work is to sort out the voices in and to record this choral identity, and it has six characteristics:

1. The revolutionary artist is a teacher.
2. The revolutionary artist is concerned with "the least glamorous stuff."
3. The revolutionary artist is involved in a process of preservation and creation.
4. The revolutionary artist might uncover tension but must temper hate.
5. The revolutionary artist gives voice to extraordinary lives in being with the People. For Walker this to be in the south and with the poor.
6. The revolutionary artist may hate what large groups stand for, but has tolerance towards individuals.[29]

Revolution and revelation are linked. The "walker" is a collector: bringing black history together bone by bone, piece by piece, and giving it life, like the word that animates the dry bones in Ezekiel 37. Walker is keenly aware of her own position in history and that these voices and others have contributed to it. In *In Search*, she locates the animating force of voice in two sources: The Civil Rights Movement, as we have seen, but also motherhood.

Most people "in place" are women in *Mother's Gardens*, and mothers play a large role in structuring the seemingly fragmentary pieces, from Walker's own mother to Walker as a mother. The mother-daughter relationship is part of the definition of womanist action. Walker's great-great-great-grandmother, whose name Walker kept, frames Walker's tribute to Martin Luther King, Jr. Her literary foremothers shape her voice. Walker's mother is with her when she is searching for Zora Neale Hurston's grave, adding her marvelous, pithy comments. Walker reveals in "A Writer Because of, Not in Spite of, Her Children" what it means to be writing as a woman with children and how that reality undercuts Western notions of how art is produced—and what art is, we would add. Walker's own pregnancy is a central event in the work. And, it ends, as it begins, with Rebecca who sees the world in her mother's eye.[30]

The mother's garden—or quilt or recipe or handmade clothes or whatever art the woman practices—is, of course, the work, the mode of expression, of the silent, brutalized black women Toomer describes and Walker names as "saints." These women, possessing an intense, deep unconscious spirituality had only gardens and kitchens in which to express their art. And there, they were beautiful—if not wholly fulfilled—as Walker's mother was in her garden.[31] In the particular domestic art, in the quotidian mystery,[32] identity was established and exercised. Many of these arts were done only to be undone or redone (like weeding the flower bed, making the bed) and as such, are related to the deep meaning of life itself: we are born to act, usually repetitiously, and flower to die. These arts, passed mother to daughter, maintain humanity, kept alive, people as well as, as Walker puts it, the notion of song.

Walker does not minimize suffering. What she argues is that suffering was and is not always mute. We just need to know where to look for agency and expression. Theologian Dorothee Soelle, in *Suffering*, argues, "one of the fundamental experiences about suffering is precisely the lack of communication, the dissolution of meaning and productive ties. To stand under the burden of suffering always means to become more and more isolated."[33] Audre Lorde argues that suffering is "unscrutinized and unmetabolized pain . . . the inescapable cycle of reliving pain over and over again when it is triggered by events or people. It is a static process which usually ends in oppression."[34] And, I would add, silence. What's more, Elaine Scarry reminds us that suffering silences language: it may not destroy, but it unmakes, de-stories the world.[35] As Soelle expresses it, such suffering may make us mute, numb, isolated, reactive, submissive, and powerless.[36] As Emilie Townes says, in such suffering,

There may be no choice involved—only survival.
   Suffering is outrageous. Suffering does not enoble, enable, or equip. . . . A life based on survival and reaction does not produce healthy minds, bodies, or souls.[37]

This is the condition of the black women that Walker is teaching in Mississippi. What womanist power offers is an alternative to the oppressive story of history, another story that liberates. Soelle calls the first movement out of suffering "psalmic language,"[38] a language that is, as Lorde puts it, "is an experience that is recognized, named, and then used for transformation. It is a dynamic process pointing toward transformation."[39] The language of and from pain is the first speaking, bringing emotion and rationality together, but an ability that is still embedded in suffering.

There is, therefore, nothing magical about moving from silence to freedom, from wound to world. The middle stage of articulation may be utopian, may involve acceptance as well as the attempt to conquer the existing structures, and may sensitize the soul to suffering in such a way that it is in more pain before that suffering can be alleviated. A key development in this stage is, Soelle argues, prayer: "an all-encompassing act by which people transcend the mute God of an apathetically endured reality and go over to the speaking God of a reality experienced with feeling in pain and happiness."[40]

Celie, in *The Color Purple*, reaches this point when she and Shug find Nettie's letters and Celie stops writing to God, the god who can be named, the limited symbol of power. This is a white, white-bearded male figure who does not transform her existence but only hears it (maybe) indifferently and who seems to accept lynching, madness, lack of relationality, and cruelty. Celie says, "You must be sleep."[41] Her subsequent letters to Nettie end with "Amen."[42] These letters suggest Celie's combination of religion with a revolutionary spirit. As Soelle suggests, "in the Christian understanding of suffering, mysticism and revolution move . . . close to one another."[43] Celie ceases to be a victim, though she remains in her situation. She moves towards a "storm of power" after which there is "elemental goodness" and the "abolition of all power by which some men dominate others."[44] Then, Celie can change, see spirit everywhere, create solidarity in her community, and accept and conquer her powerlessness.

Walker, we assert, does not "overspiritualize," to use Jacqueline Grant's term, an oppressive reality.[45] Instead, she asks how there can be not just reconciliation and peace, but also liberation and justice[46]—in a new form. That form cannot renounce its world—and this is particularly important since Walker understands the Civil Rights Movement as having reclaimed a world—but must reconstitute it. Home is "the site of speaking, the place of a shared language and of meaning, the place to find a voice to speak for those who have no home or voice."[47]

That capacity comes from unexpected sources. In *In Search of Our Mother's Gardens*, the source is the child. In a beautiful moment, Walker's Rebecca gives life to the one who has given it to her: receives her mother's gift and establishes that Walker, too, has a garden. Walker herself has been a wounded saint, feeling cut off by her scar. When Rebecca sees the world in her mother's eye, she heals an old wound: the pain of Walker's life, her difference, her marginality, and her wounded eye/I. "For the most part," Walker writes, " the pain left then . . . . There was a world in my eye. And I saw that it was possible to live it: that in fact for all it had taught me of shame and anger and inner vision, I did love it." Rebecca gives her mother her self. That night, the other dancer, the free, beautiful whole person, became, Walker concludes, concluding the volume, "me."

The possession of "me" with which so many black women's writings end—we think of *Beloved*,[48] for example—is multi-layered, and we pretend do not understand it all, but we will suggest some possibilities of meaning here. Identity is "me": the objective: establishing relation, the accusative: making a charge, and the dative, giving: doing something to or for. "Me" is a versatile, fluid mode of being. The scar that Walker was ashamed of, that so altered her being, was on the "eye/I," requiring her to find another way to be. Signifying on as well as adopting the Western, Platonic understanding of seeing as wisdom, Walker suggests that her altered vision, her view from the fracture, is the key to understanding identity in a postcolonial world. I think that she is suggesting, more deeply perhaps, that we, in the West, are all located on this site of fracture, all require this re-vision, which the slave narrative and the Civil Rights Movement represent, but that only some, those subaltern women Toomer describes, have borne its shame, and, to them, we often refuse to listen.

The shame has been given to and taken on by women who were objects of exploitation. The reclaiming of motherhood is a profound personal and political statement. It undercuts the definition of black women's identities as breeding stock, which comes from capitalist exploitation of women's reproduction in slavery, and their bodies as machines for making children who are product. This reclaiming is also a statement about identity: that it is formed in and flourishes in intimate relationships in place. Both these deconstruct the Enlightenment universal, dis-placed but powerful, "I" and its privilege. As Talal Asad suggests in *Genealogies of Religion*, the postcolonial tempers the postmodern potential to re-inscribe Enlightenment categories. To be "local" is not to be "circumscribed and limited."[49] Walker's eye does not just *see* but *is* a world. And, the meta-narrative is not unassailable: We do not just talk back to it, but we love and flourish in its presence, reforming its categories as we tell, in a revolutionary act, that revolutionary love story.

Walker, in her search for wholeness, has always used what she needed to make transformation happen. In recent years, she has turned to Buddhism as a way to see her story and through which to tell it. Buddhism, as we suggested in our discussion of Michel Foucault, offers a practice by which to combine self-examination with self-emptying. A long time practitioner of Transcendental Meditation, Walker discovered Pema Chodron when she lost a loved one and seemed unable to recover. Chodron is an American Tibetan Buddhist Nun who is the director of Gampo Abbey in Nova Scotia. Chodron's teaching focuses on *tonglen* meditation, a meditation of sending and taking.[50] *Tonglen* is a breathing and meditation practice that accepts and heals suffering. Chodron writes,

> you invite the pain in . . . by doing the practice, you awaken your heart and you awaken your courage. When I say "awaken your heart," I mean that you're willing not to cover over the most tender part of yourself.[51]

Tonglen perfectly intersects with Walker's work in her autobiographies and fiction. It involves consciously taking in all one's "conflicts, confusion, and pain" but also those of other people. One visualizes taking in pain and darkness—taking in, with every in-breath, the truth that life is suffering, "not as a mistake you made, not as a punishment, but as a part of the human condition."[52] On the out-breath, one opens, sending out light, spaciousness, and relaxation: "You connect with the feeling of joy, well-being, satisfaction, tenderheartedness, anything that feels fresh and clean, wholesome and good."[53] To do this practice and to develop *bodichitta,* the awakened and courageous heart, is finally to be able to connect with suffering in all the realms of existence, including but not particularly focusing on your own.

Suffering, Chodron argues, can harden the heart. *Tonglen* teaches one to take the moment of suffering and "flip it,"[54] making suffering the seat of compassion. The core of the practice is to start where one is. Spiritual paths, Chodron argues, generally have ideals; we feel that we have to be better than we are. Her practice "creates an emotional honesty about where you are. [You] get compassion for where you are and for all other beings."[55]

Negative emotions, therefore, are not bad. "Negative negativity," particularly uncontrollable anger, is the problem, the "spin off" we engage in when a negative emotion strikes us and we begin the internal monologue that blocks healing or that strikes out at another. Audre Lourde recognizes this dilemma in *Sister Outsider:* "Where does the pain go when it goes away?" she asks. "Every black woman in America lives her life somewhere along a wide curve of ancient and unexpressed angers."[56] Anger and other emotions, Chodron suggests, along with Walker, are wisdom in disguise. We must learn to sit with our energy to open up the heart in order to use our negative emotions as a creative force.[57] If we try to avoid pain, Chodron says, "the world becomes scarier and scarier. You don't want to go out your door."[58] One's own suffering is, therefore, the most difficult. It is where we start, as Celie suggests in *The Color Purple:* "We all have to start somewhere if us want to do better, and our own self is what us have to hand."[59] It is, however, easy to get stuck in the self, either becoming numb through suffering or aggrandizing the self, seeing the self as a martyr. *Tonglen,* as Chodron suggests, puts the "self" in its proper place, in relation: the self is only one other suffering being, neither the least nor the most important one.

This practice suggests a way to face oppression, which, we think, is what drew Walker to it. The moderator, in a conversation between Walker and Chodron, asked how *tonglen* could work in situations of oppression; what one could do when the spirit is attacked. Walker replied that one should see that the oppressor is a miserable person, though that is a leap of understanding. Chodron added that the cause of someone's aggression is his or her own suffering and that a strong sense of enemy-making closes down connection: "You can also just realize that your aggression will not help. [Practice] *tonglen* and breathe in the recognition of the oppression of all people and something different can come out of your mouth."[60] If this can be done, Walker added, "War will not be what comes out of your mouth."

The movement from war, conflict that destroys, to revolution, the conflict that transforms, is what *tonglen* can accomplish, and it parallels the work of the Civil Rights Movement and of the revolutionary artist. This teaching is, as Chodron and Walker suggest, revolutionary, and it is one that has been used by peacemakers in the twentieth century, whether it is called *satyagraha,* as Gandhi called it, or non-violent resistance. Non-violence in change, in transitivity, is where Walker begins her journey and non-violence remains a reference point along the way. Non-violence is the way that wounds become worlds, that we experience transitivity without violence, moving through pain to wholeness.

Such a practice takes courage, honesty about the self, and a willingness to suffer. Walker's work, from *In Search of Our Mother's Gardens* to *The Color Purple* and beyond, to these conversations with Pema Chodron, suggests that simply to try to reconstruct the old pieces of self and society that have crumbled under one disaster or another merely creates a Frankenstein's monster: a pieced-together horror that looks like the wounded self—and most important, a horror that we cannot love. We have done this again and again, and, now, we must embrace these flawed reconstructions before we can move to the transitive work of reconstitution.

Walker suggests that, particularly as Americans, we resist embracing what we have created. We resist change, often violently, keeping us stuck in a cycle of anger and abuse, victims and victimizers. We resist an embrace that recognizes that, as Heraclitus taught us and as Walker learned, we do step in the same river twice—the river is the same—but we do not—the river moves on. Continuity and change are principles of transitivity without violence.

To have transitivity without violence is to occupy a paradoxical "space between." That space, now called "The Black Atlantic," is where the African American was "made" and where, Walker's work suggests, we most creatively dwell and work. As Vincent Harding writes, on the rivers, where pasts were "jammed into one frightening present," something new was born, something that included pain, but also hope, movement, and transformation.[61] On the way, in the paradox, in the meantime—in the transitive space—there can be generated a site for insight and action. That is to say, Walker suggests that we must acknowledge "the imperfections and limitations of persons and of works that is the indisputable sign of being human."[62] That begun, for the task of making home is on-going, we can make wounds into worlds, suffering into compassion, through love that can look upon the horror, move us through it, and let us build reconstituted selves, communities, and loves.

This idea is a difficult one for modern people to accept: it suggests a mystical path. Nobody wins; we all journey together. All we can do is be there, present and flawed, but trying. Walker finds this in her art and in *tonglen:* as the writer, she is that being who realizes that all beings mother her into being; that being who breathes in the suffering of all around her, expresses it, and breathes out healing and love, a healing and love that comes, finally, to her own self and moves back out again to us, through the narrative. This is more than survival; it is transforming love. As Walker has always argued, that healing begins where the wound was made, just as her own healing came when Rebecca named her wounded eye a world, and love is the transitive and transforming power of the spirit.

It is this point at which we will circle back and end. The charge against the writings of black women and other women has been that to focus on the personal does not have political or epistemological efficacy. To be sure, the postmodern anxiety about memory has led, perhaps, to indulgence. This, however, may make us forget the impact of the postcolonial personal story and the moments in history when it *has had* political and epistemological impact. The slave's narrative was instrumental in abolitionist movements and in changing law, and, more recently, the Truth and Reconciliation Commission in South Africa and such commissions in other places have had a deep impact on political structures and ways of being and knowing. In all these cases, collective memory has been altered—perhaps not completely but to some degree by single testimonies. This is hard to hold to in our post 9/11, neo-con, neo-imperialistic world, but the lone voice, like Walker's, can be one for change as it intersects with other voices to (re)define community. Her courage in continuing to work and to witness—to weave the events of her life, its fragments, into story that is a public document—can be a reminder to all of us that big changes begin with ordinary people, embracing their wounds and how those wounds hurt others and claiming the spiritual power in quotidian acts. As Walker puts it, in *Anything We Love Can Be Saved,*

We have reached a place of deepest emptiness and sorrow. We look at the destruction around us and perceive our collective poverty. We see that everything that is truly needed by the world is too large for individuals to give. We find we have only ourselves. Our experience. Our dreams. Our simple art. Our memories of better ways. Our knowledge that the world cannot be healed in the abstract. That healing begins where the wound was made.[63]

CHAPTER 11

THE LIMITS OF RECONSTRUCTION: RECONSTITUTING COMMUNITY IN MARTIN LUTHER KING, JR.

Justice for black people will not flow into society merely from court decisions nor from fountains of political oratory. Nor will a few token changes quell all the tempestuous yearnings of millions of disadvantaged black people. White America must recognize that justice for black people cannot be achieved without radical changes in the structure of our society. The comfortable, the entrenched, the privileged, cannot continue to tremble at the prospect of change in the status quo.

—Martin Luther King, Jr., "A Testament of Hope"[1]

INTRODUCTION: THE PROBLEM AND ITS CONTEXT

Effective and durable social and political reform requires recognizing and maintaining a tension between what we will call *reconstruction* (efforts to restructure the formal legal arrangements of the community) and more subtle and profound efforts at *reconstitution* (allowing the fabric of the community to be reshaped by the addition of the persons and mores of formerly disenfranchised populations into the community).[2] In the United States, particularly in matters of race relations, *reconstruction* has been the paradigmatic language and mode of social reform. Our cultural reliance on the "rule of law" means that social and political reform begins and often ends with attempts to change formal legal structures in an effort to reshape the structural environment in which we live. What this formal legal effort cannot do, however, is reconstitute the community. Law can only articulate limits and suggest direction for the constitution of the community; it cannot teach people how to live together. Legal and formal attempts at reconstruction, as painful and important as they are and have been, are simply inadequate when the much more difficult task of reconstituting the community is neglected or, as is more often the case, assumed to follow on the heels of legal reconstruction.[3]

An over-reliance upon "reconstructing" the social and political environment through legal and structural changes can, we have seen, have the opposite of the desired effect. The long overdue reconstruction efforts of the Civil Rights Movement have led, rather perversely, to a mutually excluding and dual sense of entitlement demonstrated by the passage of and subsequent debate over the major pieces of civil rights legislation.[4] On the one hand, for the formerly disenfranchised, passage and implementation of the Civil Rights Act of 1964, the Voting Rights Act of 1965, and subsequent civil rights laws are formal admissions of the majority's guilt, formal recognitions that the former oppressor has many returns to pay. On the other hand, for the former oppressor, the passage and implementation of these laws is a major concession and, once undertaken, excuses or moves the community beyond culpability for past offenses, miraculously "levels the playing-field," and allows everyone to wash their hands of inequities past and present. From both positions, the real work and difficult challenges of reconstituting the community, that is, helping to create an environment of new expectations, habitable by human beings beyond racial or ethnic differences, to the degree that it is considered at all, is left to the other side. The legislation does not create dialogue, but, when assumed to resolve a difficult problem, rather shuts down that dialogue and shifts the burdens of reconstituting the community from its citizenry to the formal governing structures of that community.[5] This tendency, we would argue, is indicative, in part, of our cultural over-reliance on the rule of law. When legal change is viewed as the *only* necessary step in community reformation, legal reconstruction bogs itself down in a language of difference and animosity and ignores the important task of social and political reconstitution.[6]

We have few models of how this difficulty is to be overcome, but the work of Martin Luther King, Jr. both illustrates the problem and suggests a direction. One of the most eloquent American defenders of the rule of law, King's work also lays bare the need for efforts of reconstitution, of refashioning the community beyond whatever formal legal changes may come. This chapter will develop and explore the implications of King's attempt to move beyond *reconstruction*, that is, beyond traditional American reform methods (legal and formal), to the critical effort of *reconstituting* the American social and political community. His efforts are illustrative because he recognizes the violation of intimacy at the core all racial difficulty in the United States. Civil rights transcends questions of where one can sit, whether one participates in the political process and to what extent; it involves bringing a proud culture's darkest secrets into the light, embracing their presence, and moving on in spite of them. King suggests that the wound might be healed through the building of a community of relationships. He appreciated, in a way few of his contemporaries did, that the two modes of community-formation we consider here, reconstruction and reconstitution, are not incompatible, but necessarily must serve as complements. Of particular concern will be the theoretical and philosophical foundations of these reconstitution efforts in King's work, particularly in his "Letter from Birmingham City Jail."[7]

Reconstruction and Reconstitution: The "Role" of Law

In our tradition, the principle of the rule of law is a valued and self-conscious protection of the ruled from the arbitrary actions of those who rule. Theorists since John Stuart Mill have cautioned that despite this protection, however, when law relies chiefly on the popular will of the people as its justification, it can lose sight of what is just and become a powerful tool of oppression.[8] An appeal to the spirit of the law is insufficient when the law is bad or used to do bad things. The spirit of the law, manifest in its legislative history and philosophical justification, in the text of the law itself, and in the way in which that law is enforced, actually reflects the *real* spirit of a community. The way a community creates, interprets, and enforces its rules, that is, the way it applies its fundamental principles to mundane social and political life, is an authentic indicator of its self-understanding. In the United States, particularly in the South, the community's spirit, darkened by fear and prejudice, found reflection in both the law ("Jim Crow") and the oppressive governing style to which fearful oppressors inevitably resort. In this environment, the meaning of the abstract, if cherished, principle of the rule of law can only vacillate between corruption and meaninglessness. For example, the Fifteenth Amendment enfranchised African-Americans in no uncertain terms in the 1860s. In the aftermath of Reconstruction, however, the United States Supreme Court allowed "local" Jim Crow laws as part of the "police power" reserved to the states. Sporadically in the 1930s and in earnest after the Second

World War, the Court, at the brilliantly nagging and persistent urging of Charles Houston, Thurgood Marshall, and others, began to revisit the "Negro problem" with an emerging sense that the abstract language of the American political vocabulary, that is, the language of "freedom" and "equality" in fact applied to those whose very recent ancestors had been slaves. For Martin Luther King, as inheritor of this struggle, the principle of the rule of law remained a solid one for it provided language and direction to the Civil Rights Movement. Measuring that ruling law against the demands of justice became the movement's *modus operandi*.

King's adherence to the rule of law and use of our political vocabulary were not merely adroit political moves. King's embrace of the principle suggested an approach to the problem of racial segregation and African-American disenfranchisement in the South. Like Socrates, with whom he compared himself, King would not abandon the rule of law simply because the law was bad or poorly applied. To those who wrapped themselves in their official duties, King would point out their abandonment of the dictates of justice and, as King would point out, the demands of America's political vocabulary. This was the tack King would take in his best known critique and defense of the rule of law, his "Letter from Birmingham City Jail." This piece, written as King sat in jail for violating what he believed was an unconstitutional court order enjoining his protest activities, demonstrates the breadth of his thinking on the issue and his faith in the principle.[9] The letter, drafted by King to friends and foes alike, defends the tactics of civil disobedience and sets out his appreciation of law as not just arbiter but also its obligation to embody justice. In the letter King uses Aquinas and a natural law approach to the legal to argue, among other things, that the physical and spiritual well-being of the members of the community ("personality") should be foremost in the mind of the legislator, the judge, the police officer, and the citizen.[10]

There are three dimensions to King's analysis in the "Letter," and they illuminate his sensitivity to the reconstruction/reconstitution problem. First, as we have already suggested, there is King's understanding of the importance of *law* as a binding, shaping force of community. The law is the framework in which a community lives and grows, the arbiter of the acceptable and the unacceptable. Corrupt or unjust laws, therefore, cannot help but govern a corrupt or unjust, that is, inauthentic, community. Secondly, there is King's concern with *community formation*.[11] An inauthentic community begs for reconstitution, but King knew that these efforts must start in smaller communities, in this case, in churches. Beyond the importance of his own affiliation, King recognized the important role that churches played in the social life of southern communities. Efforts to change the attitudes of southerners about their African-American neighbors would be more compelling coming from local clergy. Reconstituting church communities, that is, reorienting and mobilizing churches against the unjust laws of the secular state would be an important step in refashioning the general social order of the south. Finally, there is the issue of *time*. King has a double consciousness where time is concerned. On the one hand, he is justifiably impatient with those who would have him "wait." King chastises those who advocated the passive acceptance of injustices that might pass away with time. On the other hand, he knows that his own work involves necessary but only preliminary steps in reconstituting southern (American) community. Time, used wisely, that is, with a sense of history, of urgency, and possibilities, is King's ally. The balance of this chapter will flesh out these dimensions of King's project and show how his project works through the tension between reconstruction and reconstitution.

LAWS JUST AND UNJUST

Law, perhaps more than any other human contrivance, orders and defines communities. In the context of the American commitment to the rule of law, King was especially sensitive to the fact that resisting law, even unjust law, risks rending the fabric of a community.[12] King understood this rending, however, as prelude to the larger task suggested by our reconstruction/reconstitution dualism. King's civil disobedience faced two principal difficulties. First, his refusal to obey the law might merely confirm the beliefs of King's opponents that "his people" were incapable of abiding by the rules of society and so were still unfit for full membership in the community. Second, there was the risk involved in judging the laws of the community to be unjust. By what criteria would King make so profound a distinction between laws that should be obeyed and laws that, because they were unjust, were no laws at all? The first difficulty is one of the "constitution" of the community, that is, the question of membership and fitness for membership, to which we will turn in the next section. The second is a philosophical as well as political question that King knew must be answered carefully if his movement was to obviate the first difficulty.

In an effort to reconcile his movement's commitment to the rule of law with his disobedience to laws that segregate and otherwise oppress, King appealed to the formulations of Thomas Aquinas, specifically his fleshing out of the Augustinian distinction between just and unjust laws.[13] As King himself was a minister, the choice of Aquinas seems obvious. From the perspective of social reform, however, the choice of Aquinas is also decisive. By using Aquinas, as opposed to, say, Thoreau, King casts what is principally a social and political question in the language of religion and morality. His purpose is to appeal to powerful religious sentiment in order to transcend the divisions in the southern community. King's argument is straight out of the *Summa Theologica*, and the formula is correspondingly simple: *just laws* are those that square "with the moral law or the law of God" and "uplift human personality" and should be obeyed.[14] Moral laws bind the individual conscience, drawing it into a relationship with other members of the community. One has both a legal and a moral responsibility to obey just laws. By contrast, *unjust laws*, those laws that are "out of harmony with the moral law," are "not rooted in eternal law and natural law," and degrade human personality should not be obeyed.[15]

King understands that, in the heat of a political struggle, categories like "harmony with the moral law" and "rooted in eternal and natural law" could be difficult to articulate and time-consuming to defend, so he adds "human personality" to Aquinas's formulation.[16] King's own formula is profoundly simple: a law that degrades human being is not in conformity with the demands of justice. Bolstered by the evidence accepted by the Supreme Court in *Brown v. Board of Education* and by his own experience, King easily concludes that "All segregation statutes are unjust because segregation distorts the soul and damages the personality. It gives the segregator a false sense of superiority and the segregated a false sense of inferiority."[17] His classical training taught King that damage to the individual soul is damage to the community. A community, he realized, consists of both the oppressed *and* the oppressor, and both necessarily participate in oppression. When governed by unjust laws, the community is duly damaged and diseased. The protests, the implication goes, seeks to save the community, not blow it apart.

There is another way in which laws may be identified as unjust: if they serve to create an imbalance in the community. Self-deceit forms the core of an unhealthy community. A merely functioning or apparently orderly community is not necessarily a healthy one. Authentic community preserves the tension between sameness (a solid, stable, shared communal identity) and difference (the uniqueness of individuals and the smaller groupings within civil society). Privileging difference by enshrining it in formal legal structures creates a destructive imbalance in the make-up of the community. In American legal theory, the guarantee of "equal protection of the laws" protects individuals and groups from the consequences of legally sanctioned imbalances like the laws of segregation. "An unjust law," King writes, "is a code that a numerical or power majority group compels a minority group to obey but does not make binding on itself." For King, "this is *difference* made legal," that is, a fundamental distinction in status enshrined in the binding laws of the unhealthy community. Much preferred, for King, "is a code that a majority compels a minority to follow and that it is willing to follow itself."[18] This second type of law, which makes of *sameness* a legal principle, is a just law. King holds this sameness before the law as the essence of the equal protection guarantee.[19]

The source of injustice in the legal systems of the south, in general, and of Birmingham, in particular, then, were easy enough for King to discern. "A law is unjust," King argues, "if it is inflicted on a minority that, as a result of being denied the right to vote, had no part in enacting or devising the law."[20] Sameness before the law, equal protection of the laws, had been denied African-Americans in that they had been unable to participate in the legislative process. To avoid appearing to advocate the wanton disregard of the law, King makes a crucial but subtle distinction between legitimate and illegitimate authority. A population given no voice in making the law with which it must live must question its actual obligation to obey those laws. But King's understanding of civil disobedience moves beyond concern with reconstructing the law; he is concerned with reconstitution, with showing that he and his people understand their obligations as citizens.

King reminds his charges, therefore, that they are bound by all just laws, whatever the injustices of the political system. "Sometimes a law is just on its face," he writes, "and unjust in its application."[21] In that case, King insists in a Socratic moment, it is the citizen's obligation to demonstrate the misapplication of the law rather than disregard the law altogether. That demonstration must include a willing embrace of the punishment accompanying the demonstration. In one of his more cogent and influential formulations, King insists that

One who breaks an unjust law must do so openly, lovingly, and with a willingness to accept the penalty. I submit that an individual who breaks a law that conscience tells him is unjust and who willingly accepts the penalty of imprisonment in order to arouse the conscience of the community over its injustice, is in reality expressing the highest respect for law.[22]

Here is an overt recognition that simply reconstructing formal legal structures (e.g., the Fourteenth and Fifteenth Amendments) is insufficient and, therefore, changing the law cannot be the sole object of civil disobedience. King argues that disobedience to unjust laws is less an attempt to change the law than an attempt to change the hearts of those who enforce it. The task of "arousing the conscience of the community," when understood as part of reconstituting the community itself is a citizen's duty and "expressing the highest respect for law." King contends that he and his followers are agents of transition in (read, transformation of) the south. Their chief goal is to make law do what law does, that is, establish justice.

COMMUNITY AND CIVIL DISOBEDIENCE

The philosophical niceties of Thomistic natural law theory could not hide what was really at stake in the direct actions of the Civil Rights Movement. There is, as Vaclav Havel notes, an inertia in comfort that makes people resist fundamental changes in the way they live their lives.[23] If the philosophical questions of the civil rights struggle were about just and unjust laws and the nature of obligation, then the practical social question voiced in both the white and black communities, as King well knew, was "Why should I risk a change in my life?" The response, in hindsight, is as simplistic as it must have been tempting for King and his fellows: sometimes sacrifices must be made for principles or, to state this more easily, sometimes doing the right thing is a bit painful. King, however, knew better than to expect this answer to suffice for either side in the struggle. His work shows an acute awareness of both the content and concerns of his diverse audience. Whatever one's motives, King knew, disobeying the law is an affront to the present constitution of the community. Refashioning or reconstituting the community in accordance with the dictates of justice would be costly and difficult and, ultimately, would require the participation of everyone. In the "Letter from Birmingham City Jail" King, therefore, identifies the various elements in the community and addresses himself to each with an eye toward bringing them together in a heretofore impossible conversation. All at once, King writes to hearten his followers, to appeal to his enemies, and to chastise those who sympathize but beg him to wait. For King, the act of writing is an assertion of the possibility of authentic community. It is an act at once defying injustice and expressing a faith in both the basic good will of human beings and in justice itself.

Freedom, King writes, "is never voluntarily given by the oppressor; it must be demanded by the oppressed."[24] The trick is to demand it in such a way as to not destroy what good will is possible between historically estranged populations. For King, this was the challenge and justification for nonviolent resistance. From the time of the bus boycott in Montgomery, King managed to communicate to his followers the importance of remaining nonviolent in their confrontation with the segregated communities of the south. In Birmingham, too, reason failed and other measures became necessary:

> Like so many experiences of the past we were confronted with blasted hopes, and the dark shadow of a deep disappointment settled upon us. So we had no alternative except that of preparing for direct action, whereby we would present our very bodies as a means of laying our case before the conscience of the local and national community. We were not unmindful of the difficulties involved. So we decided to go through a process of self-purification. We started having workshops on nonviolence and repeatedly asked ourselves the questions, "Are you able to accept blows without retaliating?" "Are you able to endure the ordeals of jail?"[25]

The methodology of nonviolence is by now so well known as to not need rehearsing. The keystone of the methods of nonviolence, however, is the willingness to submit to the judgment of an unjust legal order, thereby exposing the tensions that lie beneath the social order, beneath the apparent comfort and tranquility of the "rule of law." Despite the claims of his opponents that nonviolent civil disobedience constituted a destruction of the social order, King maintains that

> Actually, we who engage in nonviolent direct action are not the creators of tension. We merely bring to the surface the hidden tension that is already alive. We bring it out in the open where it can be seen and dealt with . . . injustice must likewise be exposed, with all of the tension its exposing creates, to the light of human conscience and the air of national opinion before it can be cured.[26]

Tension, for King, is an invitation to dialogue where before none existed. The problems of a legally sanctioned second-class citizenship revealed, exposed to a heretofore willfully blind nation, might then be addressed in an appropriate forum. Moving the conscience of a community to reconsider its very identity and bringing estranged populations into a dialogue are the real objects of nonviolent resistance and make up the reconstituting community-building dimensions of the work of the Civil Rights Movement.

It helped that nonviolent resistance was also, King reminded a hesitant nation, the best option for social and political change. The only other alternative, he writes, is the very real "force of bitterness and hatred" which elsewhere was coming "perilously close to advocating violence." "Oppressed people," King argues, "cannot remain oppressed forever.... If his repressed emotions do not come out in these nonviolent ways, they will come out in ominous expressions of violence. This is not a threat; it is a fact of history."[27] King needed to demonstrate that nonviolence could do more, however, than simply disrupt an unjust social order, so a methodology of community-formation undergirds all his protest efforts. Effective political action in a hostile environment requires a smaller touchstone community of strength and support. From Montgomery onward, King and the leaders of the movement trained protesters in the methods of nonviolence, especially careful to prepare them for the psychological and physical abuse to which they would be subject. To communicate the necessity of enduring this kind of treatment, King attaches a form of love called *agape* to the principles of nonviolence in an effort to create and bind together the smaller outward-looking communities that were essential to the transformative goals of the movement. King, ever conscious of his audience and the limitations of his followers, knew he had to demonstrate that the resisters could create and then live in authentic human communities.

In his account of the Montgomery bus boycotts, King spells out the attitude of heart necessary to confront injustice and then transform or reconstitute it in conformity with the demands of authentic justice. "When we speak of loving those who oppose us," King writes in *Stride Toward Freedom*, "we speak of *agape*."[28] Agape emerges as the fundamental principle of human community for King. Meaning "understanding" and "the redeeming good will for men," as well as suggesting the unconditional love God has for His people, *agape* concerns itself with the other. It is a form of love that recognizes the human need for others, for the help of others, for the understanding of others, and for the differences in others which force us to grow as individuals. He writes that "it springs from the need of the other person—his need for belonging to the best in the human family."[29] It connects the oppressor and the oppressed beyond the constraints of law and social custom. King writes that "Since the white man's personality is greatly distorted by segregation, and his soul is greatly scarred, he needs the love of the Negro. The Negro must love the white man, because the white man needs his love to remove his tension, insecurities, and fears."[30] The distortion of human personality, therefore, especially by the laws and mores of a community, work against the development towards authenticity of both individuals and the community at large. In its ethical dimension, then, King intends *agape* as a reaching out, an offering of authentic human interaction that may well produce a new community. King adds a religious dimension to politics.

Politics, however, while requiring the ethical, is also about reciprocity between the governed and the governors and among the governed. As a principle of community, *agape* is an active, even interactive form of love. *Agape*, King insists, is not weak or passive, but is, rather, love in action. By invoking *agape,* King, shrewdly, asks white southerners to turn belief into action; metaphysics into ethics.

Agape is love that seeks to preserve and create community. It is insistence on community even when one seeks to break it. *Agape* is a willingness to sacrifice in the interest of mutuality. *Agape* is a willingness to go to any length to restore community. It doesn't stop at the first mile, but it goes the second mile to restore community. It is a willingness to forgive, not seven times, but seventy times seven to restore community.[31]

Beyond King's argument that *agape* is a recognition of the fact that all life is interrelated, *agape* emerges here as a model of good membership. There is a challenge to his opponents in *agape* as through it he articulates a social and political ethic, a way of being that his opponents ignore at the expense of the legitimacy of their own authority and membership in the community. In Birmingham, Selma, and elsewhere King's protesters take this principle to the streets, and, in front of television cameras, they are met with the violence of coercion and arrest. In his embrace of *agape* and despite the appearance of disrupting the community, King and his followers *offer* a model of membership, a shared sense of belonging to the community. Their offer is refused in no uncertain terms by the authorities, but the new image of a reconstituted community is, nonetheless, unmistakable and appeals to many who watch it in action on television. The publicity broadens the scope of the movement and its appeal. What King offers, beyond a reconstructive change in the legal and political system, is an alternative to the old community and the old citizenship models that condoned segregation and distorted human personality.

"THE MYTH OF TIME": WAITING OR WORKING

King knew that the language of *agape* was cold comfort to those whose lives would be transformed by the actions of the movement.[32] For many in the community, King is the very embodiment of lawlessness, chaos, and even violence. His opponents believe, despite his claims to the contrary, that King's rejection of the way things have always been, his willingness to disobey the demands of the law, reflect a dangerous recklessness, a disregard for the principles by which the community defines itself. Even those who were otherwise sympathetic were disappointed by King's apparent impatience with "legal processes." Friend and foe, then, each in his own way, argued that King's impatience caused the social disruption in the south. Time, if King would allow it, would bring about any needed reform. From a distance we can see that this charge of impatience against King, particularly by "people of good conscience," is in part a fear of life-transforming change that can be justified in terms of the American faith in the rule of law. The rule of law feeds the belief that time, specifically manifest in the legislative process and legal procedure, will right the wrong, relieve the tensions, and obviate any inadequacies in the law and the way it is administered. Because both friend and foe make this argument, King knows he must be stern but cautious on the complex issue of time.[33] He appreciates the weaknesses of legal reconstruction and so opposes a passive reliance on time (manifest in legal processes or not) as the inevitable healer of all injustices. There is, as well, positive, prophetic appreciation of the need for "active patience" in King's understanding of time as well that suggests his desire to reconstitute the community.

In the "Letter from Birmingham City Jail," King subtly re-frames the question of timeliness from one of waiting to one of the appropriate time for action. Once again, he interrupts the linear Western metanarrative to insert a religious notion of time: the *kairos* moment: the moment when the right issue, right persons, and right place come into alignment for God to work through human beings to make change. Waiting, as a mode of being or as a strategy of social reform, rarely works. By the time of the Birmingham campaign it has been nearly a century since the post-Civil War Amendments enfranchised African-Americans. King expects resistance from segregationists, but can scarcely hide his disappointment with white moderates who, in the same breath, say they are committed to justice, but argue that time will change both the law and men's hearts.

The moderate, King charges, is more committed to order than to justice. The preceding century of American social and political development simply makes the notion of incremental change an unreasonable expectation in the case of the African-Americans. Instead, the attitude of these moderates reflects an older, paternalistic view of African-Americans thought to be the province of King's opponents. This older view suggests that as a group African-Americans are not ready for citizenship, that King's actions somehow indicate an impatience indicative of immaturity that precludes the white community from taking their desire for full citizenship seriously. The white moderate's belief in the goals of the movement is one thing, but the absence of courage to embrace direct action, King argues, is inconsistent with a real justice which can know no timetable. "Shallow understanding from people of good will," King writes, "is more frustrating than absolute misunderstanding from people of ill will."[34] Time, for the moderate, is as much a crutch as it is a weapon in the hands of those who oppose the movement. The difference, as King's frustration indicates, is that you can oppose an armed man because you know where he stands, but a morally crippled man is more difficult to oppose and, therefore, a much more destructive foe. "We will have to repent in this generation," King laments, "not merely for the vitriolic words and actions of the bad people, but for the appalling silence of the good people."[35]

King was neither naive nor hubristic enough to believe that the community could be reconstituted overnight. As a scholar well-read in the classics, he knew that reconstituting community in the south and elsewhere would be the project of generations, but he was equally certain that the idle ticking of a clock would not transform the way men see each other. In the "Letter," therefore, he turns the question of time and waiting into one of the eternal question of justice, for which, he claims, there should always be time. There is no intrinsic magic in the flow of time that will cure all social ills. Justice is right action in the right spirit and, he argues, "[t]he time is always ripe to do right."[36] The issue is not, as both King opponents and supporters claim, time or its passage. The issue is the persistent presence of injustice and the appropriate response to that presence in this, particular, God-defined moment. "Injustice anywhere is a threat to justice everywhere," King writes. "We are caught in an inescapable network of mutuality tied in a single garment of destiny."[37] Sensitive to the needs of community-formation, King conceives human community in terms of responsibilities owed the self and others *qua* human beings, that is, in terms nearly like those of Hannah Arendt, as a complex and interconnected web of relationships.[38] The implication of this view is profound and ethically very difficult: any human action or, for that matter, inaction, is a choice with direct implications for the entire community. No one is absolved of responsibility for their choices, particularly the choice of whether to act or not when time and circumstance demand action.

Owing to King's position and his training as a minister, there is also a prophetic dimension to his language and his understanding of time. Lewis Baldwin places King firmly in the tradition of black preachers and argues that King is a bearer of the "black messianic hope."[39]

While his goals, and often his language, are more overtly those of the social reform than of biblical prophecy, his is nonetheless a "prophetic vision" with a prophet's appreciation for the long view. The future, acted upon now in a loving, generous, and creative (read, nonviolent, extra-legal when necessary) spirit may well be redemptive:

> One day the South will know that when these disinherited children of God sat down at lunch counters, they were in reality standing up for the best in the American dream and the most sacred values in our Judeo-Christian heritage, and thus carrying our whole nation back to great wells of democracy which were dug deep by the founding fathers in the formulation of the Constitution and the Declaration of Independence.[40]

King's persistent and effective use of the language of the "mountaintop" is more than a rhetorical device.[41] Alongside his appeals to the American tradition, it offers a vision of a community reconstituted by the agency of human beings of good will and conscience as well as the passage of time. It is a corrective, redemptive vision that *demands time*, but demands that time be used wisely and diligently to ferret out the misunderstandings (and the clear understandings) and open lines of communication in the names of confession and repentance.

Whatever his status as a prophet, King was principally a social critic and reformer. He struggled to keep his redemptive vision from getting in the way of his diligence in pointing out the unacceptable social, legal, and political arrangements he saw at work in his world. In his own posthumously published work "A Testament of Hope," King reminded his contemporaries that the tradition demands the recognition that neither privilege nor oppression is necessarily a question of the color of one's skin:

> It is time that we stopped our blithe lip service to the guarantees of life, liberty and pursuit of happiness. These fine sentiments are embodied in the Declaration of Independence, but that document was always a declaration of intent rather than of reality. There were slaves when it was written; there were still slaves when it was adopted; and to this day, black Americans have not life, liberty nor the privilege of pursuing happiness, and millions of poor white Americans are in economic bondage that is scarcely less oppressive.[42]

King maintains an uneasy alliance with time. He recognizes that it can be the occasion for either building communities or keeping them divided. Patience and taking the longer view of the passage of time are not the same as waiting for some "end time" to transform men and society any more than actions taken in the present to address injustice are necessarily marks of immaturity. "Even a superficial look at history shows that social progress never rolls in on the wheels of inevitability," King told a commencement audience at Lincoln University in Pennsylvania in 1961. "It comes through the tireless effort and the persistent work of dedicated individuals. Without this hard work, time itself becomes an ally of the primitive forces of irrational emotionalism and social stagnation."[43] King tried diligently to retain the balance between patience, the patience to face down the hatred of another, to confront that hatred with agape, and urgency, the sense that change would not come without working for it in the here and now.

CONCLUSION

The impulse for this section of our work is the lamentable lack of useful dialogue on "the race question" 40 odd years after the Civil Rights Movement. Periodic "Presidential Commissions on Race," while well-intentioned, toil in the relative obscurity of C-SPAN2 and are usually academic exercises (in at least two senses of that term). In general, their outcomes are neither publicized nor made the matter of much public discussion. In addition, there are periodic rants from either side about discrimination or reverse discrimination, episodic promises from presidential candidates and other public figures to "do something" about the deep, divisive differences that remain in the aftermath of the movement, but the actual content of those rants and the absence of content in promises to "do something" engender only frustration, or worse, indifference. There is no real discussion of the relevant issues, only, and this makes this question a mere part of our generally vacuous political discourse, accusations and well-embedded misunderstandings. The questions then are how did we get here and what do we do about it? To suggest answers, we turned back to the methodology of one of the more successful figures in American history in dealing with this question.

The distinction between reconstruction and reconstitution we have identified in King's work is not intended as a rejection of the rule of law. It is, however, an implicit criticism of relying exclusively on changes in legal structures to redress social injustices. What dialogue there is on this question usually takes the form of "legalese," that is, insoluble assertions about what is or is not constitutional. While these are important matters, they channel energy away from the goal of reconstituting community, of learning about each other so that we may live together that formed the core of Martin Luther King's mission. What we have called reconstruction, efforts at changing the law and legal structures, emerges as a necessary complement to these much more difficult and time-consuming reconstitution efforts. Changing the law is difficult but doable. In our system, there are well-established procedures for changing the law, even for changing the "Supreme Law of the Land." There are no well-established procedures for a fruitful, civil public dialogue, for attempting to enter into the other's positionality to understand both that position and our own a bit more clearly, for listening, and learning to trust.

These are the values implicit in King's understanding of *agape* and they present a challenge that we have so far failed to meet. The relative ease of willful misunderstanding, the way terms like "discrimination," and "entitlement" role off the tongue like racial epithets once did, obscure the infinitely more difficult challenge of understanding and cooperation. King was not deluded, nor should we be, that a reconstituted community would emerge all at once. It remained a goal, a goal that he called "The Beloved Community." If one looks at the website, for example, of The King Center, located in Atlanta, Georgia, one sees that this structure was key to King's thought.[44] The Beloved Community is both transitive and hybrid. It is transitive, in that King understood reconstitution as ongoing: that is, the passage of time must be accompanied by directed effort (i.e., strategic, thoughtful, nonviolent, in King's case). It is hybrid in that it would be made up of all peoples and in the fact that King knew that reconstruction and reconstitution were not mutually exclusive. He believed that we are fortunate to be able to take the power of reconstruction for granted, but he understood that neglecting its necessary complement reconstitution could be disastrous.

The Beloved Community is a hybrid: it will be nonviolent, but not free of conflict. Conflict, King believed, was part of human nature; we, however, can be taught to settle conflict without resorting to violence. The Beloved community is global, but also local, in that it will come about as a variety of people from particular locations are trained in nonviolent action. Its ends are political ones—freedom, equality, and the end to poverty and war—but also religious ones—redemption. Finally, the Beloved Community is transitive: always in the making. King invites us to consider the meaning of reconstitution as a prelude and guide to direct action: reconstitution means a shared struggle, raising consciousness of that shared struggle, and the breaking down of arbitrary barriers to dialogue and to love, *agape*, and forgiveness.

CHAPTER 12

CONCLUSIONS FROM A
TRANSITIVE SPACE

We began our work saying that we discovered, in the course of our own conversations, that one of our interlocutors was Emmanuel Levinas. This discovery points to our method as scholars, as transitive and hybrid thinkers. Levinas desires to find a way to have transitivity without violence. Like Levinas, we too seek a nonviolent way. Yet that path is difficult. Levinas is clear that discourses—with their totalizing tendencies—cannot perform the act of yielding to the Face of the Other, cannot accept that freedom lies in the very act of limiting the self. The announcement of the Other, "It's me,"[1] undoes all theoretical language. For us, this undoing must await recognition of another undoing. If my sense of self is fixed and stable—most of us find comfort in assuming it is—the Other's announcement undoes that fixity and stability. Properly understood, the Other throws us back on ourselves. This encounter reveals the transitivity of our self-understandings and the hybridity of the world we move around in. To say the least, the recognition is jarring. The key to moving forward is whether we *react* like Sophocles' Creon or *respond* like Dr. King. In the former instance, we are controlled by the circumstance, reacting with the desire to control it ourselves. In the latter, we embrace and recognize the possibilities and limitations of our agency, seeing ourselves in our Other. In reaction lies violence and non-understanding; in considered response lies the possibility of peace.

While we do not agree with the Levinas of *Totality and Infinity* that language is the only hospitable interactive mode with the other—and we hope we have demonstrated this through our use of the arts, our suggestions about practices, and, like Ashis Nandy, our embrace of myth—we agree with his ultimate point: that there are always these two responses to the other, violence or welcome. On the one hand, we know that violence (from naming and controlling discourse to physical violence) distorts the self even as it seeks to preserve it in a fixed, stable form. When taking on this task, enemies abound: not merely the other but also the transitive and hybrid self that the encounter reveals. If that elusive fixed sense of self is to be preserved, the other must go. The welcome, on the other hand, while it certainly makes one vulnerable, is the gesture that opens the door of our physical, spiritual, psychic, and political dwellings.[2] It is the gesture that allows others to enter and rest and to interact, and it allows us, if necessary, to leave, to either go out in greeting, or to leave altogether. As we receive others and as we travel, to be received by others, we embrace both transitivity and risk and we make hybrids.

In this book, we have tried to suggest that hybridity and transitivity are not just postmodern constructions; they are our past and our present. Homi Bhabha is just as concerned with justice as Aristotle—and, like us, both are concerned with time. The questions they and we raise and the situations we address are perennial; the (post)modern just adds the speed and the information-disseminating possibilities of technology to the mix. We, and our thinkers, suggest that the past is never over. As Toni Morrison has Pilate say in *Song of Solomon*, " 'Nothing ever dies,' " *and* we are responsible for those we kill. And, as both Morrison and Derrida suggest, just when we think something—some person, some culture, some idea, some practice—is dead or encrypted, to use Derrida's language, it comes back, demanding to be heard. Thus, the movement in time, in space, and in character that transitivity suggests cannot be stopped or fixed, even in apparent death.

Recognizing this, we have invited in and engaged, here, a multiplicity of voices, from Aristotle to Giorgio Agamben, from Sophocles to Thich Nhat Hanh. We acknowledge our particular dwellings, in political theory and religious studies, but in our friendship, our doors have always been open to each other and to any friend the other brings along. All the voices we engage accept, as we do, that the world we live in is ours together. They accept that, as Alice Walker suggests, each individual story, no matter how seemingly insignificant, has contributed to the great story of humanity. They agree that, given the complications of transitive diaspora, we do not really know who our ancestors, biological, political, religious, and theoretical, are and that we may find connections to the "other" that we could not anticipate.

Each seeks a way out of what Edward Said called the politics of blame and confrontation, desiring instead a politics without regret for and denunciation of the past or easy and wasteful violence. "This world," he writes, "is too small and interdependent to let these passively happen."[3] The hybridity of our circumstances means that we have the opportunity, but also the obligation, of leaving childish fixity behind. As we learn about ourselves from the encounter with otherness, we must also take the corresponding step of learning about our others— in their terms rather than ours, and those terms will transcend mere language.

Levinas argues that only those who have the capacity for violence, for war, can rise to peace, can choose to do and to structure otherwise.[4] We would add to his thought that only those willing to turn from that capacity and suffer can do so. In our terms, war— risking the destruction of self for the destruction of the other—derives from reaction; peace—risking the self in the name of the possibility of the other—from response. While both are choices, the latter is the more difficult, the more humane choice. From Oedipus to Caryl Phillips, our thinkers think through, investigate, and then accept and undergo the past. Only through this suffering can we work toward, in traditional terms or not, the gift that spiritual practice gives: the peace that is unity in plurality.[5]

This unity, we contend, is not oneness. We have chosen to use the term "hybrid" because, for us, it does not suggest the loss of individual parts, like "melting pot" or "mixed," for example, might. Hybridity suggests that the edges may show and be sharp at certain moments. Though we present images of reconstitution, we want to preserve an uneasiness, one that will keep us all aware.

Levinas suggests that there is a joy in such work. To be shut off in the ego, to live in fear, is neither to enjoy anything nor to desire anything. To be is to desire and to be good for the other.[6] We would add that *to be* is also *to be good with* the other, in community, whether, as Foucault has shown us, a community constructed around the self or, as *Oedipus at Colonus* showed us, a community of the faithful around a powerful self, whether that community is temporary and transitive or transitively and temporarily stable and settled, in the case of the *polis*.

What we do know is the joy of working as scholars together, coming from our different locations and working out of our different methodologies to make interdisciplinary and hybrid readings of texts and world. We hope that our reading have efficacy, that they bring our readers into a nation of the imagination[7] that is multiple, seeking, and open, and, like Derrick Walcott's Shabine, the red nigger, comes to see

> I had a sound colonial education,
> I have Dutch, nigger and English in me,
> And either I'm nobody, or I'm a nation.[8]

NOTES

INTRODUCTION: NEGOTIATIONS IN TRANSITIVE SPACES

1. T. S. Eliot, "Tradition and the Individual Talent," in *Selected Prose of T.S. Eliot*, ed. Frank Kermode (New York: Harcourt Brace Jovanovich, 1975), 37–48.
2. Emmanuel Levinas, *Totality and Infinity: An Essay on Exteriority*, trans. Alphonso Lingis (Pittsburgh: Duquesne University Press 1969, 1992), 27.
3. Victor Turner, *The Ritual Process: Structure and Anti-structure* (Chicago, IL: Aldine Press, 1969), 95.
4. Ibid., 94.
5. Mary Louise Pratt, *Imperial Eyes: Travel Writing and Transculturation* (New York: Routledge, 2007), 34. See also, "Arts of the Contact Zone," www.essayforum.com. Accessed March 12, 2012.
6. W. E. B. Du Bois, *The Souls of Black Folk* (New York: ReadaClassic.com), p. 8; Giorgio Agamben, *Homo Sacer: Sovereign Power and Bare Life*, trans. Daniel Heller Roazen (Stanford, CA: Stanford University Press, 1998).
7. Judith Butler, *Precarious Life: The Powers of Mourning and Violence* (London: Verso, 2004), 23.
8. See Jean-Francois Lyotard, *The Postmodern Condition: A Report on Knowledge*, trans. Geoff Bennington and Brian Massumi (Minneapolis: University of Minnesota Press, 1984, 1991); Jean-Francois Lyotard, *Just Gaming*, trans. Wlad Godzich (Minneapolis: University of Minnesota Press, 1985, 1996).
9. See Jean Piaget, *The Moral Judgment of the Child*, trans. Marjorie Gabain (New York: Free Press, 1997).
10. See Immanuel Kant, "An Answer to the Question: 'What Is Enlightenment?' " in *Kant: Political Writings*, ed. Hans Reiss, trans. H. B. Nisbet, 2nd ed. (Cambridge: Cambridge University Press, 1970, 1991).
11. Guy Debord, *Society of the Spectacle*, trans. Donald Nicholson-Smith (New York: Zone Books, 1994, 1999).
12. Homi K. Bhabha, *The Location of Culture* (London: Routledge, 1994); Caryl Philips, *The Atlantic Sound* (New York: Vintage Books, 2001); Pratt, 5.

13. Yael Tamir, *Liberal Nationalism* (Princeton: Princeton University Press, 1993).
14. Michel Foucault, *The History of Sexuality, Vol. 3: The Care of the Self*, trans. Robert Hurley (New York: Vintage Books, 1988).
15. Our analysis here concerns two specific texts: Michael Walzer, *Spheres of Justice: A Defense of Pluralism and Equality* (New York: Basic Books, 1983), and Lyotard, *Just Gaming*.
16. Levinas, 278ff.

Chapter 1

1. Our analysis here deals primarily with Homi K. Bhabha, *The Location of Culture* (New York: Routledge, 1994); Caryl Phillips, *The Atlantic Sound* (New York: Vintage Books, 2001).
2. Sadly, cultural interactions too often happen in violence—physical and cultural—and feed the misinformation cultures have about one another, including the notion that cultures are monolithic, on the one hand, and superior to one another, on the other hand. The post-9/11 arguments of Jean Bethke Elshtain and Michael Ignatieff for American retaliation—in both Afghanistan and Iraq—were made and defended in terms of the "burden" of a moral duty borne by the Christian West (Elshtain) and by a willingness to get dirty hands in doing that duty (Ignatieff). Both arguments depend on an "us" and "them" distinction that is nearly absolute in its character. As Elshtain put it, "Every civilian death is a tragedy, but not every civilian death is a crime." See Jean Bethke Elshtain, *Just War Against Terror: The Burden of American Power in a Violent World* (New York: Basic Books, 2004), 4; Michael Ignatieff, *The Lesser Evil: Political Ethics in an Age of Terror* (Princeton: Princeton University Press, 2004). The difference, Elshtain holds, is in the motivation and in the reaction. She contrasts the glee of bin Laden supporters with the regret expressed by the American military over "collateral damage." Yet death at the hands of a well-meaning democracy seems scarcely better than death at the hands of a terrorist for the victim and her family. In neither case is cultural exchange or hybridity likely to result. Compelling and important counters to the Elshtain/Ignatieff line of thought have been offered by Judith Butler, *Precarious Life*; Talal Asad, *On Suicide Bombing* (New York: Columbia University Press, 2007); and Benjamin R. Barber, *Fear's Empire: War, Terrorism, and Democracy* (New York: W. W. Norton, 2004).
3. Paul Gilroy, *The Black Atlantic: Modernity and Double-Consciousness* (Cambridge: Harvard University Press, 1993), 3.
4. Ibid.

5. Ibid., 2.
6. Bhabha, 140.
7. W. E. B. Du Bois, *The Souls of Black Folk* (New York: Bantam Books, 1969), 45.
8. Gilroy, 127.
9. Bhabha, 145.
10. Ibid., 146.
11. Ibid., 148.
12. Ibid., 15.
13. Ibid., 2.
14. Ibid., 25.
15. See Lyotard, *Just Gaming*, . trans. Wlad Godzich (Minneapolis: University of Minnesota Press, 1996); Mircea Eliade, *Myth of the Eternal Return: Cosmos and History*, trans. Willard R. Trask (Princeton: Princeton University Press, 1971).
16. Bhabha, 30.
17. Ibid., 31.
18. Ibid., 36.
19. Gilroy, 111.
20. Ibid.
21. Phillips, 117.
22. Ibid., 143.
23. Ibid., 148.
24. Ibid., 148–149.
25. Ibid., 153.
26. Ibid., 173.
27. Ibid., 147.
28. Ibid., 142–143.
29. Ibid., 125.
30. Ibid., 177.
31. Ibid.
32. Ibid.
33. Ibid., 222.
34. Ibid., 223.
35. Ibid., 255.
36. Ibid., 262.
37. Ibid., 265.
38. Ibid., 275.
39. Ibid.
40. Sharon E. Greene, "An Interview with Robert Detweiler," in David Jasper and Mark Ledbetter, ed. *In Good Company: Essays in Honor of Robert Detweiler* (Atlanta: Scholars Press, 1994), 434. Detweiler tells Greene that narrative is "erotic," in the sense that one comes to be unable to think one's own story without thinking the story of the other.

Chapter 2

1. This and the preceding quote are from Edward W. Said, *Culture and Imperialism* (New York: Vintage Books, 1994), 19.

2. Ashis Nandy, *The Intimate Enemy: Loss and Recovery of Self Under Colonialism* (New York: Oxford University Press, 1988); Charles H. Long, *Significations: Signs, Symbols, and Images in the Interpretation of Religion* (Philadelphia: Fortress Press, 1986).

3. Mary Louise Pratt, *Imperial Eyes: Travel Writing and Transculturation* (New York: Routledge, 2007), 7.

4. Long, 197.

5. James Baldwin, "The High Road to Destiny," in *Martin Luther King, Jr.: A Profile*, ed. C. Eric Lincoln (New York: Hill and Wang, 1970), 95.

6. Nandy, 72–73.

7. Nandy, 2.

8. Alexandre Kojeve, *Introduction to the Reading of Hegel: Lectures on the Phenomenology of Spirit* (New York: Basic Books, 1969), 52.

9. Nandy, 32.

10. Long, 138.

11. G. W. F. Hegel, "Independence and Dependence of Self-Consciousness: Lordship and Bondage," *The Phenomenology of Mind*, www.marxists.org/reference/archive/works/ph/phba.htm. Accessed March 13, 2012.

12. Aeschylus, *Agamemnon* in *Aeschylus I*, trans. Richmond Lattimore (Chicago: University of Chicago Press, 1953), lines 341–342.

13. Ibid., lines 369–372.

14. Ibid., lines 925–927.

15. "Liberia Editrice Vaticana," Catholic Church, *Catechism of the Catholic Church*. (Vatican City: Libreria Editrice Vaticana, 2000).

16. Frederick Douglass, *Narrative of the Life of Frederick Douglass, An American Slave (1845)* (New York: Penguin Books, 2003).

17. Douglass, 113.

18. Frederick Douglass, *My Bondage and My Freedom* (1855), Chapter 17. www.crispinsartwell.com/douglass.htm. Accessed March 13, 2012. [Emphasis in text.]

19. Douglass, *Narrative*, 185.

20. Douglass, *Narrative*, 120.

21. Henry Louis Gates and Charles Davis, eds., *The Slave's Narrative* (New York: Oxford University Press, 1991), xxv, xxxi.

22. Ibid., xxvii, xxiii.

23. Ibid., xxvii.

24. Nandy, xvi.

25. Jerry Bentley, *Old World Encounters: Cross-Cultural Contacts and Exchanges in Pre-Modern Times* (New York: Oxford University Press, 1992), 6, 8.
26. Albert Murray, *South to a Very Old Place* (New York: Vintage Books, 1991), 31–32.
27. Jenny Edkins, *Trauma and the Memory of Politics* (Cambridge: Cambridge University Press, 2003), 12.
28. Ibid., 4.
29. Ibid., 8, 176–177.
30. Ibid., 14.
31. Nandy, 49.
32. Nandy, 104.
33. Bonnie Marranca, "Criticism, Culture, and Performance: An Interview with Edward Said," *Performing Arts Journal* 37 (1991), 26.
34. Ibid.
35. Albert Murray, *The Hero and the Blues* (New York: Knopf Doubleday Publishing Group, 1996), 25. Albert Murray, *The Blue Devils of Nada: A Contemporary American Approach to Aesthetic Statement* (New York: Knopf Publishing Group, 1997).
36. Nandy, 109.
37. Richard Hardack, " 'A Music Seeking Its Words': Double-Timing and Double-Consciousness in Toni Morrison, *Jazz*," *Callaloo* 18:2 (Spring 1995), 460.
38. Nandy, 111.
39. Long, 195.
40. Ralph Ellison, "Change the Joke and Slip the Yoke," in *Shadow and Act* (New York: Vintage Books, 1995), 45–59.
41. Long, 9.
42. Ibid.
43. Ibid., 60.
44. Ibid., 61.
45. Nandy, 59.
46. Ibid., 57.
47. Sharon E. Greene, "An Interview with Robert Detweiler," in David Jasper and Mark Ledbetter, ed. *In Good Company: Essays in Honor of Robert Detweiler* (Atlanta, GA: Scholars Press, 1994), 434.
48. Robert Stepto, "Intimate Things in Place: A Conversation with Toni Morrison," in Danille K. Taylor-Guthrie, ed. *Conversations with Toni Morrison* (Jackson, MS: University of Mississippi Press, 1994), 11.
49. Nandy, 108.
50. Charles Hartmann, *Jazz Text: Voice and Improvisation in Poetry, Jazz, and Song* (Princeton: Princeton University Press, 1991), 47.
51. Ibid., 41.
52. Ibid., 35.

53. See bell hooks, "Homeplace: A Site of Resistance," in D. S. Madison, ed. *The Woman That I Am: The Literature and Culture of Contemporary Women of Color* (New York: St. Martin's Press, 1994), 449.

54. Nandy, 104.

55. June Jordan, *Directed by Desire: The Collected Poems of June Jordan* (Port Townsend, WA: Canyon Copper Press), 411.

56. June Jordan, "Moving Towards Home," in *Living Room: New Poems by June Jordan* (New York: Thunder's Mouth Press, 1985), 134. This poem has been translated into Arabic and has become a "rallying point in the Middle East," www.enotes.com/june-jordan-criticism-jordan-june. Assessed March 13, 2012. See also "The Palestinian Right to Return Coalition," www.al-awda.org/until-return/june.html. Accessed March 13, 2012.

CHAPTER 3

1. 1Edward W. Said, *Power, Politics, and Culture: Interviews with Edward W. Said*, ed. Gauri Viswanathan (New York: Pantheon Books, 2001), 429.

2. Arjun Appadurai, *Fear of Small Numbers: A Geography of Anger* (Durham: Duke University Press, 2006).

3. Ibid., 20.

4. Ibid., 30.

5. Ibid., 28.

6. Ibid., 86, 36.

7. John Dunn, "Nationalism," in Ronald Beiner, ed. *Theorizing Nationalism* (Albany: State University Press of New York, 1999), 27–50.

8. Appadurai, 8, 53.

9. Ibid., 43.

10. It is stunning to note how far we have *not* come in dealing with the status of the stateless since Hannah Arendt's diagnosis of their peculiar condition. We have more categories to put them in, but are little better at redressing their circumstances. See Arendt, *Origins of Totalitarianism* (New York: Harcourt Brace, 1973), especially Chapter Nine "Decline of the Nation State and the Rights of Man," 266–302. See also for example the work of Giorgio Agamben, *Means without End: Notes on Politics*, trans. Vincenzo Binetti and Cesare Casarino (Minneapolis: University of Minnesota Press, 2000); Seyla Benhabib, *The Rights of Others: Aliens, Residents, and Citizens* (Cambridge: Cambridge University Press, 2004).

11. Jeremy Waldron, "Homelessness and the Issue of Freedom," in Robert Goodin and Phillip Pettit, eds. *Contemporary Political Philosophy: An Anthology* (Oxford: Blackwell Publishing, 1997), 446–462.

12. Ibid., 459.

13. In addition to Said's own, here the work of Rashid Khalidi is particularly instructive. See Edward W. Said, *The Question of Palestine* (New York: Vintage Books, 1992); Rashid Khalidi, *The Iron Cage: The Story of the Palestinian Struggle for Statehood* (Boston: Beacon Books, 2006).

14. Sara Roy, *Failing Peace: Gaza and the Palestinian-Israeli Conflict* (London: Pluto Press, 2007).

15. Gideon Levy, *The Punishment of Gaza* (London: Verso Books, 2010) is a particularly impressive journalistic account of the operation.

16. Yael Tamir, "The Land of the Fearful and the Free," *Constellations* 3, no. 3 (1997): 301.

17. Yael Tamir, *Liberal Nationalism* (Princeton: Princeton University Press, 1993).

18. Appadurai, 86.

19. In addition to Tamir, *Liberal Nationalism*, see also Will Kymlicka, *Politics in the Vernacular: Nationalism, Multiculturalism, and Citizenship* (Oxford: Oxford University Press, 2001); Kok-Chor Tan, "Liberalism and Cosmopolitan Justice," in *Ethical Theory and Moral Practice* 5, no. 4 (2002): 431–461.

20. For example, see Duncan Ivison, *Postcolonial Liberalism* (Cambridge: Cambridge University Press, 2002).

21. Muhammad Ali Khalidi, "Formulating the Right of Self-Determination," in Tomis Kapitan, ed. *Philosophical Perspectives on the Israeli Palestinian Conflict* (London: M.E. Sharpe, 1997), 71–94.

22. Michael Ignatieff, "Nationalism and the Narcissism of Minor Differences," in Beiner, ed. *Theorizing Nationalism*, 91–102.

23. See Ivison, *Postcolonial Liberalism*.

24. See, for example, Kai Neilsen, "Cultural Nationalism, Neither Ethnic Nor Civic" and Bernard Yack, "The Myth of the Civic Nation," in Beiner, ed. *Theorizing Nationalism*, 119–130, 103–118 respectively.

25. Michael Walzer, "The New Tribalism: Notes on a Difficult Problem," in Beiner, ed. *Theorizing Nationalism*, 205–218.

26. Ibid., 207. Emphasis added.

27. Ibid., 216.

28. Appadurai, 43.

29. Said, *The Question of Palestine*.

30. Hugh R. Harcourt, "In Search of the Emperor's New Clothes: Reflections on Rights in the Palestinian Conflict," in Kapitan, ed. *Perspectives*, 291.

31. Edward W. Said, *The Politics of Dispossession: The Struggle for Palestinian Self-Determination, 1969–1994* (New York: Vintage Books, 1995), 247–268.

32. Ibid., 256.

33. In addition to Said's own work, see Muhammad Y. Muslih, *The Origins of Palestinian Nationalism* (New York: Columbia University

Press, 1988); Rashid Khalidi, *Palestinian Identity: The Construction of Modern National Consciousness* (New York: Columbia University Press, 1997.

34. Edward W. Said, *Covering Islam: How the Media and the Experts Determine How We See the Rest of the World* (New York: Vintage, 1997); Edward W. Said and Christopher Hitchens, eds. *Blaming The Victms: Spurious Scholarship and the Palestinian Question* (London: Verso, 1988).

35. See Said, *The Politics of Dispossession* as well as Edward W. Said, *Peace and Its Discontents: Essays on Palestine in the Middle East Peace Process* (New York: Vintage, 1996); Edward W. Said, *The End of the Peace Process: Oslo and After* (New York: Vintage, 2001).

36. Said's support of Yasser Arafat and the Palestinian Liberation Organization stemmed from the organization's being in position to make this Palestinian case. To Said's disappointment, the identification of Arafat with the cause of the Palestinians has backfired. Said came to contend that Arafat's political naivete, revealed by his support of Iraq in the first Gulf War, by his agreement to the utterly inadequate, from Said's perspective, Oslo Accords, and by his governing of Palestinian territories like a Third World dictator, represented a catastrophic waste of potential. Consequently, Said became one of Arafat's most vocal critics. Arafat, through his own ambitions and limitations, let slip away his opportunity and obligation to articulate the Palestinian presence and make real demands on its behalf. See especially Said, *The End of the Peace Process* and the posthumous collection Edward W. Said, *From Oslo to Iraq and the Road Map* (New York: Pantheon Books, 2004).

37. Said, *Power, Politics, and Culture*, 129.

38. Edward W. Said, *Orientalism* (New York: Vintage Books, 1979).

39. Said, *Culture and Imperialism*.

40. Said, *Question of Palestine*. See also Michael C. Hudson, "Developments and Setbacks in the Palestinian Resistance Movement 1967–1971," *Journal of Palestine Studies* 1, no. 3: 64–84.

41. Said, *Power, Politics, and Culture*, 391.

42. Ibid., 249.

43. Appadurai, 51.

44. Said, *Power, Politics, and Culture*, 249.

45. Ibid.

46. Ibid.

47. Ibid., 250.

48. Edward W. Said, *The World, The Text, and the Critic* (Cambridge, MA: Harvard University Press, 1983). See also Talal Asad, *Formations of the Secular: Christianity, Islam, Modernity* (Stanford: Stanford University Press, 2003). This idea of a new secularism has informed a range of thinkers from the work of Ann Pelligrini and Janet Jacobson on

sexual politics in, for example, *Love the Sin: Sexual Regulation and the Limits of Religious Tolerance* (New York: New York University Press, 2008) to The Teagle Foundation's report on secularism and liberal arts education (http://www.teaglefoundation.org/learning/report/20051128.aspx).

49. The role and value of Islamic fundamentalism in this context has been contested. Roxanne Euben has suggested that Islamic fundamentalism be understood as a compelling, if potentially dangerous, vision that stands as a critique of the West, presumably including constructs like liberal nationalism. See Roxanne L. Euben, "Comparative Political Theory: An Islamic Fundamentalist Critique of Rationalism," *The Journal of Politics* 59, no. 1 (1997): 28–55. Meanwhile, Shari Berman argues that the rise of Islamic fundamentalism in places like Egypt marks a decline in the effectiveness of the state on which liberal nationalism will depend. Islamism, on this argument, takes over sociocultural spaces ceded to it by the state. See Shari Berman, "Islamism, Revolution, and Civil Society," *Perspectives on Politics* 1, no. 2 (2003): 257–272.

50. Ibid., 340.

51. Ibid., 129.

52. Ibid., 239.

53. Said, *Question of Palestine*, 59.

54. Sari Nusseibeh, "Personal and National Identity," in Kapitan, ed. *Philosophical Perspectives*, 205.

55. This commitment, derived from Said's encounter with Vico, is a theme that runs throughout his work. For an early statement, see Edward W. Said, *Beginnings: Intention and Method* (New York: Columbia University Press, 1985), 345–382.

56. Said, *Power, Politics, and Culture*, 251. [Emphasis added.]

57. Waldron.

58. Said, *Power, Politics, and Culture*, 132.

59. The property trap is the one Said suggests Arafat and the PLO fell into at Oslo. The Accords, Said argues, cost the Israelis nothing they valued and broke up any possibility of connecting the Palestinian territories into a coherent, self-sustainable whole. Arafat was granted some power to govern the territories under the auspices of the Palestinian Authority, but, as we have seen, the Israelis made no promise of non-interference, especially in the face of acts of terror designed to subvert the "Peace Process." Palestinian control, that is, their political "ownership" of the territories, is a fiction. What's worse, Arafat's "governance" of what remained of Palestinian territory bears all the earmarks, argues Said, of a failed postcolonial nationalist regime. See Said, *The End of the Peace Process* (2000).

60. The two quotes are from Said, *Power, Politics, and Culture*, 330. See Bhabha, *Location of Culture*.

61. Neil MacCormick, "Nation and Nationalism," in Beiner, ed. *Theorizing Nationalism*, 189.
62. Ibid., 201.
63. See Tamir, "Theoretical Difficulties," Nielsen, "Cultural Nationalism," and Yack, "Myth of the Civic Nation," in Beiner, ed. *Theorizing Nationalism*.
64. Appadurai, 8, 53.
65. Kymlicka, *Politics in the Vernacular*.
66. Yack in Beiner, ed., 105.
67. Ibid.
68. Tamir, "Land of the Fearful and the Free."
69. Benedict Anderson, *Imagined Communities*, rev. ed. (London: Verso, 1991).
70. Evan Charney, "Identity and Liberal Nationalism," *American Political Science Review* 97, no. 2: 295–310.
71. Tamir, *Liberal Nationalism*, 74.
72. See Appadurai, 60–64.
73. See, for example, James Johnson, "Why Respect Culture?" *American Journal of Political Science* 44, no. 3 (2000): 405–418; Geoffrey Brahm Levey, "Liberal Nationalism and Cultural Rights," *Political Studies* 49 (2001): 670–691; Emily Gill, *Becoming Free: Autonomy and Diversity in the Liberal Polity* (Lawrence: University of Kansas Press, 2001).
74. John Rawls, *A Theory of Justice*, rev. ed. (Cambridge: Harvard University Press, 1999).
75. Michael Sandel, "The Procedural Republic and the Unencumbered Self," *Political Theory* 12 (1984): 81–96.
76. Michael Walzer, *Spheres of Justice*.
77. Tamir, *Liberal Nationalism*, 156–158.
78. Ibid., 140–168.
79. See Brian Walker, "Modernity and Cultural Vulnerability: Should Ethnicity Be Privileged?" in Beiner, ed. *Theorizing Nationalism*, 141–146.
80. Gill, *Becoming Free*.
81. The connection of geography to national identity is pivotal and, Said argues, the cornerstone of the Israeli justification for the occupation of territories beyond the 1948 UN borders. The persistent assumption that a national identity requires land that one occupies and controls, Said marvels, is a cornerstone of Zionist claims. Israel knows that with each "settlement" and through legal tactics like the Right of Return, the Palestinian space to be and the corresponding claim to national political identity is profoundly diminished. This movement replicates, indeed, makes a self-fulfilling prophecy of, the all-too-familiar Lockean argument that undeveloped land is an affront to the Creator and must be redeemed. Industry is a virtue and the

willingness to develop the "fallow" land of Palestine makes Jewish emigres (settlers) worthy occupants and the only legitimate occupants of the Holy Land. There are, of course, Israeli Palestinians, but they have only minimal political rights. The land policies of "democratic" Israel continues in this vein. See Erin McKenna, "Land, Property, and Occupation: A Question of Political Philosophy," in Kapitan, ed. *Philosophical Perspectives*, 185–204. Consequently, as the Palestinian-controlled territories get smaller and more remote from one another, the very existence of a Palestinian people becomes more and more problematic. With neither real property nor political rights, the Palestinians in the Occupied Territories are left with diminishing claims to peoplehood, let alone statehood.

82. Said, *Power, Politics, and Culture*, 452.
83. Lynne Belaief, "Tragic Justice," in Kapitan, ed. *Philosophical Perspectives*, 331–342.
84. A refusal to deal with the folly of segregation is one of the problems Said had with the goings-on at Oslo and in the "Peace Process" at large. See Said, *End of the Peace Process*.
85. Said, *Power, Politics, and Culture*, 453.
86. Ibid., 455.
87. That this "fully formed identity" and accompanying assumptions about self-esteem at the individual level may in fact wind up in competition with the collective form these take is a concern. See Jeff Spinner-Halev and Elizabeth Theiss-Morse, "National Identity and Self-Esteem," *Perspectives on Politics* 1, no. 3 (2003): 515–532. Liberal nationalism, they argue, has not adequately concerned itself with this potential conflict and, therefore, rests on an unstable foundation.
88. Said, *Power, Politics, and Culture*, 450–451.

Chapter 4

1. Michel Foucault, *History of Sexuality, Volume 3* (New York: Vintage Books, 1990), 41.
2. Michel Foucault, *The Foucault Reader*, ed. Paul Rabinow (New York: Pantheon Books, 1984), 340.
3. Chantal Mouffe interrogates and rejects the idea of a non-agonistic politics. See Chantal Mouffe, *The Democratic Paradox* (London: Verso Books, 2009). Like Mouffe, we are not interested in banishing the agon, merely with learning to live in community in other ways. Unlike Mouffe, we are thinking of "politics" not in terms of an ongoing contest over the control of resources (material and linguistic) but rather in the larger Greek sense of the *polis*, that is, as a community of relationships not exclusively defined by contestation.
4. *The Foucault Reader*, 346, 366.

5. See the argument in Pope Benedict XVI, *Truth and Tolerance: Christian Belief and World Religions* (San Francisco: Ignatius Press, 2004). For a good general statement, see Francesco Follo, "Interculturation and Interculturality in John Paul II and Benedict XVI," http://www.oasiscenter.eu/en/node/5610. Interculturation is "traveling theory," in a sense, what happens when Christianity comes into the contact zones of other cultures.

6. Marcus Aurelius, *Meditations,* 11. http://classsics.mit.edu/Antoninus/meditations.11.eleven.html.

7. Locke attaches the liberal self and, consequently, its freedom, to the "rational and industrious" material transformation of nature through his notion of property as "life, liberty, and property." See John Locke, *Two Treatises of Government*, ed. Peter Laslett (Cambridge: Cambridge University Press, 1988). For his part, John Stuart Mill identifies the development of human conscience as the necessary dimension of human freedom. See Mill, *On Liberty* (Buffalo, NY: Promtheus Books, 1986).

8. Foucault, *History of Sexuality*, 45.

9. *The Foucault Reader*, 360.

10. Foucault, *History of Sexuality*, 47.

11. *The Foucault Reader*, 350.

12. Ibid., 369.

13. Ibid., 377, 369.

14. Ibid., 361.

15. Ibid., 774.

16. Foucault, *History of Sexuality*, 61.

17. Ibid., 95.

18. *The Foucault Reader*, 364.

19. Foucault, *History of Sexuality*, 51.

20. Ibid.

21. Ibid., 51, 53.

22. Ibid., 56.

23. Ibid., 65, 64, 65.

24. Ibid., 58.

25. *The Foucault Reader*, 86–87.

26. Ibid., 92.

27. Ibid., 86.

28. Ibid., 88.

29. Ibid., 377.

30. Ibid., 89.

31. Charles Taylor, *The Ethics of Authenticity* (Cambridge: Harvard University Press, 1991).

32. Ibid., 61–66.

33. Ibid., 80.

34. Ibid., especially, 57–60.

35. Ibid., 83.
36. Jacques Derrida, "Faith and Knowledge," in *Acts of Religion,* ed. Gil Anidjar (New York: Routledge, 2001), 79, 82.
37. Taylor, 85.
38. Ibid.
39. *The Foucault Reader,* 347.
40. Taylor, 88.
41. Ibid., 89.
42. Ibid., 92.
43. Ibid., 102.
44. Max Weber, *The Protestant Ethic and the Spirit of Capitalism,* trans. Talcott Parsons (New York: Charles Scribner's Sons, 1958).
45. *The Foucault Reader,* 66.
46. Ibid., 93.
47. Vaclav Havel, "Politicians' Role in a Global Civilization," *World Citizen News* (April/May 1996), http://www.worldservice.org/issues/aprmay96/politicians.html. Accessed March 14, 2012.
48. Edward Sri, *The New Rosary in Scripture: Biblical Insights for Praying the Twenty Mysteries* (Grand Junction, CO: Charis Publications, 2003), 103.
49. The Confraternity of Christian Doctrine, *The New American Bible* (Totowa, N.J.:Catholic World Press/World Bible Publishers, 2011), Luke 4.13.
50. *NAB,* Luke 22.40
51. Edward Sri, 103.
52. Ibid., 103.
53. Ibid., 105.
54. *NAB,* 2 Timothy 4.7.
55. "Afterword: A Talk with the Author," in Milan Kundera, *The Book of Laughter and Forgetting* (New York: Penguin Press, 1981), 233: "Once the dream of paradise starts to turn into reality, however, here and there people begin to crop up who stand in its way, and so the rulers of paradise must build a little gulag on the side of Eden."
56. Gene Sharp, *From Dictatorship to Democracy* (London: Serpent's Tail Press, 2012). Sharp's work is available, translated into numerous languages, and used from The Einstein Institute, his organization: http://www.aeinstein.org/organizations9173.html
57. See Thich Nhat Hanh, *Interbeing: Fourteen Guidelines for Engaged Buddhism,* 3rd ed. (Berkeley, CA: Parallax Press, 2005), summarized at http://www.religionfacts.com/buddhism/sects/engaged_buddhism.htm. See also Sallie B. King, *Socially Engaged Buddhism* (University of Hawai'i Press, 2009). Nhat Hanh lays out 14 Precepts of Engaged Buddhism (here paraphrased), which emphasize social change as beginning with oneself.

- Do not be idolatrous about or bound to any doctrine, theory, or ideology, even Buddhist ones.
- Do not think the knowledge you presently possess is changeless, absolute truth. Avoid being narrow minded and bound to present views. Learn and practice nonattachment from views in order to be open to receive others' viewpoints.
- Do not force others, including children, by any means whatsoever, to adopt your views, whether by authority, threat, money, propaganda, or even education. However, through compassionate dialogue, help others renounce fanaticism and narrow-mindedness.
- Do not avoid suffering or close your eyes before suffering. Do not lose awareness of the existence of suffering in the life of the world. Find ways to be with those who are suffering, including personal contact, visits, images and sounds. By such means, awaken yourself and others to the reality of suffering in the world.
- Do not accumulate wealth while millions are hungry. Do not take as the aim of your life fame, profit, wealth, or sensual pleasure. Live simply and share time, energy, and material resources with those who are in need.
- Do not maintain anger or hatred. Learn to penetrate and transform them when they are still seeds in your consciousness. As soon as they arise, turn your attention to your breath in order to see and understand the nature of your hatred.
- Do not lose yourself in dispersion and in your surroundings. Practice mindful breathing to come back to what is happening in the present moment. Be in touch with what is wondrous, refreshing, and healing both inside and around you.
- Do not utter words that can create discord and cause the community to break. Make every effort to reconcile and resolve all conflicts, however small.
- Do not say untruthful things for the sake of personal interest or to impress people. Do not utter words that cause division and hatred. Do not spread news that you do not know to be certain. Do not criticize or condemn things of which you are not sure. Always speak truthfully and constructively. Have the courage to speak out about situations of injustice, even when doing so may threaten your own safety.
- Do not use the Buddhist community for personal gain or profit, or transform your community into a political party. A religious community, however, should take a clear stand against oppression and injustice and should strive to change the situation without engaging in partisan conflicts.
- Do not live with a vocation that is harmful to humans and nature. Do not invest in companies that deprive others of their chance to live. Select a vocation that helps realize your ideal of compassion.

- Do not kill. Do not let others kill. Find whatever means possible to protect life and prevent war.
- Possess nothing that should belong to others. Respect the property of others, but prevent others from profiting from human suffering or the suffering of other species on Earth.

Do not mistreat your body. Learn to handle it with respect. Do not look on your body as only an instrument. Preserve vital energies (sexual, breath, spirit) for the realization of the Way. (For brothers and sisters who are not monks and nuns:) Sexual expression should not take place without love and commitment. In sexual relations, be aware of future suffering that may be caused. To preserve the happiness of others, respect the rights and commitments of others. Be fully aware of the responsibility of bringing new lives into the world.

58. See, for example Jorn Borup, "Zen and the Art of Inverting Orientalism: Religious Studies and Genealogical Networks," http://www.buddhanet.dk/zenorienteng.htm. Accessed March 14, 2012. Borup writes that Suzuki's language for speaking about Zen at the World Parliament of Religions was taken from theosophy. This Western translation led to a reinvention of Buddhism in Japan.
59. Appadurai, 20.
60. *The Foucault Reader*, 376.
61. Thich Nhat Hanh, *Interbeing*, 3.
62. Thich Nhat Hanh, *The Art of Power* (New York: HarperCollins, 2007), 1.
63. There are many translations of the Boddhisattva vow. For one translation see: http://www.katinkahesselink.net/tibet/bodhisatva.htm. Accessed August 4, 2011
64. Sallie King, *Socially Engaged Buddhism* (Honolulu: University of Hawaii Press, 2009), 150.
65. Ibid.
66. Ibid.
67. Nhat Hanh, *Art of Power*, 26.
68. Ibid., 26
69. Ibid.
70. Ibid., 27.
71. Nhat Hanh, *Interbeing*, 6.
72. In his "Letter from Birmingham City Jail" King expressed disappointment with those who believed that time would inevitably free King's charges and his white oppressors. "We must come to see that human progress never rolls in on wheels of inevitability.... We must use time creatively, and forever realize that the time is always ripe to do right. Now is the time to make real the promise of democracy, and transform our pending national elegy into a creative psalm of brotherhood." Martin Luther King, Jr. *A Testament of Hope: The Essential Writings*

and Speeches of Martin Luther King, Jr., ed. James M. Washington (New York: HarperCollins, 1986), 296.
73. Appadurai, 134.
74. *The Foucault Reader*, 360.
75. Ibid., 367.

CHAPTER 5

1. Abraham Lincoln, "Second Inaugural Address, March 4, 1865," in *Abraham Lincoln: His Speeches and Writings*, ed. Roy P. Basler (New York: DaCapo Press, 1946), 792.
2. George Steiner, *Antigones* (New York: Oxford University Press, 1986), 12, 17, 33.
3. Elizabeth Wyckoff in her *Antigone* uses the translation "alien." Elizabeth Wyckoff, *Antigone*, in *The Complete Greek Tragedies*, ed. David Grene and Richmond Lattimore (New York: Pocket Books, 1973), 161–209.
4. Steiner, 34–36: Steiner argues that Antigone also represents the hearth. In the play, Steiner argues, these binaries become non-negotiable in the conflict and come into collision. They should be, however, terms through which the self defines itself. That is to say, to arrive at oneself is to come into fertile contact with the other element. (231, 441–581).
5. Ibid., 85.
6. Ibid.
7. Sophocles, *Antigone* in *Sophocles I: Oedipus the King, Oedipus at Colonus, Antigone*, 2nd edition, trans. David Grene (Chicago: University of Chicago Press, 1991), lines 50 and 53.
8. Ibid., lines 90–91.
9. Ibid., lines 82–83 (emphasis added).
10. Ibid., line 78.
11. Ibid., line 108.
12. Ibid., lines 115–116.
13. See Steiner, 210–211.
14. *Antigone*, lines 599–601.
15. Ibid., line 610.
16. Ibid., lines 556–578.
17. See Steiner 220–221.
18. *Antigone*, line 542.
19. Ibid., line 541.
20. Ibid., line 607.
21. Ibid., lines 635–637
22. Ibid., lines 630 and 632. David Grene, for example, attributes them to Antigone (line 630) and the Chorus (line 632), while Elizabeth Wyckoff attributes them to Ismene.
23. *Antigone*, line 877.

24. Ibid., 632.

25. In Aristotle's thought, maturity displays itself in both the inner and outer movements of the mature man. In Book II of the *Ethics*, he argues that "in the case of the virtues an act is not performed justly or with self-control if the act itself is of a certain kind, but only if in addition the agent has certain characteristics as he performs it: first of all, he must know what he is doing; secondly, he must choose to act the way he does, and he must choose it for its own sake; and in the third place, the act must spring from a firm and unchangeable character." Aristotle, *Nicomachean Ethics*, tr. Martin Ostwald (Indianapolis: Bobbs-Merrill, 1962), 39. See also Aristotle's discussion of the types of friendship in Books VIII and IX of the *Ethics*, 214–272.

26. See "Pericles Funeral Oration" in Thucydides, *History of the Peloponnesian War*, tr. Rex Warner (New York: Penguin Books, 1954), 143–151 and "Apology" in Plato, *The Collected Dialogues* eds. Edith Hamilton and Huntington Cairnes (Princeton: Princeton University Press, 1961), 3–26.

27. Beginning at line 193, Creon says "It is impossible to know any man—/I mean his soul, intelligence, and judgment—/until he shows his skill in rule and law./I think that a man supreme ruler of a whole city,/if he does not reach for the best counsel for her,/but through some fear, keeps his tongue under lock and key,/him I judge worst of any." See *Antigone*, lines 193–201.

28. Ibid., lines 679ff.

29. Ibid., line 577.

30. Ibid., lines 683–688.

31. Ibid., lines 689–691.

32. Ibid., lines 717–723.

33. Ibid., line 741.

34. Ibid., lines 760–768.

35. Ibid., lines 774–778.

36. Ibid., lines 785–786.

37. Ibid., line 793.

38. Ibid., line 794.

39. Ibid., lines 799–801.

40. Ibid., lines 820–821.

41. See, for example, Wyckoff, line. 1068.

42. *Antigone*, lines 368ff.

43. Lincoln, "Speech at Indianapolis, Indiana, February 11, 1861," in Basler, 571.

44. Lincoln, "First Inaugural," in Basler, 586.

45. Ibid.

46. See Albert Camus, "Appeal for a Civilian Truce," in Camus, *Resistance, Rebellion, and Death*, trans. by Justin O'Brien (New York: Vintage Books, 1974), 136.

47. Lincoln, "First Inaugural," in Basler, 586.

48. Ibid., 588.
49. Ibid.
50. Ibid., 588.
51. Ibid.
52. See Donald Herbert Donald's biography, *Lincoln* (New York: Touchstone Books, 1996). There has been much loss: the death of Lincoln's son Willie in 1862; relieving General McClellan of his duties as Commander of the Union Army and appointing Grant; the war has long ceased to be theoretical for Lincoln because he has been to Gettysburg; he has defeated McClellan in the 1864 election but he knows that he has been elected by only half the Union he seeks to hold together.
53. See, for a discussion of the Emancipation Proclamation, Doris Kearns Goodwin, *Team of Rivals: The Political Genius of Abraham Lincoln* (New York: Simon and Schuster, 2006): 461–592; on the Thirteenth Amendment, see Goodwin 686ff. Lincoln has begun reconstructing the Union through the Emancipation Proclamation, the Thirteenth Amendment abolishing slavery in the Union, and the creation of the Freedmen's Bureau (See, for example, Donald, *Lincoln*, 563–583). While he believes these go a long way in the direction of God's will, he knows that they will make reintegrating the South into the Union painful and difficult, thus the problem of reconstituting the relationships that make up the Union.
54. Second Inaugural, 588.
55. *Antigone*, line 1317.
56. Ibid., line 1057.
57. Ibid., lines 467–469.
58. Toni Morrison, *Beloved* (New York: Plume Books, 1987), 199.
59. Elaine Scarry, *The Body in Pain: The Making and Unmaking of the World* (New York: Oxford University Press, 1985).
60. Scarry, 124ff.
61. See Judith Butler, "Violence, Mourning, and Politics" in *Precarious Life: The Powers of Mourning and Violence* (New York: Verso Books, 2004), 19–49.
62. *Antigone*, line 1071.
63. Ibid., line 1221.

CHAPTER 6

1. Sophocles, "Oedipus Rex," in *Sophocles I,* 2nd edition, trans. and ed., David Grene (Chicago: The University of Chicago Press, 1991); Lee Breuer, *The Gospel at Colonus* (New York: Theatre Communications Group, 1993).
2. Larry Watson, *Montana 1948* (Minneapolis, MN: Milkweed Editions, 2007), 82.

3. Breuer, 4.
4. Ibid.
5. Ibid.
6. Ibid., 5.
7. Alan Tate, *The Fathers* (Athens: Swallow Press, 1959), 234.
8. "Toni Morrison: Profile of a Writer," Homevision 2000.
9. Toni Morrison uses this phrase in several places, including "Toni Morrison: Profile of a Writer" and in her Tanner Lectures, "Unspeakable Things Unspoken: The Afro-American Presence in American Literature," 1988 available at www.tannerlectures.utah.edu/lectures/documents/morrison90.pdf. Accessed March 18, 2012. See also Toni Morrison, *Beloved*, 199.
10. Bernard M. Knox, *The Heroic Temper: Studies in Sophoclean Tragedy* (Berkeley: University of California Press, 1983), 154ff.
11. *Oedipus at Colonus*, line 530.
12. Ibid., lines 443–544.
13. Ibid., lines 584–586.
14. Ibid., line 619.
15. This is the concession finally made by Tarrou to the human aspiration to innocence in Camus' *The Plague*. See Albert Camus, *The Plague*, trans. Stuart Gilbert (New York: Vintage Books, 1991).
16. We are grateful to Christine Cowan for this insight.
17. Agamben, *Homo Sacer*, 25.
18. See for this argument, Joseph P. Wilson, *The Hero and the City: An Interpretation of Sophocles' Oedipus at Colonus* (Ann Arbor: The University of Michigan Press, 1997), 19–20.
19. See Dwight N. Hopkins, "Slave Theology," in *Cut Loose Your Stammering Tongue: Black Theology in the Slave Narratives*, ed. Dwight Hopkins and George C. L. Cummings (Louisville, KY: Westminster John Knox Press, 2003), 20–21.
20. Jon Michael Spenser, *Protest and Praise: Sacred Music of Black Religion* (Minneapolis, MN: Ausburg Fortress Press, 1990).
21. Ibid., 169–170.
22. Ibid., 179.
23. Ibid., 180.
24. Breuer, 24.
25. Ibid., 44.
26. Ibid., 47.
27. Ibid., 45.
28. Both quotes Ibid., 52.
29. *Oedipus at Colonus*, line 2015.
30. Breuer, 55.
31. Ibid., 4.
32. "Teaching Arts, Literature, and Religion," A Conference at Huntingdon College, Montgomery, Alabama, September 1993.

---

33. Sharon E. Greene, "An Interview With Robert Detweiler," in David Jasper and Mark Ledbetter, ed. *In Good Company: Essays in Honor of Robert Detweiler* (Atlanta, GA: Scholars Press), 434.
34. Scarry, *Body in Pain.*
35. Morrison, *Beloved*, 88.
36. Breuer, 55.

CHAPTER 7

1. Marilou Awiakata, *Selu: Seeking the Corn Mother's Wisdom* (Golden, CO: Fulcrum Publishing, 1993).
2. Ibid., 287.
3. The texts we are considering here are Robert Detweiler essays "From Chaos to Legion to Chance: The Double Play of Apocalyptic and Mimesis," in *The Daemonic Imagination: Biblical Text and Secular Story* (Atlanta: Scholars Press, 1990), 1–26; "Torn by Desire: *Sparagmos* in Greek Tragedy and Recent Fiction," in *Postmodernism, Literature, and the Future of Theology*, ed. David Jasper (New York: St. Martin's Press Inc., 1993), 60–77; Toni Morrison, *Beloved* (New York: Plume Books, 1988); Wole Soyinka, *The Bacchae of Euripides: A Communion Rite* (New York: W. W. Norton and Company Inc., 1974).
4. Euripides, *The Bacchae*, in *Euripides V,* ed. David Grene and Richmond Lattimore (Chicago: The University of Chicago Press, 1959).
5. Detweiler, "From Chaos to Legion," 11–12.
6. Ibid., 21.
7. Ibid., 18.
8. Ibid., 19.
9. Alan Tate, *The Fathers* (Athens: Swallow Press, 1959), 185–186.
10. Nandy, *Intimate Enemy*, 49.
11. Julia Kristeva, *Powers of Horror: An Essay on Abjection*, trans. Leon S. Roudiez (New York: Columbia University Press, 1982), 4.
12. Edkins, 8, 176–177.
13. Kristeva, 9.
14. Joseph Conrad, *Heart of Darkness*, ed. Robert Kimbrough (New York: W. W. Norton,1988), 72.
15. We refer to the work of Emile Durkheim, *The Elementary Forms of the Religious Life* (London: Allen and Irwin, 1915).
16. Toni Morrison, *Playing in the Dark: Whiteness and the Literary Imagination* (Cambridge: Havard University Press, 1992), 48.
17. Ibid., 38.
18. Ibid., 39.
19. Ibid., 44.
20. Ibid., 59.

21. Robert Detweiler, *Breaking the Fall: Religious Reading of Contemporary Fiction* (New York: HarperCollins, 1989), ix.

22. *The Bacchae*, lines 1115–1120.

23. Ibid., lines 1204–1205.

24. Ibid., lines 1215–1220.

25. Soyinka, 95.

26. Rodolphe Gasche, *Inventions of Difference: On Jacques Derrida* (Cambridge: Harvard University Press, 1998), 45.

27. Karla F. C. Holloway, *Moorings and Metaphors: Figures of Culture and Gender in Black Women's Literature* (New Brunswick, NJ.: Rutgers University Press, 1992), 55.

28. Toni Morrison, *The Nobel Lecture in Literature*, www.nobelprize.org/ nobel_prizes/literature/laureates/1993/morrison-lecture.html. Accessed March 18, 2012. Also published by New York: Knopf Doubleday, 1993.

29. Toni Morrison, "The Dancing Mind: Speech Upon the Acceptance of the National Book Foundation Medal for Distinguished Contribution to American Letters," www.nationalbook.org/nbaacceptsspeech _tmorrison.htm#.T2ZVwkqGbu0 (accessed March 18, 2012). Also published by New York: Alfred A. Knopf, 1996.

30. Morrison, Nobel Lecture.

31. Julia Kristeva, *Tales of Love*, trans. Leon S. Roudiez (New York: Columbia University Press, 1987), 7.

32. Ibid.

33. Ibid., 380.

34. Morrison, *Beloved*, 215ff.

35. Ibid., 164.

36. Sharon E. Greene, "An Interview with Robert Detweiler," in David Jasper and Mark Ledbetter, ed. *In Good Company: Essays in Honor of Robert Detweiler* (Atlanta: Scholars Press, 1994), 434.

37. Detweiler, "From Chaos to Legion to Chance," 21.

38. Ibid.

39. Morrison, *Beloved*, 36.

40. Ibid., 35–36.

41. Detweiler, "Teaching Arts, Literature and Religion," Huntingdon College, Montgomery, Alabama, September 1993.

42. Alice Walker, *Everything We Love Can Be Saved* (New York: Ballentine Books, 1998), 200.

43. "Toni Morrison: Profile of a Writer," Homevision, Released 2000.

44. Walker, *Everything*, 200.

45. Alasdair MacIntyre, *Whose Justice? Which Rationality?* (South Bend, IN: University of Notre Dame Press, 1989), 120.

46. Holloway, *Moorings*, 55.

47. Morrison, *Beloved*, 86.

48. Soyinka, *The Bacchae*, 76–77.

49. Toni Morrison, *Paradise* (New York: Alfred A. Knopf, 1998), 318.
50. Morrison, *Beloved*, 84.
51. Charles H. Long, "Du Bois, Race, and the Nature of Religion in the United States," *God Talk With Black Thinkers*, Drew University, 2002.
52. Alice Walker, *The Way Forward Is With A Broken Heart* (New York: Ballantine Books, 2001), 51.

CHAPTER 8

1. Jonathan Z. Smith, "Tillich ['s] Remains...," *Journal of the American Academy of Religion* 78, no. 4 (2010): 1151–1152. Smith argues that Tillich remains "the unacknowledged theoretician of [the study of religion's] entire enterprise" (1140). He shares with Voegelin an insistence on the problem of symbol.
2. Michel de Certeau, *The Practice of Everyday Life* (Berkeley: University of California Press, 1988).
3. Nandy, *The Intimate Enemy: Loss and Recovery of self Under Colonialism*.
4. See, for example, Manfred Henningsen, "The Collapse and Retrieval of Meaning," *Review of Politics* 62, no. 4 (2000): 809–817; Leela Gandhi, *Postcolonial Theory: A Critical Introduction* (New York: Columbia University Press, 1998); R. Radhakrishnan, "Postcoloniality and the Boundaries of Identity," *Callaloo* 16, no. 4 (1993): 750–771.
5. Bhabha, *Location of Culture*.
6. See Eric Voegelin, *Anamnesis*, tr. and ed. Gerhart Niemeyer (Columbia: University of Missouri Press, 1990); Eric Voegelin, *Science, Politics, and Gnosticism* (Washington, D.C.: Regnery Gateway, 1968).
7. Eric Voegelin *Order and History*, 5 vols (Baton Rouge: Louisiana State University Press, 1956–1987).
8. Gandhi, *Postcolonial Theory* and Radhakrishnan, "Postcoloniality and the Boundaries of Identity."
9. Bhabha, xxx.
10. Murray Jardine, "Eric Voegelin's Interpretations of Modernity: A Reconsideration of the Spiritual and the Political," *Review of Politics* 57, no. 4 (1995): 581–606.
11. Eric Voegelin, "Equivalences of Experience and Symbolization in History," in *The Collected Works of Eric Voegelin, Volume 12: Published Essays, 1966–1985*, ed. Ellis Sandoz (Baton Rouge: Louisiana State University Press, 1990), 133.
12. Ibid., 116.
13. Ibid.
14. Ibid., 118.
15. Ibid., 119.

16. Ibid., 120.
17. Ibid., 121.
18. Ibid., 125.
19. Ibid., 129.
20. Ibid., 133.
21. See Thomas W. Heilke, "Science, Philosophy and Resistance: On Eric Voegelin's Practice of Opposition," *Review of Politics* 56, no. 4 (1994): 727–753.
22. Voegelin, "Equivalences of Experience," 133.
23. Ibid.
24. See Voegelin, *Science, Politics, and Gnosticism*; Eric Voegelin, *The New Science of Politics: An Introduction* (Chicago: The University of Chicago Press, 1987).
25. Eric Voegelin, *Anamnesis*, trans. Gerhart Niemeyer (Columbia: University of Missouri Press, 1990).
26. Bhabha, 15.
27. Susan Searls Giroux and Henry A. Giroux, "Making the Political More Pedagogical: Reading Homi Bhabha," *Jac: A Journal of Composition Theory* 19, no. 1 (1999): 139–148.
28. Gandhi, 9ff.
29. Lawrence Phillips. "Lost in Space: Sitting/Citing the In-Between of Homi Bhabha's Location of Culture," *Jouvert: a Journal of Postcolonial Studies* 2, no. 2 (1998) [online journal]. http://english.chass.ncsu.edu/jouvert/v2i2/PHILLIP.HTM. Accessed September 21, 2000.
30. Bhabha, 29.
31. Ibid., 25 (emphasis added).
32. Ibid., 34.
33. Ibid., 109.
34. Ibid., 35.
35. Ibid., 36.
36. Ibid., 37.
37. Ibid., 109.
38. Ibid., 112.
39. Ibid.
40. Ibid., 114.
41. See Antony Easthope, "Bhabha, Hybridity, and Identity," *Textual Practice* 12, no. 2 (1998): 341–348; Monika Fludernik, "The Constitution of Hybridity: Postcolonial Interventions," in *Hybridity and Postcolonialism: Twentieth Century Indian Literature*, ed. Monika Fludernik (Tubinen: Stauffenberg, 1998), 19–53.
42. Bhabha, 115.
43. Ibid.
44. Ibid., 116.
45. Voegelin, "Equivalences of Experience," 119.

CHAPTER 9

1. Michael Walzer, *Spheres of Justice* (Oxford: Blackwell Publishers, 1983); Jean Francois Lyotard and Jean-Loup Thebaud, *Just Gaming*, trans. Wlad Godzich (Minneapolis: University of Minnesota Press, 1985). When dealing with thinkers of such broad-ranging interests, it is necessary to note that this chapter represents a comparative reading on a specific issue, that is, their theories of justice and the relationship of those theories to social and discursive spaces.

2. See Rawls, *A Theory of Justice* (Cambridge, MA: Harvard University Press, 1971); "Justice as Fairness: Political Not Metaphysical," *Philosophy and Public Affairs* 14 (1985): 223–251.

3. See Dworkin, "What is Equality? Part II: Equality of Resources," *Philosophy and Public Affairs* 10 (1981): 283–345.

4. See Sandel, *Liberalism and the Limits of Justice* (Cambridge: Cambridge University Press, 1982). An excellent introduction to approaches to justice is Serge-Christophe Holm, "Distributive Justice," in *A Companion to Contemporary Political Philosophy*, eds. Robert Goodin and Phillip Pettit (Oxford: Blackwell Publishers, 1996).

5. Niccolo Machiavelli, *The Prince* in Machiavelli, *Selected Political Writings*, ed. and trans. David Wootton (Indianapolis: Hackett Publishing, 1994). Machiavelli's prince must identify and make strategic and efficient use of the resources available to him, whether they are capacities, persons, appearances, or topography. Though it is more common to talk about amorality in Machiavelli, this work is most fruitfully seen as being about the effective management of resources in political spaces.

6. Walzer, 7.

7. This and preceding quote are from Ibid., 8.

8. Ibid., 261.

9. Ibid.., 10.

10. Ibid., 11.

11. Ibid., 31.

12. Ibid., 32.

13. Ibid., 277.

14. Ibid., 261.

15. Ibid., 121.

16. Ibid.

17. Ibid., 122.

18. Ibid., 281.

19. Ibid., 298.

20. Ibid., 310.

21. Ibid., 311.

22. See Walzer, "Response," in *Pluralism, Justice, and Equality*, eds. David Miller and Walzer (Oxford: Oxford University Press, 1995), 281–297, especially, 282.

23. Ibid., 319.
24. See Bill Readings, *Introducing Lyotard: Art and Politics* (London and New York: Routledge, 1991), xxxi.
25. See Jean Francois Lyotard, *The Differend: Phrases in Dispute*, trans. Georges Van Den Abbeele (Minneapolis: University of Minnesota Press, 1988). For Lyotard, Algeria is the *differend par excellence*. See for example the collection of essays in Lyotard, "Algerians" in *Political Writings*, trans. Bill Readings and Kevin Paul Geiman (Minneapolis: University of Minnesota Press, 1993), 165–326.
26. Lyotard, *The Differend*, xi.
27. A telling example would be the way modern government bureaucracies handle problems that arise in their jurisdictions. The first step to addressing the problem is to find a pre-established category which it might fit. The category comes with rules and procedures designed to resolve problems that arise in that category. The problem is then translated into the language of the bureaucratic category rather than being taken on its own terms.
28. Ibid., xiii (our parentheticals).
29. Lyotard, *Just Gaming*, especially 80–81.
30. This idea is one source of the proximity of the postmodern and post-colonial critiques. In his post-colonial work, Edward Said takes a contrapuntal stance, that is, he seeks to "read back" to the tradition(s) of literary and political hegemony of the West. See especially Said, *Orientalism* (1978); *Culture and Imperialism* (1994).
31. Lyotard, *Just Gaming*, 9.
32. Ibid., 19.
33. Ibid., 23.
34. Ibid.
35. Ibid., 17.
36. Ibid., 84.
37. Ibid., 87.
38. Ibid., 91.
39. Ibid., 93.
40. Ibid., 95 (emphasis added).
41. Ibid., 66–67.
42. Ibid., 98–99. For instance, in *Federalist #10*, James Madison makes a similar argument regarding "factions." Instead of arguing from our "multiple belonging" to a variety of groups, he relies on the extended physical space of the emerging republic to dilute any possibility of an emerging consensus or majority faction that will then tyrannize the minority.
43. Lyotard, *Just Gaming*, 100.
44. Ibid.
45. Ibid.
46. Michel de Certeau, *The Practice of Everyday Life, Vol. 1* (Berkeley: University of California Press, 1988), 22, 38. DeCerteau argues that

space is existential, while place is proper and ordered. Space, however, can exist in place, opening its transitive qualities.

47. See Vaclav Havel, "Six Asides About Culture," in *Open Letters: Selected Writings 1965–1990*, ed. Paul Wilson (New York: Vintage, 1992), 272–284.

CHAPTER 10

1. Alice Walker, *In Search of Our Mothers' Gardens: Womanist Prose* (New York: Harcourt, Brace, Jovanovich, 1983).
2. Kimberly R. Connor, *Imagining Grace: Liberating Theologies in the Slave Narrative Tradition* (Urbana: The University of Illinois Press, 2000).
3. Cited in Connor, 3.
4. Ibid.
5. Ibid., 4.
6. Ibid., x.
7. *The Color Purple* (New York: Warner Brothers, 1985) undoubtedly her finest work, both established and haunted Walker. It is her greatest success but also her most challenging and problematic work in its vision and in the questions it raises. The novel and film have been criticized for, particularly, their depiction of black men, but also for being ahistorical (magical, fantastic, or fairy tale) and for moving uncritically towards a "cultural nationalism" that embraces capitalism as a way out of oppression. Walker counters these criticisms in several places—first, in *Living by the Word* (1988) and then in *The Same River Twice* (1996). Walker argues that her novel combines the historical, political and spiritual in its womanist vision of community.
8. Walker, *Mother's Gardens*, 147, 148.
9. Ibid., 138.
10. Ibid., 129.
11. Ibid., 145.
12. Ibid., 164.
13. Ibid., 17.
14. Ibid., 21.
15. Ibid., 28.
16. Edward Said, *The World, The Text and the Critic* (Cambridge: Harvard University Press, 1983).
17. Walker, *Mother's Gardens*, 32.
18. Ibid., 143.
19. David Palumbo-Liu, "The Politics of Memory: Remembering History in Alice Walker and Joy Kogawa," in *Memory and Cultural Politics: New Approaches to American Ethnic Literatures,* ed. Robert E. Hogan, Joseph T. Skerrett, Jr. and Amritjit Singh (Boston: Northeastern University Press, 1996), 225.

20. Walker, *Mother's Gardens,* xi.
21. Ibid.
22. Ibid.
23. Ibid.
24. Ibid., xii.
25. Ibid.
26. Ibid., 36.
27. Ibid., 5.
28. Ibid., 17.
29. Ibid., 136–138, 176.
30. Ibid., 393.
31. Ibid. 232.
32. Kathleen Norris, *The Quotidian Mysteries: Laundry, Liturgy, and Women's Work* (New York: Paulist Press, 1998).
33. Dorothee Soelle, *Suffering,* trans. Everett R. Kalin (Philadelphia: Fortress Press, 1975), 75.
34. Emilie Townes, "Living in the New Jerusalem: the Rhetoric and Movement of Liberation in the House of Evil," in *A Troubling in My Soul: Womanist Perspectives on Evil and Suffering,* ed. Emilie M. Townes (New York: Orbis Books, 1995), 84.
35. Elaine Scarry, *The Body in Pain.*
36. Soelle, 75.
37. Townes, 90.
38. Soelle, 71.
39. Townes, 84.
40. Soelle, 78.
41. Walker, *Color Purple,* 183.
42. Ibid., 204ff.
43. Soelle, 102.
44. Ibid.
45. Jacqueline Grant, "The Sin of Servanthood and the Deliverance of Discipleship," in *A Troubling,* 203.
46. Grant, 209, 215.
47. Harriet Davidson, "Adrienne Rich's Politics and Poetry of Location," in *Contemporary Poetry Meets Modern Theology,* eds. Anthony Easthope and John O. Thompson (Toronto: University of Toronto Press, 1991), 176.
48. Toni Morrison, *Beloved* (New York: Alfred A. Knopf, 1987), 8.
49. Talal Asad, *Genealogies of Religion: Discipline and Reasons of Power in Christianity and Islam* (Baltimore: The Johns Hopkins University Press, 1993).
50. Pema Chodron, *The Wisdom of No Escape and the Path of Loving-Kindness* (Boston: Shambhala, 1991). 56.
51. Ibid., 57.
52. Ibid., 60.

53. Ibid., 12.
54. *Alice Walker and Pema Chodron in Conversation* (Sounds True Studio, 1999).
55. Ibid.
56. Audre Lorde, *Sister Outsider: Essays and Speeches* (Darlinghurst, Australia: Crossing Press, 1984), 145.
57. *Conversation.*
58. Ibid.
59. Walker, *Color Purple,* 278.
60. *Conversation.*
61. Vincent Harding, *There Is a River: The Black Struggle for Freedom in America* (New York: Harcourt Brace and Company, 1993), 5.
62. Alice Walker, *The Same River Twice: Honoring the Difficult* (London: The Women's Press, 1996), 284.
63. Alice Walker, *Anything We Love Can Be Saved* (New York: Ballantine Books, 1998), 200.

Chapter 11

1. Martin Luther King, Jr. *A Testament of Hope: The Essential Writings and Speeches of Martin Luther King, Jr.,* ed. James M. Washington (New York: HarperCollins, 1986), 314.
2. We chose these terms quite self-consciously both to point back to the catastrophic failure of Reconstruction and to suggest that the attempt to transform social attitudes and mores solely through the rule of law is bound to fail. The categories emerged in our reading of Sophocles' *Antigone* when we tried to move beyond Hegel's reading that the confrontation between Creon and Antigone was a confrontation of principles. There are lessons to be learned about right conduct and effective social and political strategy in the play as well. While avoiding the play, this essay will flesh out some of those lessons in King's work.
3. Compare Eric Foner's epic account of the failure of Reconstruction and, among others, Taylor Branch's account of the Civil Rights Movement. In both instances, the law is changed, social structures are changed, and the job is left undone. See Eric Foner, *Reconstruction: America's Unfinished Revolution 1863–1877* (New York: Harper, 2002); Taylor Branch, *Parting the Waters: America During the King Years, 1954–63* (New York: Touchstone Books, 1988).
4. Compare the spirit and consequences of the Civil Rights Act of 1964, the Voting Rights Act of 1965, the Civil Rights Act of 1968, and the Civil Rights Act of 1991 with the various manifestations of backlash (e.g., against "reverse discrimination") in the courts and in our political rhetoric.
5. See also Patricia J. Williams, *The Alchemy of Race and Rights: Diary of a Law Professor* (Cambridge, MA: Harvard University Press, 1991).

6. Malcolm X's critique of the way the governing establishment han-
   dled necessary legal reform brilliantly anticipates this problem. See
   his "The Ballot or the Bullet," in *Malcolm X Speaks: Selected Speeches
   and Statements*, ed. George Breitman (New York: Grove Press, 1994),
   23–44.
7. King, *Testament of Hope*, 289–302.
8. See John Stuart Mill, *On Liberty* (Buffalo, NY: Prometheus Books,
   1986).
9. Several years later, the constitutionality of the court order was upheld
   by the Supreme Court in a 5–4 decision, *Walker v. City of Birmingham*
   (1967). The significant product of the event, however, is not the
   Court's very close ruling.
10. The evidence introduced regarding the effects of segregation on the
    personality development of African-American children proved deci-
    sive in *Brown v. Board of Education* (1954). See Richard Kluger,
    *Simple Justice: The History of Brown v. Board of Education and Black
    America's Struggle for Equality* (New York: Vintage, 1977).
11. See Lewis V. Baldwin, *There is a Balm in Gilead: The Cultural Roots
    of Martin Luther King, Jr.* (Minneapolis: Augsburg Fortress Press,
    1991).
12. Despite challenges, King's regard for the law changed little over
    the course of the movement. See, for example, his speech on "The
    American Dream" at the June 6, 1961 commencement at Lincoln
    University in Pennsylvania and the excellent interview he gave to
    Playboy magazine in *A Testament of Hope*, 208–216, 340–377.
13. See Aquinas, *Summa Theologica*, especially Questions 90–92, 94–97.
    As one might expect, Augustine plays a role here as well. See *The Polit-
    ical Ideas of St.Thomas Aquinas: Representative Selections*, ed. Dino
    Bigongiari (New York: Hafner Press, 1953), 3–29, 42–86.
14. King, *Testament of Hope*, 293.
15. Ibid.
16. King is thinking of Martin Buber's "I-Thou" formulation and seems
    to use the term in the same way that Simone Weil does earlier
    in her essay called "Human Personality." See Martin Buber, *I and
    Thou*, trans. Walter Kaufmann (New York: Touchstone Books, 1971);
    Simone Weil, "Human Personality," in *Simone Weil: An Anthology*,
    ed. Sian Miles (New York: Grove Press, 2000), 49–78.
17. King, *Testament of Hope*, 293.
18. Ibid., 294.
19. This suggests that King would have agreed, for instance, with the spirit
    of affirmative action programs, but he might have deplored the cynical
    way they are sometimes implemented and disappointed that they are
    still necessary.
20. King, *Testament of Hope*, 294.
21. Ibid.

22. Ibid.

23. See Vaclav Havel's essays regarding the "post-totalitarian" regime in Czechoslovakia in Havel, *Open Letters*.

24. King, *Testament of Hope*, 292.

25. Ibid., 291.

26. Ibid., 295.

27. Ibid., 297.

28. Martin Luther King, Jr., *Stride Toward Freedom: The Montgomery Story* (San Francisco: HarperSan Francisco, 1986).

29. Ibid., 105.

30. Ibid.

31. Ibid.

32. These were not always easy difficulties for King to resolve for himself. See King's speech, "Facing the Challenge of a New Age" delivered before the First Annual Institute on Non-violence and Social Change in Montgomery, December 1956 in King, *Testament of Hope*, 135–144.

33. See, for instance, Martin Luther King, Jr., *Why We Can't Wait* (New York: Penguin Books, 1964) and his speech on the Vietnam War entitled "A Time to Break Silence" (1967) in King, *A Testament of Hope*, 231–244.

34. King, *Testament of Hope*, 295.

35. Ibid., 296.

36. Ibid.

37. Ibid., 290.

38. See Hannah Arendt, *The Human Condition* (Chicago: University of Chicago Press, 1958).

39. See Baldwin, *There is a Balm in Gilead*, particularly chapters 4 and 5. We are not certain that King was interested in being a prophet, but a discussion of the role of the prophet can be found in Walter Brueggemann, *Hopeful Imagination: Prophetic Voices in Exile* (Philadelphia: Fortress Press, 1986). Only memory, Brueggemann contends, allows for possibility. The future, and of this King too is certain, is inevitably tied to how we see our past.

40. King, *Testament of Hope*, 302.

41. The most famous examples of this "language of the Mountaintop" are his 1963 "I Have a Dream" speech delivered at the Lincoln Memorial and the "I See the Promised Land" speech delivered the night before he was assassinated. See *A Testament of Hope: The Essential Writings and Speeches of Martin Luther King, Jr.*, 217–220, 279–288.

42. King, *Testament of Hope*, 315.

43. Ibid., 213.

44. www.thekingcenter.org/king-philosophy#sub4. Accessed March 31, 2012.

CHAPTER 12

1. Emmanuel Levinas, *Totality and Infinity: An Essay on Exteriority*, trans. Alphonso Lingis (Pittsburgh, PA: Duquesne University Press, 1969), 296.
2. Ibid., 152–174.
3. Edward Said, *Cultural and Imperialism* (New York: Vintage Books, 1994), 19.
4. Levinas, 222.
5. Levinas, 306.
6. Ibid.
7. Derrick Walcott, "The Schooner 'Flight,'" famouspoetsandpoems. com/poets/derek_walcott/poems/11253. Accessed March 27, 2012.
8. Ibid.

BIBLIOGRAPHY

Aeschyus. *Agamemnon*. In *Aeschylus I*. Trans. Richard Lattimore. Chicago: University of Chicago Press, 1953.

Agamben, Giorgio. *Homo Sacer: Sovereign Power and Bare Life*. Trans. Daniel Heller Roazen. Stanford, CA: Stanford University Press, 1998.

———. *Means without End: Notes on Politics*. Trans. Vincenzo Binetti and Cesare Casarino. Minneapolis: University of Minnesota Press, 2000.

Anderson, Benedict. *Imagined Communities*. Rev. ed. London: Verso Books, 1991.

Antonious, Marcus Aurelius. *Meditations*. Google eBook edition. Filiquarian Publishing, http://books.google.com/books?id= GVasMH3TQ_MC& lpg=PP1&dq=meditations%20marcus%20aurelius&pg=PP1#v=onepage &q=meditations%20marcus%20aurelius&f=false. Accessed August 4, 2011.

Appadurai, Arjun. *Fear of Small Numbers: A Geography of Anger*. Durham, NC: Duke University Press, 2006.

Aquinas, Thomas. *The Political Ideas of St. Thomas Aquinas: Representative Selections*. Ed. Dino Bigongiari. New York: Hafner Press, 1953.

Arendt, Hannah. *The Human Condition*. Chicago: University of Chicago Press, 1958.

———. *Origins of Totalitarianism*. New York: Harcourt Brace, 1973.

Aristotle. *Nicomachean Ethics*. Trans. Martin Ostwald. Indianapolis: Bobbs-Merrill, 1962.

Asad, Talal. *Formations of the Secular: Christianity, Islam, Modernity*. Stanford: Stanford University Press, 2003.

———. *On Suicide Bombing*. New York: Colombia University Press, 2007.

Avineri, Shlomo. *Hegel's Theory of the Modern State*. Cambridge: Cambridge University Press, 1974.

Awiakata, Marilou. *Selu: Seeking the Corn Mother's Wisdom*. Golden, CO: Fulcrum Publishing, 1993.

Baldwin, James. "The High Road to Destiny." In *Martin Luther King, Jr.: A Profile*. Ed. C. Eric Lincoln. New York: Hill and Wang, 1970, 95.

———. "The Dangerous Road Before Martin Luther King." In *The Price of the Ticket: Collected Nonfiction, 1948–1985*. New York: St. Martin's Press, 1985, 245–262.

Baldwin, Lewis V. *There is a Balm in Gilead: The Cultural Roots of Martin Luther King, Jr.* Minneapolis: Augsburg Fortress Press, 1991.

Barber, Benjamin R. *Fear's Empire: War, Terrorism and Democracy.* New York: W. W. Norton, 2004.

Belaief, Lynne. "Tragic Justice." In *Philosophical Perspectives on the Israeli Palestinian Conflict.* Ed. Tomis Kapitan. London: M. E. Sharpe, 1997, 331–342.

Benedict XVI, Pope. *Truth and Tolerance: Christian Belief and World Religions.* San Francisco: Ignatius Press, 2004.

Benhabib, Seyla. *The Rights of Others: Aliens, Residence, and Citizens.* Cambridge: Cambridge University Press, 2004.

Benjamin, Walter. "On the Concept of History." In *Walter Benjamin: Selected Writings, Volume 4: 1938–1940.* Eds. Howard Eiland and Michael W. Jennings. Trans. Edmund Jephcott. Cambridge: Belknap Press of Harvard University Press, 2003, 401–424.

Bentley, Jerry H. *Old World Encounters: Cross Cultural Contacts and Exchanges in Pre-Modern Times.* New York: Oxford University Press, 1993.

Berlant, Lauren. "Race, Gender, and Nation in the *The Color Purple.*" In *Alice Walker: Critical Perspectives Past and Present.* Eds. K. A. Appiah and Henry Louis Gates, Jr. New York: Amistad Press, 1993, 211–238.

Berman, Shari. "Islamism, Revolution, and Civil Society." *Perspectives on Politics* 1, no. 2 (2003): 257–272.

Bhabha, Homi K. *The Location of Culture.* London: Routledge, 1994.

"The Bodhisattva Vow." http://katinkahesselink.net/tibet/bodhisatva.htm. Accessed August 4, 2011.

Branch, Taylor. *Parting the Waters: America During the King Years, 1954–63.* New York: Touchstone Books, 1988.

Breuer, Lee. *The Gospel at Colonus.* New York: Theatre Communications Group, 1993.

Brueggemann, Walter. *Hopeful Imagination: Prophetic Voices in Exile.* Philadelphia: Fortress Press, 1986.

Buber, Martin. *I and Thou.* Trans. Walter Kaufmann. New York: Touchstone Books, 1971.

Butler, Judith. *Precarious Life: The Powers of Mourning and Violence.* London: Verso Books, 2004.

Camus, Albert. "Appeal for a Civilian Truce." *Resistance, Rebellion, and Death.* Trans. Justin O'Brien. New York: Vintage Books, 1974.

———. *The Plague.* Trans. Stuart Gilbert. New York: Vintage Books, 1991.

Catholic Church. *Catechism of the Catholic Church.* Vatican City: Libreria Editrice Vaticana, 2000.

Certeau, Michel de. *The Practice of Everyday Life.* Berkeley: University of California Press, 1988.

Charney, Evan. "Identity and Liberal Nationalism." *American Political Science Review* 97, no. 2 (2003): 295–310.

Chödrön, Pema. *The Wisdom of No Escape and the Path of Loving-Kindness.* Boston: Shambhala, 1991.

Collins, Gina Michelle. "The Color Purple: What Feminism Can Learn from a Southern Tradition." In *Southern Literature and Literary Theory*. Ed. Jefferson Humphries. Athens: University of Georgia Press, 1990, 75–87.

The Confraternity of Christian Doctrine. *The New American Bible*. Totowa, N.J.: Catholic World Press/World Bible Publishers, 2011.

Conner, Bob. "How Adequate Is Secularism as a Basis for Liberal Education?" Teagle Foundation, 2005, http://teaglefoundation.org/learning/report/20051128.aspx. Accessed February 2, 2012.

Connor, Kimberly Rae. *Conversations and Visions in the Writings of African-American Women*. Knoxville: University of Tennessee Press, 1994.

Conrad, Joseph. *Heart of Darkness*. Ed. Robert Kimbrough. New York: W. W. Norton, 1988.

Davidson, Harriet. "In the Wake of Home: Adrienne Rich's Politics and Poetry of Location." In *Contemporary Poetry Meets Modern Theory*. Eds. Antony Easthope and John O. Thompson. Toronto: University of Toronto Press, 1991, 166–176.

Davis, Charles T. and Henry Louis Gates, Jr., eds. *The Slave's Narrative*. Oxford: Oxford University Press, 1991.

Debord, Guy. *Society of the Spectacle*. Trans. Donald Nicholson-Smith. New York: Zone Books, 1999.

Derrida, Jacques. *Acts of Religion*. Ed. Gil Anidjar. New York: Routledge, 2002.

Detweiler, Robert. *Breaking the Fall: Religious Reading of Contemporary Fiction*. New York: HarperCollins, 1989.

———. "From Chaos to Legion to Chance: The Double Play of Apocalyptic and Mimesis." In *The Daemonic Imagination: Biblical Text and Secular Story*. Atlanta: Scholars Press, 1990, 1–26.

———. "Torn by Desire: *Sparagmos* in Greek Tragedy and Recent Fiction." In *Postmodernism, Literature, and the Future of Theology*. Ed. David Jasper. New York: St. Martin's Press, 1993, 60–77.

Donald, Herbert Donald. *Lincoln*. New York: Touchstone Books, 1996.

Douglass, Frederick. *My Bondage and My Freedom*, 1855, Chapter 17. www.crispinsartwell.com/douglass.htm. Accessed March 13, 2012.

———. *Narrative of the Life of Frederick Douglass, an American Slave*. Ed. Houston A. Baker, Jr. New York: Penguin Books, 1982.

Du Bois, W. E. B. *The Souls of Black Folk*. New York: New American Library, 1969.

Dunn, John. "Nationalism." In *Theorizing Nationalism*. Ed. Ronald Beiner. Albany: State University Press of New York, 1999, 27–50.

Dworkin, Ronald. "What is Equality? Part II: Equality of Resources." *Philosophy and Public Affairs* 10 (1981): 283–345.

Easthope, Antony. "Bhabha, Hybridity, and Identity." *Textual Practice* 12, no. 2 (1998): 341–348.

Edkins, Jenny. *Trauma and the Memory of Politics*. Cambridge: Cambridge University Press, 2003.

Eliade, Mircea. *The Myth of the Eternal Return*. Trans.Willard R. Trask. Princeton: Princeton University Press, 1971.

Eliot, T.S. "Tradition and the Individual Talent." In *Selected Prose of T.S. Eliot*. Ed. Frank Kermode. New York: Harcourt Brace Jovanovich, 1975, 37–44.

Ellison, Ralph. "Change the Joke and Slip the Yoke." In *The Collected Essays of Ralph Ellison*. Ed. John F. Callahan. New York: The Modern Library, 1995, 210–224.

Elshtain, Jean Bethke. *Just War Against Terror: The Burden of American Power in a Violent World*. New York: Basic Books, 2004.

Euben, Roxanne L. "Comparative Political Theory: An Islamic Fundamentalist Critique of Rationalism." *The Journal of Politics* 59, no 1 (1997): 28–55.

Euripides. *The Bacchae*. In *Euripides V*. Ed. David Grene and Richmond Lattimore. Chicago: The University of Chicago Press, 1959.

Fludernik, Monika. "The Constitution of Hybridity: Postcolonial Interventions." In *Hybridity and Postcolonialism: Twentieth Century Indian Literature*. Ed. Monika Fludernik. Tubingen: Stauffenberg, 1998, 19–53.

Follo, Francesco. "Interculturation and Interculturality in John Paul II and Benedict XVI." http://www.oasiscenter.eu/en/node/5610. Accessed March 31, 2012.

Foner, Eric. *Reconstruction: America's Unfinished Revolution 1863–1877*. New York: Harper, 2002.

Foucault, Michel. *The History of Sexuality, Vol. 3: The Care of the Self*. Trans. Robert Hurley. New York: Vintage Books, 1988.

———. *The Foucault Reader*. Ed. Paul Rabinow. New York: Vintage Books, 2010.

Franklin, John Hope. *From Slavery to Freedom: A History of Negro Americans*. New York: Vintage Books, 1969.

Gandhi, Leela. *Postcolonial Theory: A Critical Introduction*. New York: Columbia University Press, 1998.

Gasche, Rodolphe. *Inventions of Difference: On Jacques Derrida*. Cambridge: Harvard University Press, 1998.

Gill, Emily. *Becoming Free: Autonomy and Diversity in the Liberal Polity*. Lawrence, KS: University of Kansas Press, 2001.

Gilroy, Paul. *The Black Atlantic: Modernity and Double Consciousness*. Cambridge: Harvard University Press, 1993.

Giroux, Susan Searls and Henry A. Giroux. "Making the Political More Pedagogical: Reading Homi Bhabha." *Jac: A Journal of Composition Theory* 19, no. 1 (1999): 139–148.

Goodwin, Doris Kearns. *Team of Rivals: The Political Genius of Abraham Lincoln*. New York: Simon and Schuster, 2006.

Grant, Jacqueline. "The Sin of Servanthood and the Deliverance of Discipleship." In *A Troubling in My Soul: Womanist Perspectives on Evil and Suffering*. Ed. Emilie M. Townes. New York: Orbis Books, 1995, 199–218.

Greene, Sharon E. "A Conversation with Robert Detweiler." In *In Good Company: Essays in Honor of Robert Detweiler*. Eds. David Jasper and Mark Ledbetter. Atlanta, GA: Scholars Press, 1994, 433–450.

Harcourt, Hugh R. "In Search of the Emperor's New Clothes: Reflections on the Rights in the Palestinian Conflict." In *Philosophical Perspectives on the Israeli Palestinian Conflict*. Ed. Tomis Kapitan. London: M. E. Sharpe, 1997, 282–296.

Hardack, Richard. "'A Music Seeking Its Words' Double-Timing and Double-Consciousness in Toni Morrison's *Jazz*." *Callaloo* 8, no. 2 (Spring, 1995): 451–471.

Harding, Vincent. *There is a River: The Black Struggle for Freedom in America*. New York: Harcourt Brace, 1981.

Harris, Trudier. "On *The Color Purple*: Stereotypes and Silence." *Black American Literature Forum* 18, no. 4 (Winter 1954): 155–161.

Hartmann, Charles. *Jazz Text: Voice and Improvisation in Poetry, Jazz and Song*. Princeton: Princeton University Press, 1991.

Havel, Vaclav. *Open Letters: Selected Writings 1965–1990*, edited by Paul Wilson. New York: Vintage, 1992.

———. "A Courageous and Magnanimous Creation." *Harvard Review* 9 (Fall 1995): 103–112.

———. "Politicians' Role in a Global Civilization." *World Citizen News*, April/May 1996, http://www.worldservice.org/issues/aprmay96/politicians.html. Accessed March 14, 2012.

Hegel, G.W. F. *Phenomenology of the Spirit*. Trans. A.V. Miller. Oxford: Clarendon Press, 1977.

Heilke, Thomas W. "Science, Philosophy and Resistance: On Eric Voegelin's Practice of Opposition." *Review of Politics* 56, no. 4 (1994): 727–753.

Henningsen, Manfred. "The Collapse and Retrieval of Meaning." *Review of Politics* 62, no. 4 (2000): 809–817.

Hitchens, Christopher and Edward W. Said, eds. *Blaming the Victims: Spurious Scholarship and the Palestinian Question*. London: Verso Books, 1988.

Holloway, Karla F. C. *Moorings and Metaphors: Figures of Culture and Gender in Black Women's Literature*. New Brunswick, NJ: Rutgers University Press, 1992.

Holm, Serge-Christophe. "Distributive Justice." In *A Companion to Contemporary Political Philosophy*. Eds. Robert Goodin and Phillip Pettit. Oxford: Blackwell Publishers, 1996, 438–461.

The Holy Bible: Containing the Old and New Testaments. Reference ed. Camden, N. J.: T. Nelson, 1959.

hooks, bell. *Black Looks: Race and Representation*. Boston, MA: South End Press, 1992.

Hopkins, Dwight N. "Slave Theology in the 'Invisible Institution.'" In *Cut Loose Your Stammering Tongue: Black Theology in the Slave Narratives.* Eds. Dwight N. Hopkins and George C. L. Cummings. Louisville, KY: Westminster John Knox Press, 2003, 1–32.

Hudson, Michael C. "Developments and Setbacks in the Palestinian Resistance Movement 1967–1971." *Journal of Palestine Studies* 1, no. 3 (1972): 64–84.

Hurston, Zora Neale. *Their Eyes Were Watching God.* New York: Harper & Row, 1990.

Ignatieff, Michael. "Nationalism and the Narcissism of Minor Differences." In *Theorizing Nationalism.* Ed. Ronald Beiner. Albany: State University Press of New York, 1999, 91–102.

———. *The Lesser Evil: Political Ethics in an Age of Terror.* Princeton: Princeton University Press, 2004.

Ivison, Duncan. *Postcolonial Liberalism.* Cambridge: Cambridge University Press, 2002.

Jacobson, Janet and Ann Pelligrini. *Love the Sin: Sexual Regulation and the Limits of Religious Tolerance.* New York: New York University Press, 2008.

Jardine, Murray. "Eric Voegelin's Interpretations of Modernity: A Reconsideration of the Spiritual and the Political." *Review of Politics* 57, no. 4 (1995): 581–606.

Johnson, James. "Why Respect Culture?" *American Journal of Political Science* 44, no. 3 (2000): 405–418.

Jordan, June. *Living Room: New Poems, 1980–1984.* Thunder's Mouth Press: Distributed by Persea Books, 1985.

———. *Directed by Desire: The Collected Poems of June Jordan.* Port Townsend, Washington: Copper Canyon Press, 2007.

Kant, Immanuel. "An Answer to the Question: 'What is Enlightenment?'" In *Kant: Political Writings.* Ed. Hans Reiss. Trans. H. B. Nisbet. 2nd ed. Cambridge: Cambridge University Press, 1991, 54–60.

Khalidi, Muhammad Ali. "Formulating the Right of Self-Determination." In *Philosophical Perspectives on the Israeli Palestinian Conflict.* Ed. Tomis Kapitan. London: M. E. Sharpe, 1997, 71–94.

Khalidi, Rashid. *Palestinian Identity: The Construction of Modern National Consciousness.* New York: Colombia University Press, 1997.

———. *The Iron Cage: The Story of the Palestinian Struggle for Statehood.* Boston: Beacon Books, 2006.

King, Martin Luther, Jr. *Why We Can't Wait.* New York: Penguin Books, 1964.

———. *Stride Toward Freedom: The Montgomery Story.* San Francisco: HarperSan Francisco, 1986a.

———. *A Testament of Hope: The Essential Writings and Speeches of Martin Luther King, Jr.* Ed. James A. Washington. New York: HarperCollins, 1986b.

The King, Martin Luther, Jr., Center. "The King Philosophy." www.
thekingcenter.org/king-philosophy. Accessed March 31, 2012.

King, Sallie B. *Socially Engaged Buddhism*. Honolulu: University of Hawai'i
Press, 2009.

Kluger, Richard. *Simple Justice: The History of Brown v. Board of Education
and Black America's Struggle for Equality*. New York: Vintage, 1977.

Knox, Bernard M. *The Heroic Temper: Studies in Sophoclean Tragedy*. Berkeley:
University of California Press, 1983.

Kojève, Alexandre. *Introduction to Reading of Hegel*. Ed. Allan Bloom. Trans.
James H. Nichols. Ithaca, NY: Cornell University Press, 1980.

Kristeva, Julia. *Powers of Horror: An Essay on Abjection*. Trans. Leon
S. Roudiez. New York: Columbia University Press, 1982.

———. *Tales of Love*. Trans. Leon S. Roudiez. New York: Columbia
University Press, 1987.

Kundera, Milan. *The Book of Laughter and Forgetting*. New York: Penguin
Press, 1981.

Kymlicka, Will. *Politics in the Vernacular: Nationalism, Multiculturalism, and
Citizenship*. Oxford: Oxford University Press, 2001.

Levinas, Immanuel. *Totality and Infinity: An Essay on Exteriority*. Translated
by Alphonso Lingis. Pittsburgh: Duquesne University Press, 1969/1992.

Levey, Geoffrey Brahm. "Liberal Nationalism and Culture Rights." *Political
Studies* 49 (2001): 670–691.

Levy, Gideon. *The Punishment of Gaza*. London: Verso Books, 2010.

Lincoln, Abraham. *The Collected Works of Abraham Lincoln IV, 1860–1861*.
Ed. Roy P. Basler. New Brunswick, NJ: Rutgers University Press, 1953a.

———. *The Collected Works of Abraham Lincoln VIII, 1864–1865*. Ed. Roy
P. Basler. New Brunswick, NJ: Rutgers University Press, 1953b.

Locke, John. *Two Treatises of Government*. Ed. Peter Laslett. Cambridge:
Cambridge University Press, 1988.

Long, Charles H. *Significations: Signs, Symbols and Images in the Interpretation of Religion* Minneapolis: Fortress Press, 1986.

Lorde, Audre. *Sister Outsider: Essays and Speeches*. Darlinghurst, Australia:
Crossing Press, 1984.

Lyotard, Jean-Francois. *The Differend: Phrases in Dispute*. Trans. Georges Van
Den Abbeele. Minneapolis: University of Minnesota Press, 1988.

———. *The Postmodern Condition: A Report on Knowledge*. Trans. Geoff
Bennington and Brian Massumi. Minneapolis: University of Minnesota
Press, 1991.

———. "Algerians." In *Political Writings*. Trans. Bill Readings and Kevin
Paul Geiman. Minneapolis: University of Minnesota Press, 1993, 165–326.

———. *Just Gaming*. Trans. Wlad Godzich. Minneapolis: University of
Minnesota Press, 1996.

MacCormick, Neil. "Nation and Nationalism." In *Theorizing Nationalism*.
Ed. Ronald Beiner. Albany: State University Press of New York, 1999,
189–204.

244   BIBLIOGRAPHY

Machiavelli, Niccolo. *The Prince* in *Machiavelli, Selected Political Writings*. Trans. and Ed. David Wootton. Indianapolis: Hackett Publishing, 1994.

Malcolm, X. "The Ballot or the Bullet." In *Malcolm X Speaks: Selected Speeches and Statements*. Ed. George Breitman. New York: Grove Press, 1994, 23–44.

Marranca, Bonnie. "Criticism, Culture and Performance: An Interview with Edward Said." *Performing Arts Journal* 37 (1991): 21–42.

McKenna, Erin. "Land, Property, and Occupation: A Question of Political Philosophy." In *Philosophical Perspectives on the Israeli Palestinian Conflict*. Ed. Tomis Kapitan. London: M. E. Sharpe, 1997, 185–204.

Mill, John Stuart. *On Liberty*. Buffalo, NY: Prometheus Books, 1986.

Morrison, Toni. *Beloved*. New York: Plume Books, 1987.

———. "Interview with Bill Moyers." *The World of Ideas*. PBS, September 14, 1990.

———. *The Nobel Lecture in Literature*. www.nobelprize.org/nobel_prizes/literature/laureates/1993/morrison-lecture.html. Accessed March 18, 2012. Also published by New York: Knopf Doubleday, 1993.

———. "Intimate Things in Place: A Conversation with Toni Morrison." In *Conversations with Toni Morrison*. Ed. Danielle Taylor-Guthrie. Jackson, Mississippi: University of Mississippi Press, 1994, 10–29.

———."The Dancing Mind: Speech Upon the Acceptance of the National Book Foundation Medal for Distinguished Contribution to American Letters," www.nationalbook.org/nbaacceptsspeech_tmorrison.htm#.T2ZVwkqGbu0. Accessed March 18, 2012). Also published by New York: Alfred A. Knopf, 1996.

———. "Unspeakable Things Unspoken: The Afro-American Presence in American Literature." Tanner Lectures, 1988. www.tannerlectures.utah.edu/lectures/documents/morrison90.pdf. Accessed March 18, 2012.

Mouffe, Chantal. *The Democratic Paradox*. London: Verso Books, 2009.

Murray, Albert. *South to a Very Old Place*. New York: Vintage Books, 1991.

———. *The Hero and the Blues*. New York: Knopf Doubleday Publishing Group, 1996.

———. *The Blue Devils of Nada: A Contemporary Approach to Aesthetic Statement*. New York: Knopf Publishing Group, 1997.

Muslih, Muhammad Y. *The Origins of Palestinian Nationalism*. New York: Colombia University Press, 1988.

Nandy, Ashis. *The Intimate Enemy: Loss and Recovery of Self Under Colonialism*. Delhi: Oxford University Press, 1988.

Neilsen, Kai. "Cultural Nationalism, Neither Ethnic Nor Civic." In *Theorizing Nationalism*. Ed. Ronald Beiner. Albany: State University Press of New York, 1999, 119–130.

Nhat Hanh, Thich. *Interbeing: Fourteen Guidelines for Engaged Buddhism*. 3rd Ed. Berkeley, CA: Parallax Press, 2005.

———. *The Art of Power*. New York: HaperCollins, 2007.

Norris, Kathleen. *The Quotidian Mysteries: Laundry, Liturgy, and Women's Work*. New York: Paulist Press, 1998.

Nusseibeh, Sari. "Personal and National Identity." In *Philosophical Perspectives on the Israeli Palestinian Conflict*. Ed. Tomis Kapitan. London: M. E. Sharpe, 1997, 205–220.

Palumbo-Liu, David. "The Politics of Memory: Remembering History in Alice Walker and Joy Kogawa." In *Memory and Cultural Politics: New Approaches to American Ethnic Literatures*. Eds. Robert E. Hogan, Joseph T. Skerrett, Jr. and Amritjit Singh. Boston: Northeastern University Press, 1996, 211–226.

Phillips, Caryl. *The Atlantic Sound*. New York: Alfred A. Knopf, 2000.

Phillips, Lawrence. "Lost in Space: Sitting/Citing the In-Between of Homi Bhabha's Location of Culture." *Jouvert: a Journal of Postcolonial Studies* 2, no. 2 (1998) [online journal]. http://english.chass.ncsu.edu/jouvert/v2i2/PHILLIP.HTM. Accessed September 21, 2000.

Piaget, Jean. *The Moral Judgment of the Child*. Trans. Marjorie Gabain. New York: Free Press, 1997.

Plato. "Apology." *The Collected Dialogues*. Eds. Edith Hamilton and Huntington Cairnes. Princeton: Princeton University Press, 1961

Pratt, Mary Louise. "Arts of the Contact Zone." *Profession* 91 (1991): 33–40.

———. *Imperial Eyes: Travel Writing and Transculturation*. New York: Routledge, 2007,adhakrishnan, R. "Postcoloniality and the Boundaries of Identity." *Callaloo* 16, no. 4 (1993): 750–771.

Rawls, John. "Justice as Fairness: Political Not Metaphysical." *Philosophy and Public Affairs* 14 (1985): 223–251.

———. *A Theory of Justice*. Rev. ed. Cambridge: Harvard University Press, 1999.

Readings, Bill. *Introducing Lyotard: Art and Politics*. London and New York: Routledge, 1991.

Roy, Sara. *Failing Peace: Gaza and the Palestinian-Israeli Conflict*. London: Pluto Press, 2007.

Said, Edward W. *Orientalism*. New York: Vintage Books, 1979.

———. *The World, The Text, and The Critic*. Cambridge, MA: Harvard University Press, 1983.

———. *Beginnings: Intention and Method*. New York: Columbia University Press, 1985.

———. *The Question of Palestine*. New York: Vintage Books, 1992.

———. *Culture and Imperialism*. New York: Vintage Books, 1994.

———. *The Politics of Dispossession: The Struggle for Palestinian Self-Determination, 1969–1994*. New York: Vintage Books, 1995.

———. *Peace and Its Discontents: Essays on Palestine in the Middle East Peace Process*. New York: Vintage Books, 1996.

———. *Covering Islam: How the Media and the Experts Determine How We See the Rest of the World*. New York: Vintage Books, 1997.

———. *The End of the Peace Process: Oslo and After*. New York: Vintage Books, 2001a.

———. *Power, Politics and Culture: Interviews with Edward W. Said*. Edited by Gauri Viswanathan. New York: Pantheon Books, 2001b.

———. *From Oslo to Iraq and the Road Map*. New York: Pantheon Books, 2004.

Sandel, Michael. *Liberalism and the Limits of Justice*. Cambridge: Cambridge University Press, 1982.

———. "The Procedural Republic and the Unencumbered Self." *Political Theory* 12 (1984): 81–96.

Scarry, Elaine. *The Body in Pain: The Making and Unmaking of the World*. New York: Oxford University Press, 1985.

Sharp, Gene. *From Dictatorship to Democracy*. London: Serpent's Tail Press, 2012. See also Albert Einstein Institution, 2010, http://www.aeinstein. org/organizations/org/FDTD.pdf. Accessed February 2, 2012.

Smith, Jonathan Z. *Map is Not Territory: Studies in the History of Religion*. Chicago: University of Chicago Press, 1993.

———."Tillich ['s] Remains." *Journal of the American Academy of Religion* 78, no. 4 (2010): 1139–1170.

Soelle, Dorothee. *Suffering*. Trans. Everett R. Kalin. Philadelphia: Fortress Press, 1975.

Sophocles. *Antigone* in *The Complete Greek Tragedies, Volume 3: Sophocles I*. Trans. Elizabeth Wyckoff, eds. David Grene and Richmond Lattimore. New York: Pocket Books, 1973, 161–209..

———.*Sophocles I: Oedipus the King, Oedipus at Colonus, Antigone*. 2nd ed. Trans. David Grene. Chicago: University of Chicago Press, 1991.

Soyinka, Wole. *The Bacchae of Euripides: A Communion Rite*. New York: W. W. Norton and Company, Inc., 1974.

Spenser, Jon Michael. *Protest and Praise: Sacred Music of Black Religion*. Minneapolis, MN: Augsburg Fortress Press, 1990.

Spinner-Halev, Jeff and Elizabeth Theiss-Morse. "National Identity and Self-Esteem." *Perspectives on Politics* 1, no. 3 (2005): 515–532.

Sri, Edward. *The New Rosary in Scripture: Biblical Insights for Praying the Twenty Mysteries*. Grand Junction, CO: Charis Publications, 2003.

———. "Christ the Obedient Son: Lessons From the Agony in the Garden." *Lay Witness Magazine* (May/June, 2004): 4–5, 47.

Stepto, Robert. "Intimate Things in Place: A Conversation with Toni Morrison." In *Conversations with Toni Morrison*. Danille K. Taylor-Guthrie. Eds. Jackson, MS: University of Mississippi Press, 1994, 10–29.

Steiner, George. *Antigones*. New York: Oxford University Press, 1984.

Tamir, Yael. *Liberal Nationalism*. Princeton: Princeton University Press, 1993.

———. "The Land of the Fearful and the Free." *Constellations* 3, no. 3 (1997): 296–314.

———. "Theoretical Difficulties in the Study of Nationalism." In *Theorizing Nationalism*. Ed. Ronald Beiner. Albany: State University Press of New York, 1999, 67–90.

Tan, Kok-Chor. "Liberalism and Cosmopolitan Justice." *Ethical Theory and Moral Practice* 5, no. 4 (2002): 431–461.

Tate, Alan. *The Fathers*. Athens, GA: Swallow Press, 1959.

Taylor, Charles. *The Ethics of Authenticity*. Cambridge: Harvard University Press, 1991.

Thucydides. *History of the Peloponnesian War*. Trans. Rex Warner. New York: Penguin Books, 1954.

Townes, Emilie. "Living in the New Jerusalem: the Rhetoric and Movement of Liberation in the House of Evil." In *A Troubling in My Soul: Womanist Perspectives on Evil and Suffering*. Ed. Emilie M. Townes. New York: Orbis Books, 1995, 78–91.

Turner, Victor. *The Ritual Process: Structure and Anti-Structure*. New York: Aldine de Gruyter, 1969, 1995.

Voegelin, Eric. *Order and History*, 5 vols. Baton Rouge: Louisiana State University Press, 1956–1987.

———. *Science, Politics, and Gnosticism*. Washington, D.C.: Regnery Gateway, 1968.

———. *The New Science of Politics: An Introduction*. Chicago: University of Chicago Press, 1987.

———. *Anamnesis*. Trans. and Ed. Gerhart Niemeyer. Columbia: University of Missouri Press, 1990a.

———. "Equivalences of Experience and Symbolization in History." In *The Collected Works of Eric Voegelin, Volume 12: Published Essays, 1966–1985*. Ed. Ellis Sandoz. Baton Rouge: Louisiana State University Press, 1990b, 115–133.

Waldron, Jeremy. "Homelessness and the Issue of Freedom." In *Contemporary Political Philosophy: An Anthology*. Eds. Robert Goodin and Phillip Pettit. Oxford: Blackwell Publishing, 1997, 446–462.

Walker, Alice. *In Search of Our Mothers' Gardens*. New York: Harcourt Brace Jovanovich Publishers, 1983.

———. *Living by the World*. New York: Harcourt Brace Jovanovich Publishers, 1988.

———. *The Same River Twice*. New York: Schribner, 1996.

———. *Anything We Love Can Be Saved*. New York: Ballantine Books, 1998.

———. *The Way Forward Is With a Broken Heart*. New York: Ballantine Books, 2001.

Walker, Brian. "Modernity and Cultural Vulnerability: Should Ethnicity Be Privileged?" In *Theorizing Nationalism*. Ed. Ronald Beiner. Albany: State University Press of New York, 1999, 141–166.

Walzer, Michael. *Spheres of Justice: A Defense of Pluralism and Equality*. New York: Basic Books, 1983.

———. "Response." In *Pluralism, Justice, and Equality*. Ed. David Miller and Michael Walzer. Oxford: Oxford University Press, 1995, 281–298.

———. "The New Tribalism: Notes on a Difficult Problem." In *Theorizing Nationalism*. Ed. Ronald Beiner. Albany: State University Press of New York, 1999, 205–218.

Watson, Larry. *Montana 1948*. Minneapolis, MN: Milkweed Editions, 2007.

Weber, Max. *The Protestant Ethic and the Spirit of Capitalism.* Trans. Talcott Parsons. New York: Charles Scribner's Sons, 1958.

Weil, Simone. *Simone Weil: An Anthology.* Ed. Sian Miles. New York: Grove Press, 2000.

Wilson, Joseph P. *The Hero and the City: An Interpretation of Sophocles' Oedipus at Colonus.* Ann Arbor: University of Michigan Press, 1997.

Williams, Patricia J. *The Alchemy of Race and Rights: Diary of a Law Professor.* Cambridge, MA: Harvard University Press, 1991.

Yack, Bernard. "The Myth of the Civic Nation." In *Theorizing Nationalism.* Ed. Ronald Beiner. Albany: State University Press of New York, 1999, 103–118.

NAME INDEX

Subject Index